The Year of
Reading Proust

A Memoir in Real Time

Phyllis Rose

SCRIBNER

SCRIBNER
1230 Avenue of the Americas
New York, NY 10020

Copyright © 1997 by Phyllis Rose

SCRIBNER *and design are trademarks of*
Simon & Schuster Inc.

Designed by Brooke Zimmer
Set in Janson
Manufactured in the United States of America

1   3   5   7   9   10   8   6   4   2

Library of Congress Cataloging-in-Publication Data

Rose, Phyllis, date
The year of reading Proust: a memoir in real
time/Phyllis Rose.
p. cm.
Includes bibliographical references.
1. Rose, Phyllis, date. 2. United States—Biography. 3.
Authors, American—20th century—Biography. 4.
Proust, Marcel, 1871–1922—Criticism and
interpretation. I. Title.
CT275.R7827A3   1997
818'.5409—dc20   97–17700
[B]   CIP

ISBN 0-684-83984-9

The author is grateful to Chatto & Windus, the Estate
of Marcel Proust, and the translators, for permission to
quote from In Search of Lost Time *by Marcel Proust,*
translated by C. K. Scott Moncrieff, Terence Kilmartin,
and Andreas Mayor, revised by D. J. Enright. All quo-
tations are from the Modern Library edition in six vol-
umes (New York, 1992).

To Wendy Gimbel

"And surely this was a most tempting prospect, this task of re-creating one's true life, of rejuvenating one's impressions. But it required courage of many kinds, including the courage of one's emotions. For above all it meant the abrogation of one's dearest illusions, it meant giving up one's belief in the objectivity of what one had oneself elaborated, so that now, instead of soothing oneself for the hundredth time with the words: 'She was very sweet,' one would have to transpose the phrase so that it read: 'I experienced pleasure when I kissed her.' "

Time Regained

Contents

Our Hearts Were Young and Gay

"The things about which we most often jest are generally . . . the things that worry us but that we do not wish to appear to be worried by, with perhaps a secret hope of the further advantage that the person to whom we are talking, hearing us treat the matter as a joke, will conclude that it is not true."   *The Captive*

SOME TIME AGO, ABOUT TO GIVE a lecture which my conservative audience would find daring and controversial but which I myself thought obsequious and inconclusive, I looked in the mirror to check my appearance. At first what I saw satisfied me. I was well groomed, well dressed: a pleasant-looking middle-aged woman. I looked again in horror. I was Cornelia Otis Skinner.

In the 1950s, when my mother was in her prime and I was a teenager, Cornelia Otis Skinner was a prized speaker at Book and Author luncheons. Poised, genteel, and articulate, she embodied post–World War II literary culture. Her books were witty, sometimes rueful accounts of the mild difficulties of her privileged life. I scorned her. She was the idol of my mother's set—therefore, to my teenaged self, middlebrow, mediocre, banal.

Cardinal Newman, in his earnest Victorian autobiography, describes the awful moment of realizing, from a look at himself in a mirror, that he was a monophysite. Whatever a monophysite was, clearly it horrified Cardinal Newman to be one. It was something he had never expected to turn into, any more than I had expected to become Cornelia Otis Skinner or Gregor Samsa had expected to become a bug. We work so hard to avoid moral pitfalls, professional debasements, intellectual fallacies, only to find ourselves metamorphosed, as we never could have predicted, into alien beings. We are caught at the foot by traps we overlook while keeping branches away from our eyes.

One winter day in Key West with time on my hands, I went to the library to find out what I could about my double, listed in the computer catalog as Cornelia Otis Skinner, 1901—. I compiled a list of books I had not heard of, *Nuts in May*, *The Ape in Me*, *Madame Sarah*, *Elegant Wits and Grand Horizontals*, *The Pleasure of His Company*, and one book I had heard of, *Our Hearts Were Young and Gay*, written with Emily Kimbrough. This was a book my mother had loved. It was published in 1942, the year I was born, and for all I knew, my mother's enthusiasm for it had played a part in my childhood fantasies of being a writer. I was eager to look it over.

Our Hearts Were Young and Gay is about Cornelia Otis Skinner's trip to Europe with her friend Emily Kimbrough just after World War I when they were barely twenty. Their contrasting personalities form the narrative's core. Cornelia studies voice with an actor of the Comédie Française. Emily decides she wants lessons, too. A flibbertigibbet who doesn't study her lines until the last minute, Emily can recite page after page of French verse, while Cornelia, who takes the recitation seriously and works hard at it, performs poorly. This is the pattern: Emily is offhand and dazzling; Cornelia is earnest and earthbound.

In London they live in a dreary room in Tavistock Square. It is cold. They are told to feed money to the geyser to get hot water. Emily looks in vain for the old man they're supposed to tip, the geezer. Ha ha!

They see rabbit capes for sale for £30–10s–6d. Emily asks Cornelia how much 30 ells, 10 esses, and 6 dees come to. They both buy capes in the voluminous shapeless style then popular, feel they are very beautiful, cause everyone around them to laugh hysterically.

In Rouen they stay in a lovely hotel which turns out to be a brothel. Ha ha!

It is all well told and well written. They don't rub in the ironies. Their friendship is lovable. Then why did this book depress me so? First: despite its many charms, it's a textbook example of "dated." How totally they assume their own centrality, their cuteness, when what seems cute and central has changed. Some books are undermined by history, able to speak to one decade or generation but not the next, their limited depth and range revealed in time.

After that, the charm itself—the effort to charm, the girlish compulsion to solicit approval, the impulse to mist, at the end of almost every paragraph, an unspoken "Am I not lovable?" In every feminine attempt to please and amuse, I saw a hated reflection.

I had other books by Skinner on the table before me in the Key West library, including *Nuts in May*, a collection of essays. I had published a collection of essays, and many of our subjects were the same. My son appeared in the essays at different ages, just like hers. I liked to write about the impossibility of getting anything done in France, due to a culturally enforced absence of the can-do spirit and a perhaps genetically encoded mean-mindedness. So did Cornelia. For touches of humor, I liked a bit of literal translation from the French. So did she. Some of my favorite aperçus were hers as well—the inability of children to accept the sexuality of their parents, the performer's fantasy of appearing naked.

I also had before me *Elegant Wits and Grand Horizontals*, a panoramic history of the Belle Époque. Through biographical portraits of flamboyant figures like the dancer Cléo de Mérode, the courtesans Liane de Pougy, La Belle Otéro, and Emilienne d'Alençon, and the dapper man about town, Robert de Montesquiou, who served as a model for Proust's Charlus, my double built up a picture of the social life of Paris in the 1890s. I had used the same method in a book which created a general view of the institution of marriage by portraying the marriages of five Victorian writers. I recognized the impulse to divide and conquer, climb the mountain by looking only at the next step, pile up one chapter after another. It was an essayist's way to write a book.

One phrase in the jacket copy for *Elegant Wits* struck me to the quick: it said the book was "as effervescent as champagne." I had written a biography of Josephine Baker (in itself, a project that might have appealed to Skinner), and it went through some hard times before it was published. Among other things, it was rejected by an editor who said it wasn't "bubbly" enough. A book about Josephine Baker, she said, ought to be "as effervescent as champagne," and mine was not. Evidently, Cornelia Otis Skinner's would have been.

We were both mothers, Francophiles, biographers, essayists. But she was also a celebrated actress who had popular one-woman shows. Her books were best-sellers. She was a certified humorist. I was flattering myself to think I was Cornelia Otis Skinner. I looked myself up in the catalogue. Out of the six books I'd published, the Monroe County Public Library had only one. I followed out the implication: I am not nearly as renowned in my time as Cornelia Otis Skinner was in hers, and she is almost totally forgotten. I would be lucky if my writing pleased before it passed, but pass it probably would, leaving no ideas behind, stirring no one up, changing nothing, evanescent as the bubbles in champagne but not as bubbly.

Before this epiphany, I believe I could have called myself a modest person, with a firmer grasp of my insignificance than many writers. I knew I was, critically and commercially, very small potatoes. Yet simultaneously I had always thought my work would live forever. Just as my humility came in part from knowing distinguished writers, so did my chutzpah. I cooked, dressed, talked as well as they did. It didn't strain belief that I could write as well, too. In Key West, where I'd spent the past five winters, where so many writers have won the Pulitzer Prize that local newspapers seem to use the adjective "Pulitzer Prize–winning" before the noun "author" more often than not, I felt that I must be a prize winner, too. The only difference between me and Richard

Wilbur, Alison Lurie, James Merrill, and Annie Dillard, was that their prizes were in the past and mine was in the future.

This deeply buried, deeply arrogant level of consciousness was the one outraged and traumatized by the fear that I was a feeble copy of Cornelia Otis Skinner. I fell into an existential sinkhole. The bottom of existence I'd thought was there—my ultimate, enduring achievement—no longer was. I had always believed that someday, perhaps after my death, my work would be classic. I had never doubted that what I wrote would eventually find a place on the bookshelf of every literate reader. I could afford to twit my friends who thought our correspondence would be published because I knew it really would be. I lived very comfortably with my humility, but my humility rested on the bedrock of my arrogance.

The evening of my epiphany in the Key West library, I was feeling very low when I made my nightly phone call to my mother in New York. My mother would have loved to be with me in Key West, but the previous winter the prospect of making the trip, especially of changing planes in Miami, so frightened her that her already weak heart failed again. So she sat in her apartment and at six o'clock I would take the cordless phone to the seawall and describe the sunset to her: "There's a band of orange all along the water line and the water is silver," or "The sun is a huge orange ball." She really didn't care what I said. She liked the sound of my voice. She called me her dessert because my call usually came as she was finishing her dinner.

My mother's approval was new, a miraculous late growth, like the flower of a century plant. I don't mean to say she ever disapproved of me or found what I accomplished insufficient. She always approved, but she was tight-mouthed. Now, whether it was the mellowing of age or the antidepressants she'd been on for two years, something had loosened her tongue. In our daily conversations, the river of praise was unstoppable. I bathed in it. If I used a metaphor of life-giving water for her, hers for me was life-giving sun. "Your calls warm me." "Hearing your voice at the end of the day is like sitting in the sun." We were having a late romance, my mother and I.

That night it was too cold and overcast to have my drink and call her outside. I lay on the sofa, my legs up on the arm, listening to her description of the frigid weather in New York. There were blocks of ice in the East River. There was frost on her windows on the twenty-fifth floor. It was the coldest day on record in the history of New York City. She went out for ten minutes, because she was feeling so cooped up, but she wore a ski mask to protect her face.

After some spirited talk about the vulgarity of Tonya Harding, she said, "I'm reading your book again, your book of essays. It's wonderful, wonderful. I'm amazed at your wisdom."

I sat up. "You really like it?"

"More than like it, darling."

"It's good?" I wouldn't let it go.

"Better than good. It's a *meikhl*. You know what a *meikhl* is? A treat."

I was more than fifty years old and at one level knew better, but at another my mother's praise seemed just and accurate, keener than the book reviews, swifter than the prize committees.

"Do you remember Cornelia Otis Skinner, Mother?"

"Of course I do. She wrote that wonderful book—what was it called? with her friend—what was her name?"

"*Our Hearts Were Young and Gay*. Emily Kimbrough."

"Emily Kimbrough. That's it. A charming book."

"I remember you liked her. But nobody reads her anymore."

That was as close as I could come to telling her about the large blow to my self-esteem I had come that day to absorb or to mentioning the great themes that were oppressing me—the pitfalls of ambition, the fleeting nature of fame, the extremely slim odds of one's work surviving.

"Nobody reads her?" said my mother, providing both balm for my pain and, as she often did, the last word. "Their loss."

I

Reading Proust

"We guess as we read, we create; everything starts form an initial error. . . . A large part of what we believe to be true . . . with an obstinacy equalled only by our good faith, springs from an original mistake in our premises."   *The Fugitive*

For A LONG TIME I USED TO TRY to read Proust. At first I could not. Like a heavy car with a tiny engine, I charged up the hill again and again only to stall around page 50, somewhere within the exhausting story of young Marcel's getting to sleep one night in Combray. Who can have reached adulthood in our times in literate circles without knowing how much Marcel wanted his mother to come upstairs and kiss him good night? But fewer people may know the subsequent, perverse emotion: that when Marcel's whining succeeds in getting his father to send his mother to spend the night in his room, he feels somewhat discomforted. To have his mother with him all night is too great a gift, a humiliating sign his father thinks him a sickly child who might as well be indulged. Moreover, having secured his mother, Marcel no longer wants her so much. As he will discover over and over in love, what is imagined and yearned for is more exciting than what is possessed; anticipation is a more pleasurable state than occupation. Almost all the love affairs in Proust are variations on Groucho Marx's insight that any club that wants you is not a club you want to join.

The opening section of *Swann's Way* seemed so slow, so static, so filled with tedious description and irritating embellishment, I was always so fatigued by the immense work of reading which evidently lay ahead of me, that either I would fall asleep myself reading how Marcel did or I would put the book aside with a mixture of irritation at Proust's demands on me, shame at my own feeble powers of response, and the whoopdedoo exhilaration of a schoolkid at recess, only to pick it up and try again, perhaps in a different paperback edition, a different translation, years later, and have the same thing recur.

Once or twice, however, with my foot pressed even harder on the accelerator, I would chug uphill to the story of Uncle Adolphe, between pages 99 and 110. There I stalled again, but for a different reason. Worldly Uncle Adolphe, knowing that his family disapproved of the actresses and courtesans he enjoyed entertaining, contrived to keep their visits strictly separate from the visits of his family, but young Marcel, eager to meet such women, managed to burst in on his uncle on one of the forbidden days. So he got to meet the adorable lady in pink, and although his uncle suggested he keep news of this meeting from his parents, Marcel was so excited that he told them all about it, causing a rift between them and Uncle Adolphe. Later Marcel encountered his uncle on the street, riding in his carriage, and he was so moved by his uncle's kindness and so remorseful for having caused the family rift that he considered merely raising his hat to him an inadequate gesture. So he did nothing, turning his head away. Uncle Adolphe, concluding that Marcel was acting on his parents' instructions, never forgave them, and Marcel never saw his uncle again.

To be so moved that you don't even make a gesture of common courtesy is a morsel of typically Proustian paradox: it is normal to express your feelings by gestures which seem to express their exact opposite. Anyone who has never answered a letter that especially pleased them will understand. You might think from my stopping my reading at Uncle Adolphe that I wasn't enjoying it, as had been the case earlier on, when I read about Marcel's efforts to go to sleep. But it was exactly the opposite. I savored the moment so much that I could not continue. The result was the same—I stalled—but the process was different, for in the second case I was re-enacting the perverse logic of Marcel's snub of his uncle: I felt too much to make the simple gesture of continuing to read. If I moved on, I would leave behind the section I so much enjoyed. Yet if I didn't abandon the beloved part, how would I ever come to know the whole of the novel? I was like a traveler who arrives in Rome in the first days of a lengthy tour of Italy, falls in love with the city, and is tempted to cancel the rest of his travel plans, even though he knows he would thereby deprive himself of the certain delights of Venice and Florence; he finally continues his trip, but never experiences exactly the same pleasure, always feels a certain regret, comparing the joys of the next city to the joys he knew in Rome, which are augmented by memory, and finding the subsequent pleasures lesser.

Well, I exaggerate. I went on to experience the same joys I had in reading about Uncle Adolphe and more in my year of reading Proust. Just now, writing, I got carried away by my exercise in Proustian style, of whose chief elements—paradox, inclusiveness, and simile—simile was the horse that took me off on that wild ride to Rome, Venice, and Florence. I will try to rein him in. But in discussing the pain caused by moving forward in enterprises we love, I might have gone on to mention the regret of the mother who, no matter how much she loves her grown son, always suffers from the loss of the adorable baby he once was and which, of the successive incarnations that form what we call for convenience a person, was the one she first fell in love with. Had I done so, I would have made a complete Proustian circuit—from a solitary mental event (reading) to a physical activity (in this case travel, which for Proust is often an enactment of desire) to a human relationship (the feelings of mother for son) considered in time. Such spirals replace in Proust the straight-line narrative of the traditional novel.

•   •   •

Yes, I read Proust for a year. More than a year. In fact, as I write this, I am still reading him. I have not yet begun the final volume of *In Search of Lost Time*, the sixth, which contains, I know, Proust's account of sitting down to write his masterpiece and the final party, given by the new Princesse de Guermantes, highest-ranking member of the most exclusive circle in Paris, whom we first meet as middle-class, affected Madame Verdurin. No one reads Proust for the plot. Still, I maintain a kind of skepticism that substitutes for narrative momentum. Madame Verdurin becomes the Princesse de Guermantes? I'll believe it when I read it.

Unpropelled by narrative, caught in the spirals or circles of reference which generate his depth and amplitude, every reader of Proust has to find his or her own reason for moving ahead. I myself began by ignoring what was unique to Proust, reading him as though he were a nineteenth-century novelist, like Tolstoy or George Eliot or Stendhal, with whom I already felt comfortable. So I read quickly and as if with half-closed eyes those sections in *Swann's Way* about sleep and landscape which I found static and woke up when I got to the "story" (for story it blessedly was) of Swann's obsession with Odette ("Swann in Love"). Swann is among the most refined men in Paris, and Odette is no better than a high-class call girl. (She will turn out to have been Uncle Adolphe's lady in pink.) Swann loves Odette almost because she is not his type, his love fueled by jealousy. This was matter I could understand, more paradoxical than Madame Bovary's love affair or Julien Sorel's or Fabrice del Dongo's, but still in the great French tradition of writing about love.

And so I arrived, panting and gasping as from a long-distance race, at volume 2. On a practical note, I must add that I would never have reached this level of achievement had I not made the reading of Proust the central business of my life, the work I turned to when I first got up in the morning. I had begun, as usual, doing my own writing in the morning and reading Proust in the afternoon or in bed before I went to sleep. That proved impossible. Proust declined my peripheral attention. He wanted, he demanded, he got my best thought, my best energy, the best of my day.

I had read *Swann's Way* so conscious of my own pleasure or lack of it that I could hardly enjoy it. I was so amazed to be reading the book at all, to have moved beyond Uncle Adolphe, that the feeling of amazement overwhelmed all my other responses, as when a person who for the first time skis or drives a car is too astonished to find himself successfully propelled through space, too absorbed by the difficulties of movement, to take in the scenery. Focused on the success or failure of my own activity, I was largely unable to study the verbal scenery of volume 1. But by volume 2, I was steady enough on my feet to look around.

What I noticed first, unfashionably enough, was Proust's wisdom. Generations of critics have told us we are not supposed to read novels for what they have to tell us about life, but Proust seemed to have many things he wanted to say, or rather to explain, about human nature, and I wanted to hear. At the start of *Within a Budding Grove*, we find Swann, who had been the model of tact, friend of duchesses and princesses who prized his discretion, now married to Odette and become a vulgarian who boasts when some junior government official's wife pays a visit to his. Proust is eager to explain why. Have we noticed the way artists, as they age, pride themselves on their secondary talents? A great writer will imagine he pleases his friends with gifts of his mediocre paintings, or a brilliant theoretical chemist will want to be admired for his efforts at poetry. The principle is the same in social life. We know the standards of the arts we practice. Outside our own area, our taste and discretion go astray and we ascribe to our least efforts, all the more precious to us because marginal, an importance they don't have. So Swann, who would never have boasted of his friendship with duchesses, boasts of his wife's visits from Madame Bontemps.

To my astonishment Proust, who I'd been led to expect looked always into himself, seemed to be looking at other people's behavior, explaining, understanding, generalizing from particular cases, or predicting the particular from an understanding of the general. In the first section of *Within a Budding Grove*, Marcel is obsessed with getting to know Madame Swann and Gilberte, her daughter. When he meets the diplomat, the Marquis de Norpois, who is a friend of Madame Swann, he steers the conversation around to her, gets the marquis to say that he will mention him to Madame Swann, and has the ridiculous urge, instantaneously suppressed, to kiss Monsieur de Norpois's hand in gratitude. He is so embarrassed at having almost done this that he convinces himself Monsieur de Norpois didn't notice. But Monsieur de Norpois had noticed, even remembers the gesture years later and recalls it to Marcel. And of course, seeing how important it is to Marcel that he mention him to Madame Swann, he resolves by no means to do so.

This small, well-observed transaction becomes the subject of a discourse on the effects of magnification. How could Marcel have convinced himself his gesture was too small to be seen? We often think we are invisible, either because we underestimate our size in other people's eyes or because we overestimate the number of gestures—the size of the world—most people take in. Proust moves easily from Marcel and the Marquis de Norpois to "we" or "people" or "one," the level of generalization.

Generalizations about "we" are so thick throughout *Lost Time* that for the sport of the thing in discussing them I will limit myself to volume 2, where my notes were not so voluminous as they later became. Very often these generalizations are cast in an epigrammatic form that links Proust to Montaigne: "The time which we have at our disposal every day is elastic; the passions that we feel expand it, those that we inspire contract it, and habit fills up what remains." (p. 257) "We understand the characters of people we are indifferent to." (p. 648) "Pleasure is like photography. What we take, in the presence of the beloved object, is merely a negative which we develop later, when we are back at home, and have once again found at our disposal that inner darkroom the entrance to which is barred to us so long as we are with other people." (pp. 616–617) "The true secret of giving ourselves pleasure . . . is not to aspire to it but merely to help ourselves pass the time less boringly." (p. 728) Sometimes, rarely, there's a hortatory note, and epigram shades into essay, as in his portrait of the friendship of Marcel and the aristocratic Saint-Loup and the ensuing discussion of the rewards of friendship versus those of art. Sometimes the generalizations take the form of references to human traits we are all presumed to know about, references that breathe a French worldliness, like similar references in Colette, as when he mentions "that subservience of refinement to vulgarity" which is the rule in many households (p. 126), or "that anxiety . . . that desire for something more, which destroys in us, in the presence of the person we love, the sensation of loving." (p. 139)

It was no surprise to me, it confirmed what I'd been sensing, when Marcel refers to himself toward the end of *Budding Grove* as a "human naturalist." Darwin, during his travels on the *Beagle*, collected specimens of bird and animal life which later, a housebound recluse in England, he sifted mentally in order to write *The Origin of Species*. So too Proust, in his years of social observation and activity, collected examples of human behavior which later, immured in his cork-lined bedroom in Paris, he sifted and studied in order to find general, unifying laws. The title of Proust's masterpiece, *A la recherche du temps perdu*, currently translated into English as *In Search of Lost Time*, has inspired a good deal of talk about time *(temps)*—time lost, time scanned, time recovered—but critics have paid less attention to Proust's *recherche*, which evokes for me research as well as searching. Proust is a researcher, happiest when, between two sensations, experiences, or pieces of behavior he finds a common element, when, beneath particular examples, he discerns a connective law. After all, what is simile, that cornerstone of Proust's style, but a way of finding a connection between two seemingly dissimilar things?

Proust is hardly alone among epic writers in obtaining denseness of texture, denseness of reference, a sense of felt life, from those surprising, sometimes far-fetched similes which have been used to deepen description as far back in western literature as Homer and which are therefore called "Homeric." By comparing something to something very different, you incorporate two layers of life in your work within one description. So in Homer one finds soldiers in ambush compared to wolves preying on sheep, and thereby the reader has both the farmyard and the battlefield called to mind. By the same token, Proust describes the way the Marquis de Norpois listens motionless when someone talks to him in the manner of people who are used to controlling conversations and who are often asked for advice. Then suddenly he "falls on you like an auctioneer's hammer." In one sentence you have the world of the salon and the world of the auction. Monsieur de Norpois sends Marcel to pay a visit on a writer whom he very much admires but little thought to meet, plunging him into as great anxiety "as if he had told me I was to embark the next day as cabin boy on a wind-jammer." Salon widens into seaport. The degree to which Proust relies on simile to open out his work is, I think, unprecedented in the novel, merely hinted at even in so insistently comparative a work as *Middlemarch*, and is the point at which his aesthetic impulses, that is, his impulses as a writer of poetic prose, and his scientific impulses, his way of proceeding as a "researcher" into human nature, intersect and reinforce each other.

The final step in any scientific investigation is, of course, the application of the principles discovered to new data—in other words, further experiments. Rapidly, I began applying the fruits of Proust's research to my own life.

An old friend, a man who had felt compelled to side with my husband's first wife when they were divorced but continued to wish us well, visiting our town, pleasantly accepted an invitation to dinner at our house then canceled a day or so later on a notably feeble pretext. Was I puzzled? No. Proust had explained his behavior: "The Princess never liked to tell people that she would not go to their houses. Every day she would write to express her regret at having been kept away—by the sudden arrival of her husband's mother, by an invitation from her brother-in-law."

Another friend would taunt me periodically with the names of people she'd been seeing, people who didn't seem so eager to see me. It made it easier to bear to know that Madame Swann, too, had collected friends as though she were conducting a colonial campaign of annexation. I told myself that if my friend bothered to taunt me with her new colonies, at least that made me Germany to her France or Spain to her Netherlands.

A new couple came to town and made their way with unprecedented swiftness into our little circle of writers and painters. Although their impact as artists and their charm as friends was considerable, a distinguishing feature of these newcomers was their wealth. But you'd never have known this from hostesses who invited them to parties and then extolled their talents to the other guests. I understood because Proust had revealed that when people were admitted to the witty Guermantes circle because they were wellborn, as happened now and then, the Guermantes would always protest that the initiates were really very witty.

Increasingly I saw similarities between our town and Balbec, the seaside resort where Marcel goes in the second half of *Budding Grove* (and where I'd been reluctant to follow him, so entranced was I by the matter of Marcel and Madame Swann, Marcel, and Gilberte). Proust explained the social dynamics of places like Balbec, Martha's Vineyard, and Key West. According to the Proustian paradox that what should be marginal to people is often central to them, life in vacation spots matters more to many people than life in the city. And this is true to such an extent that some will cultivate in the city individuals they would otherwise not have bothered with in order to see them in the vacation spot, where, because of local hierarchies, they enjoy much greater status.

Proust had shown me the underlying laws. Like the Marxist who boasts that if you really understand history you can predict it and sneers at those who, not understanding it, are condemned to repeat it, like the Freudian smug in the face of human aberration because he thinks he can explain what produced it, I felt privileged, exempt, suddenly the master of the life I was observing. I had been given a key, a free subscription to some hitherto locked-out cable channel which in front of my eyes lost its frustrating distortion and transformed itself from blurred, wavy, taffy-pull mystery shapes into a clear and enjoyable picture.

When my son complained about a feeling of oppression upon starting his first job, despite the fact that he liked the job very much, I sent him, hoping to do for him what Proust had done for me, a Xerox of two paragraphs about Marcel's anxiety when his father agrees to let him abandon diplomacy and devote himself to literature, saying to Marcel's mother, among other things, "He's no longer a child. He knows pretty well now what he likes." The passage explored various anxieties his father's response aroused in Marcel, starting with the question of whether his writing deserved that much generosity. More deeply, he had always thought of himself as standing on the threshold of life, with that life before him. Now, it appeared, it had already begun. When would the fun start? Time had him in its grip. Soon he would be old. My son had a hard time with the passage, whose complexity and length I cannot reproduce without quoting the whole thing and disastrously tearing the fabric of my own discussion (Proust is deeply competitive: it's always a choice between yourself and him), but eventually he understood it and appreciated the consolation that parallel experience provides.

By the start of volume 3, I felt so solid on my sea legs that I could even—and easily—distinguish between "good Proust" and "bad Proust." The opening of *The Guermantes Way* was bad Proust. The sentences were short and jumpy, lacking associative flow. The similes, of which I now considered myself a connoisseur, seemed conspicuously forced and arid, comparing Marcel's experience not to other experience, but to Greek myth or the Bible—literary events not lived ones. A person having to return to his seat after the intermission at the theater, parting the crowd, is compared to the Hebrews in the Red Sea. Boo! Marcel's idea that a certain gentleman in the audience was the Prince of Saxony on his way to see the Duchesse de Guermantes accompanied this gentleman like a deity who, invisible to everyone else, accompanies a Greek soldier in battle. Hiss!

As I review these opening sections of *The Guermantes Way* now, I see no lapse. Marcel and his family have moved to Paris and are living in the same building as the Guermantes. Marcel begins his ascent into the Guermantes circle. The somewhat stilted similes I noted are there, but so is much else that is marvelous. Why did I focus on the glitches? To signify that a new stage had been reached in my reading of Proust? That I was not merely capable of enjoyment but of discernment as well? Because, in the continuing underlying competition between us, a competition in which

I'd had to begin by ceding him the supremacy, not just reading him entirely on his terms but giving over my life to him, I could regain power over Proust by rejecting parts of him? In this ostensibly responsive but subconsciously hostile mode, I conceded ("Even I have to admit") that by page 108, Proust was back in form. This was, I noted, "prime Proust," condescending praise which while seeming to award the Artist five points awards the Critic ten. The passage I liked so much described—remembrance of things past—Marcel falling asleep. See how far I had come? I might have flunked that exam the first time around, but this time I would get an A+!

Falling asleep now, Marcel is older, no longer a child at Combray longing for his mother, but a young man visiting his friend Saint-Loup, who is with his regiment in a town called Doncières. Marcel has gone there to escape from his obsession with the Duchesse de Guermantes but also to solicit Saint-Loup's help in arranging an introduction to her. The regimental band plays outside his window, sometimes interfering with sleep, sometimes absorbed into the process. The description of falling asleep is about 1,500 words long, that is about the length of this chapter up to the paragraph starting, "I had read *Swann's Way* so conscious of my own pleasure or lack of it that I could hardly enjoy it." It presents the gradual detachment of the mind from everyday reality and its entry into another world where problems that have been addressed over and over by the conscious mind throughout the day are solved in another way.

Sometimes the experience of reading Proust is like the experience—were we ever to subject ourselves to it—of watching a feature-length movie in slow motion. He pays such minute attention to the sequence of emotions and experiences which constitute any psychological event, he breaks down all psychological movement into so many component parts that all motion seems suspended, and what we see, however fascinating, is no longer sequential action but a series of static gestures. A visual analogy exists in the photographs of Eadweard Muybridge, showing, for example, a woman walking up a ramp or a horse running in frames of split seconds, each allowing us to understand locomotion in a way we never had before. Describing how the mind blurs, softens, and distorts as we fall asleep, gradually escaping from the world of reality into the world of dreams, Proust isolates the moment at which we notice with glee a sudden lapse in logic in our own obsessive thoughts. This moment signals the opening of a door into the other world. His description of it makes me recall the famous freeze-frame in Muybridge's study of animal locomotion by which he proved Leland Stanford's hunch that at some point a running horse has all four legs off the ground. I think, too, of Harold Egerton's strobe photo of a milk spill, proving that a splash, random and sloppy to the unassisted eye, forms a perfect circle in scientific reality. I have known that moment of glee at the advent of illogic, but I've never read about it, never seen it reconstituted as literature, and hence have never really been sure of its existence outside my own experience. Thanks to the literary equivalent of the freeze-frame, one has the exhilarating feeling over and over in reading Proust of coming into undiscovered country, of reading about experiences never written about before, even though the experiences he writes about—falling asleep or falling in love—are about as basic as human experience gets.

Although most literature represents a radically condensed and speeded-up version of life, so that the baby of page 1 is the dying old man of the final chapter of a book we read in a month at most, the pace of life is generally faster than the pace of Proust and generally more even. I had been reading Proust for four months before I reached the end of volume 3, with the Guermantes's party especially slow going. I zipped through the opening of *Sodom and Gomorrah*, which introduces Charlus as a homosexual, takes us back to Balbec, describes Marcel's affair with Albertine as well as Charlus's affair with the violinist Morel. But it took me five months to read the account of Monsieur and Madame Verdurin's party in that volume. Admittedly that was a bit much: I was distracted; I had other work to do; I went on some travels. But I defy anyone to read that section in the matter of hours which the Verdurins's party in reality might have occupied. No more than *Ulysses* can be read in a day. Like other modernist innovators in the novel—James Joyce and Virginia Woolf—Proust compressed the time of the "action" (Bloom's day in Dublin leading up to his meeting with Stephen, Mrs. Dalloway's day in London leading up to her party) in order to anchor the narrative while the prose line wandered in time and space, with any moment in the present acting as a kind of diving platform offering access to a lake of memory, anticipation, and association.

Roger Shattuck, in his "Modern Masters Series" book on Proust, frankly lists the parts of *Lost Time* he thinks you can skip. He wants to suggest a kind of minimal investment that will nonetheless allow you to experience Proust's masterpiece. I think this is brave of him and kindly meant. Sometimes I consult his list to check my progress and the coming attractions. According to Shattuck, you must read most of *Swann's Way* and part 2 of *Within a Budding Grove*. In *The Guermantes Way*, he finds essential only chapter 1 of part 2. In *Sodom and Gomorrah*, only the first thirty and the last thirty pages. In *The Captive*, only the first thirty pages and the two hundred pages on the concert.

Ahead of me I saw next to *The Fugitive* the single, uncompromising word "omit."

Omit? Omit the whole volume? What was the problem? I could hardly wait to get to *The Fugitive* and see for myself. Perhaps unsurprisingly, given what we know about perversity and paradox, this was among my favorite sections of *Lost Time*. Albertine, the zesty young woman who beomes Marcel's mistress, lives in his Paris apartment in a state of virtual captivity created by his jealousy. Eventually she leaves him and dies soon after in a riding accident. Even better than the brilliant section on Marcel's grandmother's death, *The Fugitive* describes what it is like to have a loved one die. In Proustian detail, which is to say slowly, patiently, imaginatively, thoroughly, bringing everything in his mind to bear on each observation, comparing, contrasting, contextualizing, historicizing, drawing out of his inner darkness the precise words needed to render the emotion in all its particularity as it's never been rendered in words before, he presents the stages of Marcel's grief and the process of recovery.

I was so taken with this section that, whenever a conversation could be crowbarred around to Proust or death or literature, I would recount whole chunks of it, citing in pedantic detail what Proust had to say about the process of detachment. "Proust says you have to trace your steps backward to where you were before you knew the person who died. That is, you have to forget them in order to accept that they're dead. If you still actively love them, it's too painful."

"I don't feel that way about Jimmy," said Alison Lurie one day over lunch in Key West, applying what I'd said Proust said to the death of her friend, the poet James Merrill. "I just feel that he's gone some place very far away. Like Australia."

I felt foolish, so reasonable was Alison's attitude. My own explanation of mourning seemed labored and tortuous compared to "I just feel he's in Australia." To excuse myself, I can only say I was thinking of my father, whose death, unlike James Merrill's, was no surprise and whom I could in no way imagine as having gone to Australia. At his age? In his state of health? Without my mother?

Still, I was beginning to wonder if I had a mind of my own or if I was just a puppet speaking for Proust. If a friend consulted me on a question of human behavior, I would search my notes and my memory to see if Proust had anything to say about it. Was there anyone in literature, Wendy asked, who could make sense of her friend Irene? Was there any character who varied as much as Irene did between charm and relentless vindictiveness? Yes. In Charlus, as Proust explains, the desire to charm produced extreme alternations between affection (if you were charmed) and hatred (if you seemed immune). What should my son do about the downstairs neighbor, who constantly and unreasonably complained about noise? Neurotics, Proust counseled, are irritated at the slightest provocation by inoffensive enemies, but as soon as anyone takes the offensive against them, they become meek. So I advised my son, who had gone out of his way to be polite, to change tactics and stand up to the neighbor. The harrassing calls stopped.

I was twelve months into my project, almost through volume

5, which contains *The Captive* and *The Fugitive*, and reading Proust had become as much a way of life as a literary pastime, closer to a religious practice than to the usual discrete encounter with a single work of art. I retreated into my communion with the text as a way of vacationing from daily life, as a Sunday worshipper might put aside routine concerns on entering a church, returning to the way I'd read as a fifteen-year-old, when, since I had no date for New Year's Eve, to bury my chagrin, to keep from thinking of the fun I was missing, I immersed myself in *Gone With the Wind* and finished it in one long celebratory night. Now, if I was distracted by social demands, household chores, bills to pay, calls to return, supplies to restock, I could momentarily suspend my obligations to the world of the living by picking up Proust, the essential escapism of what I was doing neutralized by the belief that I was enlarging my understanding of the world as well as renewing my zest for it. Proust was solving my problems, structurally, by providing an alternative activity, and substantively, by functioning as a sourcebook, the Whole Earth Catalogue of Human Emotions, the sacred text that seers consult for answers, the chicken entrails they read. Moreover, Proust's style had permeated my mind and changed my literary taste. A mixed blessing: everything I'd written before, whose chief virtues were clarity and brevity, now seemed pinched and parsimonious.

At the start of my project, I had turned down the corners of pages to mark passages I especially liked or wanted to remember: I would come back to them some time in the future. With volume 2, I started writing notes in the blank pages at the back of the book, jotting down page numbers, saying to myself, "Quote this," but not writing down what I wanted to quote. By volume 5, my notes were so extensive that I ran out of blank pages at the back of the book and then at the front of it, too. I was copying out whole passages. Passage after passage. I responded so thoroughly to Proust by this point that there was almost nothing I didn't think worth coming back to. I had to start reading at the computer, so I could transcribe the beloved passages quickly enough to move on.

Eventually it struck me that nothing less than total transcription of the text would do. Anything more condensed was inadequate tribute, inadequate understanding, unworthy of its subject. Like the hero of Borges's story, "Pierre Menard, Author of the Quixote," I didn't want to write a contemporary appreciation of Proust, or my version of Proust, I wanted to write Proust over from the beginning, word for word, and have it be mine. I had run into the fundamental problem of criticism as an account of literature, and it reproduced the problem of literature as an account of life. A translation, a reduction, a condensation, an approximation, a metaphor is the best that can be achieved in art, no matter how inclusive, as an account of life, and the same is true for criticism as an account of art. No matter how full we make our accounts of reading, no matter how hard we try to make our style sympathetic to the work under discussion and not to violate it by analysis, what we produce is less than the text it describes. Just as there is no way to live a life except minute by minute, there is no way to experience a novel except word by word, and when I reach the end of Proust, the only thing for me to do will be to start to re-read.

I am almost afraid to say how much I like the even tenor of my days in this year of reading Proust. Insofar as I possess a religious sense, and I think that in a citydweller's wary way I do, I believe in the odds, a powerful force whose vagaries the wise person seeks to understand but which he or she must ultimately learn merely to accept. "The odds" dictates constant change in human affairs. Nothing lasts. Fashions change. The stock market goes up and down. Men wear long hair or short. Japanese cars replace American cars and are in turn replaced by European cars. People fall in love and marry, then divorce. Artists dazzle for awhile with their inventiveness then fall into self-repetition or sterility and sometimes, to our amazement, dazzle afresh. The odds are that as soon as I praise the uneventfulness of my life that very quality will disappear.

From superstitious dread, I can hardly bring myself to name the ways in which my life's placidity could be violated, yet at the same time I believe that if I name enough of them, I can ward off the evil, or at least be exempt from those I name. Someone I love could die, be seriously injured, become blind or incontinent or paralyzed from the neck down, have a stroke or cerebral hemmorhage or heart attack, get cancer or Alzheimer's or multiple sclerosis. I myself could get sick. I could lose my job. I could be swindled and lose my savings. I could be stalked. I could be mugged. I could stand up on a leg that had fallen asleep, lose my balance, fall, and rip my knee apart. I could realize that I'd been abused as a child. I could become bitter and depressed. I could be sued. I could spend the rest of my life in a jail or a courtroom or a hospital. My house could burn. The United States could go to war. There could be civil war, riots in New York, student rebellions, military coups. There could be floods, droughts, hurricanes, fires, even earthquakes. Clouds of insects could swarm up from South America: killer bees, gypsy moths. All the trees could die. All the vegetables could be blighted. Bats could be overharvested in the Far East, causing the rain forests to die, land to erode, seas to rise, global warming to increase, and before you know it we could all be extinct.

Somewhere in the world, something awful is happening every minute. You have only to pick up a newspaper or a history book or watch the nature programs on TV to learn specific examples of the Platonic forms of catastrophe. The fire in the charity bazaar in Paris in 1896 in which duchesses were trampled and burned is the fire in the Triangle Shirtwaist factory in turn-of-the-century Manhattan is the fire in the Latino social club in the present-day Bronx. People are trampled and burned. Duchesses and seamstresses, dowagers and teenagers. No one is exempt. Planes crash. Cars go off the road. Boats overturn. Scuba equipment fails. Swimmers get caught in riptides. Climbers fall off mountains.

I live with the fear of disaster. In every situation I imagine what can go wrong. There's magical thinking here: if I imagine it, it won't happen. And psychic preparation, like the air-raid drills in my childhood, when we all filed into the hall and stood with our heads bent against the wall and arms crossed behind our necks, actions which could hardly have helped in the event of a nuclear fireball, but which helped our teachers and parents get through the atomic traumas of the 1950s. What can be imagined, we think, can be endured. We're emotionally prepared. But sometimes I wonder which is better: this imagination of disaster, which lives in advance through terrible things that never occur, or the perpetual outrage and surprise of the innocent mind.

Just as some people prefer smooth peanut butter to chunky, I have come to prefer an even-textured daily life to excitement alternating with boredom, anxiety with depression. It's a taste that comes with middle age.

When I was young, I wanted peak experience, intensity, every moment crammed to the edges with incident. I wanted passion and exaltation. I wanted every summer day to be spent at the beach. I wanted to fall in love over and over and to make love every day. Now I want familiar people around me. I like dinner parties where all the other guests are known. The time of each day I spend asleep has come to seem sensuous and deeply pleasant, a joy in itself, not the necessary but tedious period of restoration I saw it as when I was young. I spend my summers anywhere other people are not. The beach seems too crowded. I experience it as relief that I no longer need to be in the ocean. The same is true for sex.

When I turned fifty, my mother said, "This is the best decade. You don't have to be afraid anymore." I instinctively felt these words made sense but didn't articulate to myself the sense they made, putting that off for later. First, I savored them. I knew they were a great gift, a blessing. Their force, as it turned out, was pre-scriptive. By saying, "You don't have to be afraid," my mother, like some shimmering Good Fairy in a tulle ball gown, tiara, and magic wand, made me not afraid, wafted over me the gift of confidence. Later, when I tried to understand exactly what she meant in saying "You don't have to be afraid anymore," my mother's words appeared more and more sibylline. The more I sought to confront their truth, the more their truth receded, like the Bonairean flamingo, standing one-legged in a shallow pond, who allowed me to see his outline but flew out of sight when I tried to get closer.

What is it I no longer have to be afraid of? The threat of nature, random violence, and civil disturbance is always there.

The threat of illness and declining power only increases with age. Perhaps she means my life is established. I've made my mark, whatever it is, however eccentric or private or small. I have my family. I no longer have to try to impress people: I am who I am. Perhaps she means, "You no longer need be afraid to die. You don't have to fear you haven't lived."

Thoreau wanted to live deliberately so that when the time came for him to die, he would not discover that he had not lived. By living he meant "seeing deeply," understanding from within the life of nature. My own fear of the unlived life was less intellectual. I felt it whenever a plane I was traveling in hit a bump and I thought we were going down. My stomach fell away from itself like an elevator moving fast. I'd pray, "Not now. Let me not die a virgin." Or later, "Let me not die before I get married." Or later, "Let me have a baby first." Or, "Let me write a book." Or, "Let me see Teddy into college." Now, when the plane loses altitude, my stomach still tightens—it's instinctive; I love life—but the horror of the unlived life doesn't follow. Biological necessity has released me. I have swum upstream and spawned. I can paddle around happily for a long time yet, but speaking of myself as an organism in nature, it's okay for me to die.

I could, of course, ask my mother to explain what she meant. She's eighty-eight and gets mentally sharper as her body gets weaker. The baby of her large Russian-Jewish family, the first to be born in America, formerly frail and dependent, she has survived to this great age to her own and everyone else's surprise, shrunk to two-thirds her former size, her cardiac organ failing, but with miraculously increased courage and wit. She would happily explain what she meant. But I won't ask for an explanation, fearing that if I emphasize the expository function of her words, they will lose their magical power, or perhaps turn out to have a quite specific—and negligible—meaning. I prefer to keep them as a banner over my fifties: thou shalt not be afraid.

2

TV Guide

"A simple slice of bread, but one that we eat, gives us more pleasure than all the ortolans, leverets and rock-partridges that were set before Louis XV, and the blade of grass quivering a few inches in front of our eyes as we lie on the hillside may conceal from us the vertiginous summit of a mountain if the latter is several miles away." *The Fugitive*

WHEN I WAS WRITING MY first book, I had a love affair with a man in publishing. He was short, pudgy, owl-eyed, but so smart and funny, so much fun to be with, that he had no trouble attracting women, even if he didn't like the terms on which he attracted them and made it even worse by imagining that the women who loved him were gritting their teeth and ignoring his person in order to avail themselves of his clout. So of course I did the worst thing I could have and submitted my book to him as a potential publisher. Both of us now were convinced that I was interested in him only for what he could do for me. It was a toss-up which of us thought worse of me. I hoped I hadn't gone to bed with him only to get something out of him, but who was I to know if I had or hadn't? It seemed all too likely. "You have so much going for you. Why do you have to imagine you're a writer?" my lover said in revenge. And: "Some men give diamonds. I'll give a book." But in the end, he refused even to give me the book, implying by his action, about which he wrapped a good deal of anguish, that he was finally too principled and my book too dreadful to go through with the sleazy bargain we'd struck, and making of me not just a hooker but a hooker who'd been stiffed.

Two events helped me out of this depressing situation. First, I went to a psychiatrist, an old woman on Central Park West, who, hearing about my worries and his worries, suspecting the ways in which I must be hurting him if he was hurting me in the ways he was hurting me, said, "You don't sound like a very good couple." This was news to me. I had always thought up to this time (I was in my mid-thirties) that a girl should find a guy whose mind operated more or less on the same wavelength as hers but who was smarter than she was. My lover loved books and was smarter than I was, therefore we made a good couple. No one ever told me about the strange needs people bring to sex, and I don't mean for bondage or abuse, but for simple erotic attraction. No one convinced me that a girl might not be attracted by the smartest guy in sight. I truly expected the psychiatrist to be impressed with my lover because his Freudian credentials were so good, as witnessed by books he'd published whose titles I was prepared to cite. It amazed me that she didn't seem interested, that she thought him a bad match for me.

The second event happened early on in the affair, but I didn't realize its importance until Dr. S. told me we weren't a good match. Then it all made sense. I had gone to see Brian De Palma's film, *Carrie*, and had loved it, scared silly by the telekinetic teenager who makes knives fly out of the kitchen drawer to crucify her own mother and who wreaks a terrible revenge on the school friends who humiliate her. My lover was full of scorn. Why was I wasting my time with junk like that? I would destroy my mind, rot it out, if I didn't pay more attention to what I exposed it to. At the time I felt puzzled, the same bewilderment as when, a six-year-old, I took an intelligence test that demanded I match complementary objects—broom and dustpan, paper and crayon, frying pan and spatula (the kind of test whose embedded cultural biases we have since learned to mistrust) and at the end of the test was left with a needle and teapot. A deeply uneasy feeling of things not fitting, things not belonging together. When Dr. S. said, "You don't sound like a good couple," I remembered what my lover had said about rotting my brain and suddenly understood: I didn't belong with a man who looked down on popular culture. I should never ally myself, however temporarily, with a man who doesn't like scary movies and junk TV.

"And . . . if I found Saint-Loup a trifle earnest," wrote Proust, "he could not understand why I was not more earnest still. Never judging anything except by its intellectual weightiness, never perceiving the magic appeal of the imagination that I found in things which he condemned as frivolous, he was astonished that I—to whom he imagined himself to be so utterly inferior—could take any interest in them." (Vol. 2, p. 428)

No matter how much time I've spent this year reading Proust, I've spent more watching television. Every evening when we're at home, after dinner L. and I go up to our bedroom, lie on our bed, our backs propped up by the pillows, no doubt causing spinal damage, and watch TV, a 20-inch Mitsubishi with a color screen and remote control. I hold the remote, which has become an indispensable part of TV watching; we use it to mute the ads and to channel surf. I don't like the ads muted: I consider advertising an art form of sorts and prefer to take in the whole work of art, but L., whose French ears can stand only so much English, insists on it. He doesn't like channel surfing. For his sake I mute the ads, and for mine he allows channel surfing.

We rarely comment on what we see. We don't discuss characters, motives, plots, and drama. We go for hours without talking beyond, "I'm going to the kitchen. Would you like something?" Yet these silent hours are times of intimacy. My friend David, who has no TV in our hometown, Middletown, Connecticut, occasionally asks to join us for some indispensable show like *NYPD Blue*, and sometimes we feel we have to let him; the request is so modest, so reasonable, to refuse so churlish. But really, like Garbo, we prefer to be alone.

Watching TV, we do different things, according to our natures. I am a narrative junkie. I consume stories in all forms. TV shows, novels, dreams, newspaper accounts of kidnappings, murders, heroism, panic, disaster: they all feed the habit. In a way they're all the same. When my son Teddy was a little boy, he used to tell me his dreams at breakfast. "Any interesting dreams last night?" I asked one morning, and he replied, "Nothing but commercials." In whatever form, there's a million gazillion stories out there, and Teddy and I both need our daily fix of them.

Not L. He doesn't tune into the narrative. He watches images, colors, and shapes. If, while we're watching TV, I go to the bathroom or take a phone call and ask him what's happened when I was gone, he has no idea. The complicated, allusive screenplays that delight me irritate and frustrate him. For him, the TV is a meditative object, like a stone in a Japanese garden. As I move rapidly from one thing to another, compulsively switching channels, he brings to bear a Zen monk's tolerance. *Murder, She Wrote* or *L.A. Law, Gone With the Wind* or *Terminator 2, 60 Minutes* or the evening news, it's all spume and delusion to him, a flickering picture, a dance of pixels. At most he takes in genre and setting. He enjoys certain settings more than others: New York a lot, a tropical reef most of all, and he refuses to watch shows set in hospitals. L. can't understand why anyone would want to spend more time in a hospital than they have to.

Aside from that one prohibition, I wield the control. I choose what we watch. I determine the pace of transitions. My channel surfing seems random but it isn't entirely. Just as I wouldn't serve my shrimp with rum and mint preceded by a cucumber soup with mint or a tomato-based fish stew before a pork roast with ratatouille, I wouldn't alternate between two police shows or follow one nature program with another. In channel surfing as in menu planning, refreshment of the palate is the principle. One tomato dish, one coconut dish, one mushroom dish is enough for any dinner. So is one wildlife program, one history program, one sports event, one costume drama, one fifties film, one homicide, or one courtroom enough for an evening's entertainment.

Recently we watched the third episode of *Pride and Prejudice* alternating with *NYPD Blue*. Either one would have been enough.

In fact, I would have preferred to devote my full attention to *NYPD Blue*. But *Pride and Prejudice*'s conclusion overlapped. We had no choice. We had to watch both. For a while it gave me a tremendous sense of power and privilege to be in two worlds simultaneously. According to Proust, the automobile in its early days gave people just such an exhilarating sense of simultaneous access. They were able to be in two places on the same day which had never before been seen on the same day, even with the help of the fastest horse. Television extends access over time. I was simultaneously in contemporary Manhattan and in Regency England, to say nothing of my actual location in Key West, Florida. When the shows ended, however, I experienced a double loss, deprived not just of one world but two. I had to tune into an old episode of *Law and Order* to come down, as experienced druggies will use one drug to help them come off another, a little pot to end an acid trip, heroin to ease off cocaine.

On a typical night, it is 1942, the year of my birth, "The Year of the Generals" on The Learning Channel. General MacArthur is in the Philippines. Manila falls to the Japanese. The Americans retreat to Bataan and Corregidor. The soldiers have no food, no supplies. They can't hold out. General MacArthur is ordered to leave, too much a symbol of American power for FDR to let him be captured by the enemy. Bataan falls, later Corregidor.

Survivors of Bataan marched sixty-five miles to the camps, starving. They fell from exhaustion and were shot or bayoneted by the side of the road. As the march continued, the Americans walked past a trail of corpses of fellow soldiers. One man who spoke, now old and overweight, tears in his eyes, his voice choked, recalled helping and being helped on the Death March by a buddy who died minutes after reaching the camp.

Next, Nimitz and the Battle of Midway. Wave after wave of American planes shot down. Only the last made it through, released their torpedos, blew up the Japanese carriers, turned the tide of the Pacific war. One navy fighter pilot watched from the water, his plane shot down, surrounded by Japanese warships aflame, fearing to be saved by the wrong side, rescued rightly, and flown to Washington to tell the President the tale of our first Pacific victory. He was the only man in his squadron to survive and the only man who saw the whole battle.

Tears in my eyes now. Too moved to channel surf during the commercials, I merely mute them, thinking of the goodness of my countrymen, the joy and pain of surviving, the awful democracy of combat, the majestic war games of the generals, the weekly TV series on the Pacific war when I was a child called *Victory at Sea*, whose theme song was by Richard Rodgers, my brother in his white navy uniform graduating from Dartmouth in 1954 and going off to Korea, hearing on vacation in the South of France in the summer of 1990 the news of the invasion of Kuwait by the Iraqis, fearing a war in which Teddy would have to serve.

Time to go back to the generals, now Patton and Eisenhower. Patton the bad boy, condemned onscreen as a slaughterer of soldiers by Andy Rooney, who began his career covering the invasion. Eisenhower the good, the humble, the political animal, the coalition leader, *his* early moves covered by Walter Cronkite. Every general has his attendant journalist as the shark has its remora. Ike in despair over the invasion of North Africa, not wanting to invade Europe in such a roundabout way, bowing to Monty. Mother always told me how the fleet was massing under her window at Doctors' Hospital for the invasion of North Africa when I was born, but I'd never known the invasion of North Africa was, from a military point of view, probably a mistake, an example of British caution triumphing over American guts.

I flip through a few channels finding Cary Grant and Deborah Kerr in gorgeous late 1950s Technicolor, she in gray slacks and a yellow V-neck sweater in a stately room with pale blue walls. Soon Robert Mitchum blunders in, an American tourist. It is clear that he and Deborah Kerr are going to have an affair. I can't bear to watch her leave Cary Grant, an elegant but impoverished English earl, for Robert Mitchum, a brash American millionaire, so I switch back to the war. Patton is racing across Sicily with Monty right behind. We watch the Italians, tired of war, welcome the Americans. But the commercials are coming more quickly and getting longer. Back to Deborah, Cary, and Bob.

Sure enough. She can't get him out of her mind. She goes up to London, ostensibly for the hairdresser. Cary Grant knows why she's really going but escorts her gallantly to the train. "I'll be back tomorrow, darling," she says. He says, "I'll expect you when I see you, darling."

The Allies are at Messina. The war is moving quickly toward the Normandy landings, which we just saw a few weeks ago, and the commercials, for interactive CD-ROM versions of great battles, are getting intolerable. We switch forever from war to adultery.

Deborah Kerr has stayed in London with Robert Mitchum, as Cary Grant knew she would. Mitchum wants to marry her, offering her an easy, beautiful life. She is tired of raising mushrooms for a living and making ends meet. Cary Grant invites the millionaire back to the estate for the weekend and challenges him to a duel. Although both of them shoot to miss, Grant is lightly wounded, and all Kerr's love for him returns.

Kerr and Mitchum starred together in one of my favorite movies of childhood, *Heaven Knows, Mr. Allison*, in which he, playing a marine, and she, playing a nun, are stranded together on a Pacific island occupied by the Japanese. It had the sexiness of renunciation and impossibility, still understood in 1950. In this movie, they have no chemistry at all, but there is a kind of sexiness for me—that of the resolved chord—in the fact that the chain of associations has led me back to where the evening began, an island in the Pacific during World War II.

Winding down, I flip around the channels. TLC now shows helicopters, naked Asian children running down a jungle path, people fleeing rice fields, Schwarzkopf and his remora Dan Rather, both young.

"No, no!" says L. in horror. "Not Vietnam!"

I find some figure skating on ESPN, a women's competition at San Jose. We have missed Bobek and Kwan, but we see someone surpass herself and someone else fall on every jump, so the range of emotions is covered.

Now and then I run into TV people in real life. L. and I went once to a New York City cocktail party where Tom Brokaw was also a guest. There were some four dozen people, few of whom I knew. But Tom Brokaw, at that time, we watched every night delivering the news. I saw him more often than I saw my own mother, my own son. I spent thirty pleasant, effortless minutes with him a day, during which he looked me directly in the eyes and spoke to me about important matters. Nightly we extended to him the intimacy we denied, except on rare occasions, to our good friend David. He came into our bedroom. I felt completely comfortable with him. So when I saw him at the Bernsteins's party, my first impulse was to go right over to him. Then I realized he was not my good old friend but a TV celebrity. Our intimacy was entirely one-sided. I drew back, betrayed. In some way, I felt he had no business showing up at parties like an ordinary person. He ought to stay on the screen. Not to stay there was as confusing to those of us who watched as when, in Woody Allen's film, *The Purple Rose of Cairo*, the explorer comes out of the movie into the audience and seduces Mia Farrow, taking her out to dinner with only play money to spend.

My life as a conscious being is more or less coterminal with broadcast TV in America. One of my earliest social memories is sleeping at a friend's house to watch the election returns when Truman defeated Dewey. I was six. I didn't care, nor did my friend, whether Truman defeated Dewey or Dewey Truman. On the edge of our seats, we were watching the medium itself, the pure miracle of instantaneous visual information.

Shortly after the 1948 elections my family got its own TV, a Magnavox with a small screen in a large wooden cabinet. It was placed in a room we called "the library," because it had bookshelves. It was actually the family entertainment room, holding my father's stamp collection, my trading card collection, and the square table on which my mother played canasta and mah-jongg with her friends. Its floor was green-and-tan linoleum tile squares in a checkerboard pattern. It was wallpapered in bamboo trellises and ivy.

Many of the rooms in our thoroughly middle-class house, a white brick structure in Dutch Colonial style, in a densely settled

South Shore Long Island suburb forty-five minutes from New York City, bore names more appropriate to the English country house of the Clue board. In addition to the library, there was a breakfast room, an entrance room, a butler's pantry, and a solarium, as well as the more usual living room, dining room, kitchen, and bedrooms. Nothing was grand about these rooms except their names, and perhaps the perception of them held by my mother, who had started life in an unheated railroad flat in the Bronx.

The breakfast room, for example, where we ate not just breakfast, but lunch and dinner as well, had, like the library, color-coordinated linoleum floor and papered walls, in this case a ruby red floor and paper with berries. It was a squarish room, with the table in the middle, an oak octagonal table in the so-called Early American style so precious to the postwar generation. On the wall hung a beaten brass decorative platter and a cuckoo clock, treasures brought back by my parents from a Caribbean cruise as impetuously as Hearst gathered art for San Simeon.

The cuckoo clock, if you pulled its chain every day to wind it, worked very well, and a wooden bird popped out of a little birdhouse every hour on the hour and said "*Dong!* Cuckoo!", while on the half hour the mechanism chimed. Why we needed our days chopped up into such precise and little pieces I do not remember, unless perhaps it was to listen to the radio, which was prominently placed in the breakfast room in a niche of the built-in hutch. On Sunday nights, when family radio was best, we sometimes listened to the radio through dinner, seated around the table. Otherwise we would pull our chairs close to the radio and focus our eyes on it as though we were in a theater and could see Jack Benny, Rochester, and the rest in the little Bakelite box.

There was nothing as gripping on early TV as the finely wrought programs of late forties radio, *The Shadow*, *The FBI in Peace and War*, and *Batman*. So the radio days didn't end immediately with the coming of the television set. But inevitably programming improved, and the library became the center of family life and the TV the hearth, rather than the breakfast room and the radio. There came a time when we abandoned Fred Allen and Jack Benny and gathered instead in front of the TV to watch Sid

Caesar and Imogene Coca, *The Camel News Caravan*, *The Hall-mark Hall of Fame*, *What's My Line?*, and *I Love Lucy*. My father never missed *Perry Mason*, ostensibly to learn from the portly lawyer how his clients expected him to behave. My own personal favorites were Howdy Doody, Hopalong Cassidy, and Tom Corbett, Space Cadet.

If that house saw one pivotal night in my childhood like the night that Proust recalls at such length, when he wished his mother to come upstairs and kiss him good night, it was a night when, telling myself stories in my head before I fell asleep, I worked myself into a state of terror and cried for my father. It was winter, and the steam heat was coming up in the radiators, making knocking and clanking sounds. I convinced myself that there was a ghost in the radiator making the noise. In another thirty seconds, the ghost would get out of the radiator and grab me. Part of me knew there was no ghost in the radiator yet wanted to act as though I thought there was in order to see if someone would come and save me from it. If I sounded an alarm, I could have my own private fire drill. I sounded the alarm. I screamed. I screamed with all my heart and lungs. Immediately I heard galumphing footsteps on the staircase. My father was beside my bed, my brother Richard right behind him. Both assured me there was no ghost in the radiator. My father sat in a chair next to the bed until I calmed down and went to sleep. The fire drill never had to be repeated.

My father was the one who read to me before I went to sleep at night. He especially liked *A Child's Garden of Verses* and a Golden Book of no special distinction containing 365 stories, one for each night of the year. After he left me and turned out the light in my room, I would often take the book into the tent I made of my covers and read by flashlight the next night's story. For whatever reason, I was given remarkably little literature for children. No Winnie the Pooh, no *Wind in the Willows*, no Uncle Wiggily or Mary Poppins, no Peter Rabbit or Alice. About the only children's books my parents gave me were the five *Babar* books by Jean de Brunhoff, which were relatively new in America when I was a child. My imagination attached itself passionately to the little elephant. I had no trouble identifying with a little male pachyderm, no more than I would have trouble identifying with cowboys. I identified with Babar as he made his way from the jungle to the city, was befriended by the old lady, discovered clothing and elevators and all the blessings of civilization. He beckoned me toward the future. I, too, could make it from the scary jungle of my own magical thinking into the clarity of grown-up thought. I, too, could advance from the helplessness of the very small and uncoordinated child into mastery of the physical world. These optimistic books offered me the hope of progress, of growing up as growing better, more in control, whereas the English tradition, when I later encountered it, always seemed to me stupidly to idealize the state of being a child, and to inhabit self-consciously imaginative worlds which I found creepy. I much preferred the elephants who went to the theater and watered their gardens with their trunks.

When Babar married his cousin Celeste and they started having children, I stopped identifying with him and started thinking of him as my father. But I could go back to the other identification easily, depending on which book I was reading. Babar was me, struggling to grow up and master the world. Babar was my father, the devoted family man, cuddly, protective, unthreatening.

My father was a devoted family man because his own father hardly ever came home in the evenings except to sleep. His father, Meyer Davidoff, was an intellectual, more of one than I will ever be. I like reading books. He liked discussing ideas. He had been studying to be a rabbi in Vilna when he chose to emigrate rather than serve in the czar's army, a common enough story among Eastern European Jews at the turn of the century. On the long crossing of the ocean, my grandfather was converted from his Old World faith, threw his religious paraphernalia into the water, and landed in New York a socialist. He went into the insurance business, which I always thought an odd choice for a socialist but my father assured me was not: "Somebody had to do it." He insured the immigrants' organizations which he helped to found, notably the

Workmen's Circle. He was also one of the founders of *The Jewish Daily Forward* and the International Ladies' Garment Workers Union. How did he do all this founding? Apparently by sitting around and gabbing with other intellectuals on the Lower East Side. The subject of their endless discussion, according to my father, was the difference between socialism and communism and which one was superior. My grandfather spent decades of happy evenings working through this issue at the Café Royal.

When Grandpa made enough money, he moved my grandmother and their eight children from the Lower East Side where he and all the other Jews had plopped down upon arrival in New York, uptown to the tonier neighborhood of Harlem. But he himself still spent most of his time on the Lower East Side, pondering, arguing, doing business, and shmoozing. Only on the Sabbath did he dine at home. For this reason, his children, growing up, hardly ever saw him, and my father vowed that he would live differently, priding himself on always being home for dinner, never doing business in the evening. Five days a week he took the Long Island Railroad home in the evenings and back into the city in the mornings. Later, he had a little red Plymouth convertible and did the same thing by car. I don't remember him ever missing a night.

He had been a skinny young man with wire-rimmed glasses. He studied accounting at NYU and then astounded his family by wanting to leave New York to go to law school. He chose Harvard, when it was still up to the student to choose a school and up to him, too, to avoid flunking out. My father, though he claimed to have spent much of his time in Cambridge playing pinochle (a very Harvard pose, that of casual scholarship), managed to graduate and went back to New York to practice law in 1929. At first, the only job he could get was with Legal Aid, for no pay. My mother, as a teacher in the New York City school system, had prize Depression employment and supported both of them.

My mother's family had consisted more of artists than of businessmen and scholars. Her father, who'd been a goldsmith in Russia, did not prosper in America. From master goldsmith, he became a jewelry repairer. He spoke only Russian and Yiddish, never learning English. They were abysmally poor. My aunt

Molly, my mother's older sister, worked in a kind of sweatshop. It was a time when elder children were sacrificed for the younger ones. My mother was the first in her family to go to college—Hunter, the immigrants' daughters' school of choice.

A Hunter classmate, one of my father's sisters, introduced them. My father, then in his third year at NYU, was immediately smitten with this blonde and blue-eyed beauty, a Jewish girl who somehow had ended up looking like Leni Riefenstahl. He asked her to the junior prom. She already had a date. He pursued her. He asked her out for New Year's Eve. He couldn't wait to show her off to his family. Wouldn't they be surprised that he could get a date with such a good-looking woman! Mother, for her part, thought my father was the smartest man she'd ever met. For her, it worked.

When my father was at law school, my mother took the boat that went from New York to Boston through the Cape Cod Canal to visit him. She took the bus, an eleven-hour trip. She took the train. They were "secretly married" by a justice of the peace in Boston in the spring of 1928. When my father came to New York, Mother told her parents she was spending the weekend with her friend Leona, and she and my father would check into a sleazy hotel in the theater district. It was to do this that they had secretly married. "The difference between sex then and sex now," said my mother, telling me about this many years later and expressing herself like the classics major she had been at Hunter, "is like the difference between alpha and omega." Their public marriage took place in February 1930 at a synogogue in the Bronx. They served sandwiches and soda at the party afterward, and one of my father's friends thought the refreshments so meager that he ran out to buy a bottle of wine.

Mother supported them, teaching at a school in Long Island City. She had to take the subway and a trolley car to get there from Lexington and Sixty-eighth Street, where they lived in one room of a brownstone, sharing the bathroom in the hall with two other tenants. When my brother Richard was born in 1932, they moved to a two-bedroom apartment in the Bronx and hired a woman to look after the baby, cook, and do the laundry. By now, my mother was assigned to one of the best schools in New York, at Amsterdam and Ninety-third Street. It shocked me when I learned not long ago that between the birth of my brother and that of my sister Susan five years later, my mother had gotten pregnant and had an abortion, in order not to have to give up her job at this wonderful school. It shocked me not because I disapprove of abortion, but because my mother was so completely comfortable with what she'd done, regarded the procedure as so routine, that she hadn't even found occasion to mention it for over fifty years.

As soon as my father began making enough money, about the time Susan was born, soon after they had moved to Far Rockaway, Mother quit teaching. It was daring enough to give up secure employment in those hard times, and she went even further, trading in her pension for a phonograph and a Persian lamb coat. My parents' goals were refreshingly materialistic. Walking down Fifth Avenue once, my father gestured toward the window of Saks and said to Mother, "Some day I'll buy you all that."

I was born five years after my sister, and when I was three, the family moved again, to Woodmere. In its way, our house there was a paradise, with fruit trees, peony beds, a trellis covered with roses, a little pond for goldfish, all packed into a half-acre plot. But my parents were New Yorkers in their souls. Suburban life was a sacrifice they made for the sake of us children, and as soon as I, the last child, went to college, they sold the house and moved back to the city.

By the standards of both their immigrant families, my father prospered. He started gaining weight. His income made him the patriarch of both families, a flock of sisters and brothers, sixteen between them, that produced for my sister, my brother, and I, a herd of cousins. Large family parties were almost always given at our house, the cousins at one big table, the aunts and uncles at another. For extra-special events, like major anniversaries, my mother gave two parties on successive days, one for family, one for friends. The dining room—the room we did not use for daily family dining but only for special occasions—could seat twenty-four people and often did.

My father's general practice was to law what the family physician's practice was to medicine, a little of this, a little of that, and house calls. His job, he said, was to help people run their businesses, and since many of his clients were dress manufacturers, he spent much of his time over at the cutting rooms and showrooms of Seventh Avenue. I got all my clothes wholesale until well into my twenties and was taught to regard the buying of apparel at retail prices as an extravagance and waste akin to using sirloin steak for stew.

Occasionally my father would run into someone who, having known *his* father as a union man and socialist, would say, "If your father knew what you were doing, he'd be turning over in his grave," or "How can you look yourself in the eye representing manufacturers when your father *blah blah blah*." My father was never upset. He knew he'd have his father's blessing. Grandpa's old labor pals didn't know that in his later years, he had had a second conversion. Like many ideologues, he thought his way clear through to the other end of his conviction and emerged a devoted capitalist.

As an old man, my grandfather wore three-piece pinstripe suits with a watchfob across the vest and, one-upping John D. Rockefeller, who gave out pennies, gave dimes to all his grandchildren. This made him beloved as well as notable, and I was very sad when he died, the only one of my grandparents I knew. He lived to see my brother's graduation from college, traveling up to New Hampshire for it and staying at the Hanover Inn. He sat on the front porch, reading his newspaper, which was in Yiddish, but if you didn't notice that, he was otherwise indistinguishable from the other old graduates of Dartmouth back for their fiftieth reunion, bony of face and conservatively dressed.

"Class of oh four?" one gentleman inquired.

My grandfather shook his head and said matter-of-factly, "Aught aught. Kovna Yeshiva."

In our Woodmere house, Mother liked to sit in the entrance room, which might with equal justice and equal pretension have been called either the sewing room or the music room, for it was there, in the room you entered when you entered the front door of the house, that the phonograph stood, waist-high, polished mahogany, with a lid you lifted for access to the turntable on the left, the controls and radio on the right, over the single gigantic speaker. In an Early American barrel chair with red leather seat and back, Mother listened to the entire original cast albums of the new Broadway musicals, getting up every fifteen minutes or so to put another stack of 78 rpm records on the turntable or to turn one over. Sometimes she sewed. She seemed always to have buttons to sew on or hems to let down and pull up again. Fashion was always changing; my sister and I were always growing; clothes were always being handed down.

Because my mother had worked so hard in the early years of her marriage, she enjoyed her leisure and had no illusions about the fulfillment to be found in work. But I think she would have liked to be a lyricist. She admired Oscar Hammerstein more than any artist of the time. She took us into New York to see *Carousel*, *Oklahoma*, and *South Pacific*, and then played the songs until I knew the words by heart, the way Teddy knows the Beatles and much of the Stones. During the war, she and some other ladies from the community had put on a musical comedy for the soldiers at a nearby army base. Later she did theatricals for the PTA, always either as director or lyricist. These are among her favorite memories.

She took a visual artist's pleasure in entertaining. She liked to see the table in the dining room set with her good Wedgwood china, her faceted Stuart crystal, the Jensen silver, the crescent salad plates, crystal finger bowls on one side, and little silver salvers for salt. She liked the room when it was full of gaiety. *Gay* was a straightforward word in those days and gaiety a desirable trait; people worked hard to achieve it. Mother, who drank almost no alcohol, tried to produce gaiety through a combination of hospitality, goodwill, and simulation. She always held a glass of gin, although she rarely drank from it. After an hour or so of a party, gaiety started to flow from her, as Proust says of Albertine, like juices from an orange when its skin has been pierced. My father didn't even pretend to drink, saying, as though he were talking of novocaine before a dentist's drill, "I don't need it."

There was no problem in those postwar years in getting domestic help, and Mother had plenty of help with her parties, at first refugees from the war, later refugees from rural poverty. Hers may have been the last middle-class generation in America to rely routinely on domestic servants and also to feel comfortable with them. She hired people as an act of kindness, whereas Teddy's generation seems to think that all such employment is exploitation and is ashamed to have people work for them.

Out of kindness, she hired a German-Jewish couple, Simon and Hannah, who had been in a concentration camp. Desperate, unsmiling, more than half-crazed, Hannah and Simon lived in rooms on our third floor, and I was afraid of them. I thought Hannah in particular was a witch. Hannah let my mother know that the Rosenthal china she had had in Germany was better than my mother's Wedgwood, and to this day, Mother remembers that Hannah's china was Rosenthal, so often was the name thrown in her face. One night Hannah called the police and accused my mother of poisoning her food, although Hannah herself did all the cooking. My mother thought I was attached to Simon and Hannah and worried about telling me the news that they would be leaving. But I, who had seen *The Wizard of Oz*, knew what to do and danced in glee that the witch was, as far as our household went, dead.

My mother always thought my heart kinder than it was, my motives better. When I was perhaps four, she bought me a new pair of black patent-leather shoes, Mary Janes as they were called. We went all the way to Far Rockaway to get them, to a shoe store with an X-ray machine that let you see the bones in your own feet, so you could see for yourself that they were growing well. Mother always made me walk around the store several times to make sure shoes fit, but no matter how much I walked around in the store, I was never completely certain about the matter and left the store in some anxiety. In the case of the Mary Janes, I knew as soon as we got home that they were too tight, so I walked into the goldfish pond and ruined them. Whether I did this because a part of me has always thought water the solution to all problems or because I flat out wanted to destroy the shoes, I honestly could not say. But my mother, to my amazement, suspected no dark motives at all. At first she thought I had fallen in the pond by accident and was frantic for my safety. But when she learned I was in no danger and had in fact walked into the water on purpose, she generously concluded that I had wanted to show off my beautiful new shoes to the goldfish.

It was on a shopping trip to Far Rockaway that for the first time I saw people whose skin was not the same color as mine. "Why are those people brown?" I asked my mother, thinking I was asking a question on the order of, "Why is the sky blue?" which would produce a simple, scientific explanation which I would not be able to remember but would find reassuring. I remember distinctly her reply. "You don't say they're brown, dear. They're black." This left my question unanswered and confused me further. The people I saw in Far Rockaway were not black, they were brown. And my mother had clearly said "we don't *say* they're brown," with a tone indicating that although they were brown, it was not polite to say so. Her afterthought, "Sometimes we say they're colored," confused me even more, because to me colored people were the people whose outlines were printed in my coloring book and whose solid masses I crayoned in. On the whole it may have been an appropriate introduction to the mystery of race relations in America.

The colored person who came to live with us when I was eight was Lily McAllister. Lily came from Starr, South Carolina, where her husband, Taft, was a farmer. They had three children, but Lily had to leave them in South Carolina, to be raised by her mother and Taft's, while she raised me in the North. She sent home the money my parents paid her, along with long letters, written on ruled paper in a hand as rounded and hearty as Lily and a style as cheerful. She would never risk her correspondents not getting a joke and wrote after every one of them "(ha ha!)". I had Lily to mother me and only me for several happy years. Then she told my mother she was quitting, she was too lonely, and my mother, both in her kindness and in her concern for the good functioning of her household, offered to hire Taft.

So Taft came to live with us, too, and to work as our "chauffeur," although he did not know how to drive and by the time he came to us my brother was away at college and my sister had her own driver's license. When Taft in due course mastered our ship-like Oldsmobile, one of his principal jobs became driving me to school. His tendency in driving, like mine in ice skating, was to hug the rails, and I was terrified to be driven by him as well as mortified. Sometimes I actually hid in the backseat, not wanting to be seen with this "chauffeur." Almost always I made him drop me off a couple of blocks from school. The embarrassment was twofold. It was bad enough to be driven around by a chauffeur, which was "different" at a time when difference was not admired. Mothers or car pools were supposed to drive you to school, not chauffeurs. It was also clear to me, although I had never seen a chauffeur except in the movies, that Taft was not a real chauffeur. A chauffeur was above all competent and intrepid, whereas Taft was timid and tentative in everything he did. My mother gave him a chauffeur's hat to wear, but I knew that this was a charade being carried on for the benefit of Taft and Lily for which my father was footing the bill but I was paying the worst price, humiliation.

In retrospect I envy the well-run household over which my mother presided. Every morning as I got dressed I could hear the sound of Lily or Taft vacuuming the living room carpet. There was freshly squeezed orange juice for breakfast. Laundry was done on a regular basis. When I got home from school in the afternoon, Lily would pour me a glass of milk and give me some cookies or cake or chocolate pudding. She was a fine cook, but my mother orchestrated the meals, and under her baton, chopped liver might precede spaghetti with meatballs and Vita herring, Southern-fried chicken. Mother and Lily did better on Jewish holidays when the menu was traditional and gefilte fish followed matzoh ball soup and was followed in turn by pot roast or turkey.

When I look at my parents as parents, when I compare their child-rearing with my generation's, I see in them a blessed absence of narcissism which is no doubt allied to the materialism that so distressed me as a high-minded and judgmental adolescent. They had a focus on their children which my friends and I, seeing our careers as an end in themselves and not a means to the end of family life, had a hard time achieving, even in part. Many of my friends have had no children. Many of us could manage just one. Most of us never wanted to reproduce the placid bourgeois households of our childhood. We grew up resenting the attention that was lavished on us. We ignored the Chinese wisdom that wishes a friend not to live in interesting times. We wanted more excitement, more interesting lives than our parents had had. The childhood my parents gave me could not have been more privileged. Yet for many years, in the fashion of spoiled middle-class girls of my generation, that was exactly what I held against them.

Take Goldie. For my sixth birthday I had asked my parents to give me a trip to Texas as a birthday present. I wanted to tie my horse to a hitching post, watch gunslingers walk the streets, and meet Bobby Benson, young hero of the radio show *Bobby Benson and the B-Bar-B Riders*. I myself wanted to be a cowboy. I knew what I'd be getting into from Tom Mix comics, the Lone Ranger on radio, Roy Rogers and my beloved Hopalong on TV, and from countless westerns seen in movie theaters. My parents told me Texas wasn't as I imagined it and gave me instead a canary which, without much thought, I named Goldie.

I hated Goldie from the first time I had to clean his cage, sandpapering the wooden bars to remove the bird shit and replacing the dirty paper at the bottom with fresh. Nothing about that canary gave me aesthetic pleasure. At night I had to cover his cage with a plastic wrapper whose very smell and feel offended me. Goldie's song I found insipid. Like my mother, I was interested in lyrics, and "instrumentals" bored me. Goldie was kept in the same room as the radio, which stimulated him to song. Often we had to cover his cage before his bedtime, so we could listen to our shows without his caterwauling in competition. I hated Goldie all the more because he was what I had gotten instead of the trip to Texas. I hated him from the time I was six, and I waited for him to die, but he lived on and on. He was still alive when I got out of elementary school and started high school. He was still alive when I went to college and my parents sold the family house. Goldie had to be given away. Eventually it occurred to me to remark to my mother on the longevity of this extraordinary bird, and eventually she thought I was old enough to know the truth.

"There wasn't just one Goldie, dear, there were several. They died every few years. Canaries don't live that long, you know. But Daddy and I thought you'd be upset, so we replaced each one with another as quickly as we could, and you never noticed the difference."

Never noticed the difference! No wonder! I hated the damned thing! Never gave it a glance, if I could avoid it. For years I held Goldie against my parents, especially my mother. Look at the gilded cage I lived in! I said to whoever would listen. Look how they kept me from reality! It was my equivalent of the story of Dickens being put to work in the blacking factory at the age of twelve, deprived of his education, hopeless, abandoned by his parents who had turned the world upside down and relied on him to support them. As I'd learned long ago from Edmund Wilson, all of Dickens's novels had proceeded from this experience. Why didn't I have something awful like that in my past? Instead I had Goldie. No wonder I hadn't written Dickens's novels. My parents hadn't allowed me to suffer.

I was a difficult, ungrateful child, and this lasted well into my forties. It wasn't until I told this story to another Dr. S., a wise man in New Haven, that I got a handle on it. I told it to him as an example of how I'd been coddled as a child, trying to gain his sympathy. ("Poor little fly on the wall," I can hear my mother say. "Nebbish!") Wasn't it at least partly my parents' fault if I hadn't yet written what I wanted to write? Hadn't my parents deprived me of the pain I needed to be nourished as an artist? Dr. S. said, with the insight and subtlety achieved only after the most sophisticated theoretical and orthodox Freudian training, "She sounds like a very good mother."

Why is it the psychiatrists I have consulted in my times of trouble might as well have been village yentas? I brought them problems I assumed were as hard to resolve as the next person's. I went prepared to scour my dreams, my childhood, my transference, ready to scrutinize my own words and my unheeded gestures, to search for the faultlines in my character. They gave me advice I might have found in a fortune cookie. The better they were, the less afraid they seemed to be of making simple pronouncements.

I told Dr. S. all the ways in which my mother didn't understand me, disappointed me, embarrassed me, and he told me all the ways in which she nurtured me and provided a model of creativity. I went to him parading my wounds, scouring my pleasant life for distress. I looked high and low for problems. My own happiness stared me in the face. What was unique about me was that no one had hurt me.

One day in therapy when I was kvetching as usual, or rather trying to kvetch in ways I thought might conceivably be "interesting," Dr. S. surprised me by saying, "You talk like someone who's been abused." I think now he meant something like this: "Why do you talk as though you were abused when in fact you had such an easy childhood?" But at the time I thought he was offering a diagnosis: I talked the way I did because I had been abused. I was shocked. I immediately jumped to my parents' defense. "Oh no, nothing like that," I said. "Unless, of course, I don't remember it." Could I have been the victim of abuse and repressed memory? It was flattering to think so.

I never "understood" my childhood because I never understood what a happy childhood it was. I had my parents' love and attention. There was no story to tell except a happy one, and I had been led by whatever theories or literary models to think that only unhappy childhoods counted. In that way, too, Proust helped. Say what you will, Proust's was a happy childhood. His biggest problem seemed to be his mother's not kissing him good night exactly when he wanted her to. And look what he made of it.

So now, looking back, Proust's masterpiece my madeleine, the key to memory, I see the duck fly down, Loretta Young sweep into the room, Roy Rogers's horse rear back and paw the air, the curtains part for *Your Texaco Show of Shows*. I see my childhood pass, a mishmash of movies, TV shows, radio programs, comic books, a moving frieze of card games, trading cards, jump rope sessions, potsy matches, shopping trips, bicycle rides, school lessons, gym classes, birthday parties, chocolate pudding, chopped liver, grapefruit halves, so untroubled that I hardly noticed it, so undramatic that I didn't value it, so uninteresting to me that I didn't see what a good childhood I'd been given, looked for what was wrong until, emerging from adolescence in late middle age, I understood that the only thing wrong was my feeling that something should be.

3

Ancient Glass

"The Duchess . . . extended to the persons who surrounded her the instability of viewpoint, the unhealthy thirst, of the caviller who, to slake a mind that has gone too dry, goes in search of no matter what paradox that is still fairly fresh, and will not hesitate to uphold that thirst-quenching opinion that the really great *Iphigenia* is Piccini's and not Gluck's, and at a pinch that the true *Phèdre* is that of Pradon."

The Guermantes Way

EASTER SUNDAY IN CENTRAL Park. L. and I, out for our Sunday morning constitutional, walk past hillsides of daffodils. Following the lead of André, Pete, and other tennis greats, I wear elasticized bicycle pants under shorts, a look that flatters no one, not even Pete and André. L. is in sweatpants and Polartec. I am attuned to the poetry of our outfits from reading James Merrill's "Self-Portrait in Tyvek (TM)." I think that if Milton had lived in the 1990s, he'd have found a way to mention in pentameter Tyvek, Spandex, Polartec, and Lycra.

We walk fast around the reservoir where Jackie Kennedy took her final walk. Apparently, not fast enough. "One side," say joggers.

I carry a $9.95 panoramic camera bought by mail from Mystic Color Labs. Now and then I stop to photograph the cherry and apple trees in flower.

"Flowering? What is that in French?" I ask L. *"Fleurissant?"*

"There is no word in French. You have to say '*en fleur*,' as in *A l'ombre des jeunes filles en fleur.* How do you say that in English?"

"*Within a Budding Grove* in the Moncrieff translation. But I think that's flowery. And it drops the *jeunes filles* entirely, unless 'budding' is a reference to young girls, as in budding breasts."

"Flowering is a nice word," says L., a connoisseur of English.

Where did *fleurissant* come from? I must have made it up on the model of *florissant*, because a group called Les Arts Florissants, led by William Christie, looms large in today's *New York Times.* Flourishing Arts. What a name for an orchestra. When I was in graduate school at Yale, I knew William C. slightly, then a student of the harpsichord and Chinese cooking. Now his hair is white. He is a famous conductor, easy in a tuxedo, the man who brought Lully to Brooklyn, made dead arts flourish. He's had a flourishing career.

As we reach the far side of the reservoir, walking on the cinder path, I laugh, remembering that when my copy of the second volume of Proust arrived at Barnes and Noble, a saleswoman called and left a message: "The book you ordered is in. *Within a Budding Groove.*"

Rollerbladers, hunched, awkward, sinuous, jerky, rollerbladers in every size and style stream past when we leave the reservoir and cut over to the drive, which is closed to traffic on weekends so bikers, skaters, runners, and walkers can take over. A woman, thirty or so, skates by us towing a little girl in kneepads, maybe seven. "I want to go home, Mom." "Hold on, honey." The mother pulls her along festively, like a small plane trailing an advertising banner. The sun is shining. There are people on the tennis courts. Life flows around the edge of the park, counterclockwise. Panoramic is the proper mode, wide and horizontal. Everything streams past in bands: joggers, bikers, skaters, women on horses.

A young German tourist asks us for directions. It takes me a second to place him as a German tourist. At first I start, apprehensive to be addressed by a stranger in the park. Then I take in his accent, his close-cropped hair, his toned flesh and fitness level, his trendy army fatigue clothes, and his plausible request to know what street we are at, which way Tavern on the Green might be. I summon my courtesy to answer him. I remember German tourists murdered in Miami, a woman lost near the airport, her rental car rammed by another car, run over when she stepped out and tried to hold onto her bag, her mother and children looking on. I feel I must right that wrong by telling this German tourist how to find Tavern on the Green.

As we walk, L. and I do not talk. We think our separate thoughts. I am thinking now about urban crime. A year ago my wallet was stolen at the corner of Park and Fifty-eighth Street, lifted out of my shoulder bag. A man in front of me stumbled, dropped his parcel, spilling things on the sidewalk, turned around to ask me for help. I recoiled, spotting the setup, backing right into the accomplice's pocketpicking hands it seems, for when I arrived at Mother's apartment, still congratulating myself on my street smarts, I noticed the flap on my bag was undone and realized my wallet was gone. The ploy is so standard it has a name, "the Good Samaritan." I've since seen warning posters at the bank explaining how it works. City life, nonetheless, seems worth it. A stolen wallet now and then seems not an unreasonable price to pay for urban energy, I think, as we head out of the park just north of Seventy-ninth Street.

From a vendor in front of the Metropolitan Museum, I buy for a dollar apiece two old copies of *National Geographic*, which he, half-nuts, calls the National Sympathetic. One, which I will give to David, has pictures of India. One has pictures of the new Saigon. I will give that to Bob.

This year Easter, Passover, and tax time all come together. *The New Yorker* has run a cover by Art Spiegelman showing an Easter bunny crucified on a tax form. A lot of people are upset by it.

Teddy has two friends staying with him, home from graduate school for the holidays. They eat the pot roast I made last night and was saving to warm up for tonight's dinner. I feel irritation toward the young who seem to think I am here on their behalf.

Everything I see in Central Park sends me the same message: if I were to disappear, I wouldn't be missed. If I die, the bicyclists and rollerbladers will still stream counterclockwise, new incarnations of the colorful Central Park crowds Prendergast painted a hundred years ago, American, democratized versions of the strollers in the Bois Proust described. Polartec and Gore-Tex will give way to fabrics even lighter, warmer, more resistant to moisture, and friendlier to the environment. Teddy, at twenty-three, with two months' experience, can produce a TV show. Another twenty-three-year-old has published a splendid book on Internet culture, according to today's *Book Review*. People much younger than me are fully competent teachers, lawyers, doctors, policemen. People my age are ready to be revered. I recall Yeats's self-portrait in "Among School Children" and get his age wrong by ten years: "A fifty-year-old smiling public man," I think. But I'm jumping the gun. Yeats was sixty when he realized it was "Better to smile on all that smile, and show/ There is a comfortable kind of old scarecrow."

At dinner we discuss Vietnam. The war, not the tourist destination. McNamara's book has just come out, confessing it was all a big mistake. "You can't imagine what America was like before Vietnam," I tell Teddy. "Everything changed. The way life is now is all connected to what they did then, even things that don't seem connected, like a mother in South Carolina drowning her babies."

As a commentator on public affairs and the course of history, I'm a fraud. Nevertheless I feel driven to instruct my son. He shouldn't let McNamara be exonerated by the second-rate culture of confession his war helped create. Don't ask me how.

"These days everybody wants to live in Disney World," I say to Teddy.

In bed, I flip through the *National Geographics*. The one with pictures of Saigon has an article on classical bronzes discovered on the ocean floor near Brindisi—a giant elbow, a foot, the heads of a philosopher, a prince, and a young girl. An odd collection, odder yet because the bronzes date from different centuries, and although they all lay on the ocean floor the same amount of time, show different degrees and patterns of decay. One hand has lost its copper and turned into a hideous blackened claw. The philosopher's head is intact but the prince's is attacked by sulphurous patches. They think the ship that threw these pieces overboard was an ancient version of a scrap metal barge, bringing worn-out statue fragments from the eastern provinces to the foundries of Brindisi for recycling when it was hit by a sudden storm and needed to lighten its load. The fragments lay on the ocean floor for two thousand years until they became objects of interest if not beauty in their own right, recycled by time, sea-changed into something rich and rare.

I put the magazine aside, deciding not to give it to Bob after all. Why should I give Bob a present? I stop myself on the verge of feeling vexed with my friend because I've decided not to give him a magazine I bought on the street for a dollar and which he probably doesn't want anyway. Why? Because I feel time passing and have nothing to show for it. Because if I make every nice gesture that crosses my mind, I'll never get anything done. Because the bronze relics on the ocean floor could be me if I don't get a move on.

In January, when I started reading Proust, I had already been feeling dry and identifying with antiquities.

Alison's house guest Dina G. offered me a free session of the therapy she practices, called "Image Work." I took advantage of it, as we sipped rum punches by the sea wall in our molded resin chairs and shouted to be heard over the roar of the Jet Skis and the parasailing motorboats on the water. Dina's therapy consists of asking you to produce an image and then essentially to free associate about it. I've always been afraid of free associating, afraid I had nothing to say. But whether it was Dina's talent, the rum punch, or the untherapeutic setting, I found myself talking more easily than I ever had in psychotherapy.

"Clear your mind," she said. "Fill your body with light. Each part of your body hums a different note. Hum the note. Hear the different sounds. Imagine a shelf. Place your cares on it. Animal, vegetable, mineral. What do you see?"

"An Egyptian statue. A woman in profile. Hair black. Dress blue. Flat. A bas-relief."

"Imagine yourself inside," said Dina. "How do you feel?

"Flat. Constricted. Captive."

"What's good about your situation?"

"I'm beautiful," I said. "I'm a work of art. I will live forever. People admire me."

"People see you?"

"Tourist groups. They come to look at me. They listen to lectures."

"What's beneath you?"

"Byzantine rubble. I'm from an earlier period than what's underneath me. It doesn't make sense."

"Were you always the way you are?"

"No. Once I was part of a temple. People worshipped here. I had a context. I wasn't just a work of art."

"And then?"

"The civilization ended. The religion was replaced by Christianity. I was buried in the sand for two thousand years."

"How did you emerge from the sand?"

"French or Italian explorers dug me up about a hundred years ago."

"Let's get back to how you look. You are beautiful and unique."

"Yes. Sometimes I worry I'm too unique. Too colorful. I think I may be a fake. The real thing would be more faded. I'm afraid I'm a tacky reproduction in an Egyptian restaurant on First Avenue and not an ancient work of art after all."

"Imagine yourself in a larger setting. Tell me where you are."

"There's a river, the Nile, with the Valley of the Kings on one bank and Luxor and Karnak on the other. I am in Luxor or Karnak."

"Can the river help you?"

"Yes. I feel dry. The river can moisten me. But wait! I see catastrophe. The river floods. I'm covered up. I'm underwater."

"Let the waters recede. Imagine yourself as you were. What would you tell yourself?"

"Hard to imagine advice. What options do I have? Endure. I'd tell myself things aren't bad, and I'm going to live forever."

"So even though you feel occasionally you may be a fake, you're basically sure of your quality."

"Yes."

"What would improve your situation? If you could do any-thing to make yourself feel better, what would it be? Remember it doesn't have to be logical or possible. What would you, this flat Egyptian statue, do to make yourself feel better?"

"I'd blast off and orbit the earth. I'd go around and around, like something from *2001* or *Star Wars* or *Star Trek*. Shooting through the universe."

"After that, how would you feel?"

"Better. Exercised. Exhausted."

"Anything else you would do?"

"Well, yes. If I could, I would spend my summers in the Met-ropolitan Museum, so I could be with others of my kind."

"I'm going to count to five, and you will gradually come back to yourself. How do you feel?"

It was the start of the winter in Key West. My semester of teach-ing was over. I was free now to write but feeling sterile, empty, with nothing to say—"flat, constricted." I was aware of the figure I cut in the world, but felt that there was nothing inside it, hence the identification with a bas-relief. I felt confident of my social self, my self in the world, but not of my own creativity.

Things used to be better, but I don't know if the Golden Age I imagine, when I was part of a temple where people worshipped, refers to my childhood (I doubt it) or an earlier stage of my life when I was more creative and harder-working than I've been for the past five years. I feel I'm putting on a show, entertaining peo-ple, a dedicated hostess ("tourist groups come to look at me").

The rubble image comes from a Byzantine building practice. Medieval builders used stones from ancient temples to fill in the walls and foundations of their own structures, which to us seems a sacrilege, but to them seemed a sensible way of saving the labor and expense of cutting new stones. It's an image of the way each generation builds on what has come before, consuming its par-ents to construct itself. The hungry generations are treading me down.

Those "French or Italian" explorers? They were French.

They were L.! He dug me up out of the sand and brought me to life. And it was ten years ago exactly, not one hundred.

As for the river, well, all the places I like best in the world have that clarity of geographic structure, either an island between two rivers, like Manhattan, or a valley between two mountain ranges, like Napa, or a river between two clearly divided banks, like the Nile between Luxor and the Valley of the Kings. I like to know where I stand. The places where I feel most comfortable on earth present no mysteries of orientation. At the same time, my deepest happiness depends on transitions. Another way of explaining why I like Napa, the Nile Valley, and Manhattan, is that transitions are easy to come by—between the mountains and the valley, the river and the desert, the East Side and the West Side.

It's banal of me to want to be bathed in the river, much more typical that I fear being flooded, losing control.

I want to blast off and circle the earth because I'm not completely looking forward to this winter. I wish I were traveling. I'm envious of friends who are orbiting the globe. Bob and Janice Stone are in Vietnam. David has been there, too, and is going on to India.

As for wanting to spend the summer at the Met with others of my kind, that's exactly what I'm doing in Key West, only it's the winter I'm spending with others of my kind, who are not works of art, but art workers.

I spend this winter reading Proust, mastering e-mail, cooking, and writing letters to David in India. Every morning I sit at the computer and think about writing—nonfiction, fiction, it doesn't matter what. I end up checking my e-mail. I'm just going to check, I tell myself, to see if something is there, nothing more. After that (I tell myself) I'll get to serious work. Before I know it, the rest of the day is gone, answering e-mail, paying bills electronically, figuring out how to send a letter on Winfax so I don't have to bother printing it out and sending it by regular fax or mail.

It's amazing how quickly hours evaporate. I spend one hour in the morning having my coffee, reading *The Miami Herald*, looking at the ocean from the porch of our house. At lunchtime I may spend another hour getting some sun on the upstairs porch. Two times a week I work out at the gym. There's the occasional hour with the ball machine at the tennis court. The hours between five and seven are very busy: L. and I make ourselves drinks, carry them out to the seawall, and watch the sun go down, if there is sun, if not, we watch the water. Either before or after that, I call Mother. Then we see the news.

Just as Marcel convinces himself that it is better not to signal to Uncle Adolphe at all than merely to lift his hat, so I manage daily to convince myself that it is more of a tribute to literature to write nothing than it would be to sit down and write. Looked at from the outside as I sit at my desk for hours staring at the computer screen, it seems that nothing is happening, but that is not true. Powerful forces—despair, fastidiousness, ambition—on one side are warring against ambition in another form and hope. Every day hope loses to despair, fastidiousness prefers the uncreated to the created, the size of what I want to accomplish sends the desire to accomplish anything at all back into its hole. A massive battle takes place every day in the time it would take, unblocked, to write eight pages. If I could just sit down and do it! Instead I think of all the excellent books I've read and think how unlike them a book of mine would be. I imagine my friends reading it dutifully. I imagine strangers picking it up and throwing it down in disgust.

Into my letters to David I put some of my failing literary energy. I try out what I consider a Proustian style but can't sustain it for more than a line or two. The patience that goes into it is beyond me. I can't make the effort it takes to pursue truth underneath the description of appearances or resist the mere naming of names. "We had dinner last night with Bob, Rust, and Joy. I served picadillo." For me the distinctness of these three personalities is evoked merely by naming them, the yumminess of the dinner by the word *picadillo*. When I say Bob, for example, I see a relaxed, white-bearded, middle-aged man encasing an intense and straggle-haired hippie, a man who can explicate corporate shenanigans, corruption in Vietnam, terrorism in the Middle

East, medieval Jewish mysticism, or drug use on shrimp boats, while playing poker in a good-natured, less than cutthroat fashion, a man who is rarely less than fascinating himself, but who listens benevolently and nods encouragingly to the dumbest things I say, Ancient Mariner and Santa Claus rolled into one brilliant, driven, easy-going, affectionate drinker of beer and lover of hot pepper sauce. But it takes work to reproduce the effect he has on me in someone else. In a way the whole of *Lost Time* is an effort to reproduce in the reader what Marcel felt when he ate the tea-soaked madeleine and recaptured his past. That is what literary work is about, and it *is* work. I avoid it whenever I can.

"Bob looks well," I wrote David. "He recently returned from being the lecturer on a Yale alumni trip to Vietnam and Cambodia. He hadn't been in Vietnam since 1971 and found the place immensely seductive although the government is completely corrupt. A friend of his bought Ming porcelain from a man on the street for thirty dollars but was stopped by customs when he tried to take it out of the country. He claimed it was a copy but the customs agent insisted it was real and that there was a fine for trying to take ancient works of art out of the country. The customs agent collected a 'fine' of ten dollars from Bob's friend but let him take the piece out of the country! Sound familiar? It seems you overpaid!

"In the middle of dinner Teddy called. He was still at work, writing copy about the trial for murder of a former policeman. He wanted to know what a word was for not just breaking the law but showing complete lack of respect for it. He needed to know right that minute. I put the question to the table, all writers, but speaking for myself I had already had a rum punch and a glass or two of wine. I came up with the word *flaunt*, and everyone agreed it was the right choice. Later in the evening, I even used it in a sentence, as our elementary school teachers told us we should. We were talking about the tunnels in which the Vietcong lived and how they were infiltrated by small Americans who used gas until the army's lawyers informed them that gassing the enemy was a violation of the Geneva Convention. 'They were flaunting the Geneva Convention,' I said. Everyone agreed. Then this morning I woke bolt upright and realized the word was *flout*. I called Teddy in panic, but fortunately that whole section of what he'd written had been cut."

A month later, I was up to the second half of the second volume of Proust and my third exchange of letters with David. My style was improving. Now I had another of the Proustian elements—paradox. That was my mount, my steed, more like John Travolta's mechanical bull in *Urban Cowboy* than a normal trail or pack horse. It whipped my body every which way, lurched me from one insight to the next. I didn't care what I said, so long as it was the reverse of what you'd think. It led me to trash one of my dearest friends in a letter to David.

"Annie gave a singing party the other night. Why she picks from all others this form of hospitality is a mystery to me. I have to assume it is the most coercive."

Once you get the hang of paradox, it's hard to stop.

If she smiled, her smiles were so pronounced as to be hurtful, suggesting that you were one of those dolts to whom false kindness must be shown because they inspire no real affection and who are so dumb they can not tell the difference.

If she shakes your hand, it is to hold you at a distance, so as not to have to kiss or hug you.

If she says that a mutual friend is especially keen to see you, you can be sure that that person has by word spoken or word omitted suggested precisely that she couldn't care less if she ever saw you again, for such is Annie's sense of her centrality that it's not only for herself she makes the biggest show of what she least feels; she does the same for others.

Paradox always leads you to a sort of truth, for it gets at truth's many-sidedness. But the tone of what I wrote David, although it amused him, was not Proustian. There's a sweetness that comes with complex understanding, and I didn't have it. The bitterness of my sterility flowed into the style, creating of Annie, whom I sometimes loved, sometimes scorned, sometimes envied, sometimes resented, sometimes relished, and sometimes pitied, a creature of blanket unattractiveness and of myself uncomplicated malice. David claimed to like this catty narrator but I was ashamed of her.

• • •

Except in writing, I've always loved accidental effects. Back in my twenties, when I was married to Mark Rose, I used to fool around with ceramics in my mother-in-law's studio. I liked glazes because when you painted them on they were one color but after the pieces were fired they turned into something else. I never knew exactly what. Green became brown. Dull and matte became glossy and glassy. The glazes I liked best were the raku glazes that fire differently at different temperatures and under different atmospheric circumstances, so even experts do not know how the piece will turn out. How can you not be intrigued by how essence and circumstance together produce appearance: a face as it ages, the scratches on a dining room table and its sheen, the way a book looks after it's read? My favorite snapshots from our travels are of restaurant tables after meals, the Pellegrino bottle half empty, the pizza crust with jagged edges against the white plate, the rumpled napkin.

What first drew L. and me to antiquities were accidental effects—in Roman glass, the weathering. "Very little ancient glass has survived with its original surface intact," says one of our books on the subject. "Moisture and acids act on the surface to cause chemical decomposition known as devitrification or 'weathering.' This decomposition produces a change of color in the surface layers, often turning them white, light brown, or iridescent. Though prized by collectors, the iridescence and effects of weathering were never intended by ancient glassmakers."

L. and I are among those perverse collectors who prize the iridescence that ancient glassmakers never intended. There are other qualities to admire in ancient glass. Other people collect examples of different glassmaking techniques, like threading, pinching, marbling, and mosaic, or different shapes, like sprinkler jars, jugs, unguentariums, and vases, or different colors, amber, green, and blue. But for us, whether with sprinkler jars or jugs, amber glass or green, what we can't get enough of is the play of light on the unpredictable and unstable surface.

I have reached the age when collecting is the stage on which I enact desire, for the feel of promiscuity—if that is what one needs to feel alive—is the same whether the object of desire is a man or a sprinkler jar. I want, therefore I am. I am, therefore I acquire. In the old days, sex was amusing as much for possibilities never acted on as for fulfillment. At any moment an encounter might turn erotic, a man's eyes would light up or mine would. There were many drawbacks to that life and I vastly prefer being married, but one thing I regret is the loss of universal eroticization—the world charged with possibility. This I now find in collecting.

That I want things so often and so passionately is one of the reasons L. and I get along so well. Every time I express a passionate desire—whether for a new life or for coconut ice cream—it causes him joy. He takes every craving as a sign of both vitality and imagination. He himself wants very little and feels this as a deficiency.

The first piece of Roman glass we bought we found in the indoor flea market on Twenty-sixth Street in New York City. I was certainly not looking for it. It's as hard to know what made me notice it as it would be to explain why someone I met at a dinner party, who didn't even sit next to me at the table, is someone I knew immediately I could spend my life with. I must have been in that heightened state of receptiveness that precedes all love and creativity.

It was in a glass case with some neolithic iron idols, which looked like flattened nails, some terracotta figurines, Etruscan stone carvings, Egyptian scarabs, all the stuff that had always looked to me like nothing, the detritus of the ages, ancient bric-a-brac, no better than Toby jugs. It was a greenish flask encrusted with gold iridescence, about eight inches tall with a long tapering neck rising from a globular base.

The dealer was a dark and diffident man, who made no effort to sell but seemed at the same time untrustworthy. I asked him the price. He named one. I said, "Can you do better?" He came down about 20 percent and said, "That's a good price. Believe me." He had auction catalogues and catalogues from Madison Avenue antiquities dealers and showed me how much similar pieces were selling for.

The price was high for something I knew nothing about, but didn't seem high for something so beautiful and two thousand years old. I felt I was buying not just the object but all the years it had lasted. In fact, I was buying my own imaginative response to the piece. Anyone else would have seen an awkward green bud vase, too expensive to use for flowers.

We agreed on a price. I paid quickly and left with my treasure. I wanted to get away before the dealer realized what a mistake he'd made in parting with it.

When we got home, I put the piece on the coffee table where we could stare at it from every angle. It took perhaps half an hour for me to see that the object I'd purchased with such palpitating joy resembled a vitrified upside-down horse penis.

In the story of this purchase, I see all the stages of desire. First comes The Sighting, when your heart does the flip-flop that signals compelling desire. *My* heart, at any rate, flip-flops. Others' may do something else. For at this point you must be in close touch with yourself. Signs of arousal vary. You must know your own: the sense of time standing still, the sudden irradiation of the atmosphere, perhaps a tingle up the arm. For me, it's the heart beating faster or turning a somersault. The next moment I call The Revelation, and it may be even more exciting than The Sighting. It's when you glimpse the possibility of possession: This man—or object—can be mine! This man wants me as much as I want him! I can afford this object! The Revelation usually follows soon after The Sighting and is succeeded by The Negotiation, which is cleaner and clearer in relation to objects than men, the terms being entirely expressed in money, and the proprietorship thereafter being absolute. The Enjoyment which follows may be more satisfying with a man than an object, but then again it may not. But however great The Enjoyment, however long it lasts, with men and objects there comes inevitably the moment of Disillusionment, which represents the end of the first stage of a relationship, whether or not it goes on eventually to long-term satisfaction. With the Roman flask, I went the complete cycle from infatuation to disillusionment in a couple of hours.

It wasn't long before I came to terms with the unfortunate

shape of my Roman flask. I taught myself to concentrate instead on its beautiful surface. Proust says we get used to the defects of the people we love and learn to see more of their virtues in time. That the flask couldn't speak up and tell me it wanted to be loved for its shape made things even simpler.

L. and I also collect prints, and our idea of a good time in the city is to drop in on Mr. Schab, who deals in Old Masters. He has an enormous collection of art monographs in German, French, and Italian, as well as English, and his place of business is lined with bookshelves from ceiling to floor, so it resembles a library more than an art gallery. From a flat file he takes out the Piranesis, Stefano della Bellas, or Callots about which he will tell you in detail, filled with an excitement that seems more of the university than the marketplace. His manner is European. When he cites a source in Italian, he reads it to you in Italian, as though you could understand it perfectly.

"I have something very special to show you, something I have never seen in my entire career. These are very precious, perhaps the first prints ever made of the inside of the ducal theater in Verona. Do you see how the curtain is light in color here? I have never seen it in that state. Later Callot darkened the curtain by etching in more lines. This is extremely rare. The National Gallery itself does not have this set of prints, and they have the best Callot collection in the world. In fact, if you were to purchase these prints, I should like it to be on the condition that when you die, they go to the National Gallery."

My own interests in subject matter and what I'm ashamed to call beauty seem hopelessly vulgar next to Mr. Schab's interests. It is always humiliating to visit him. Yet we continue to go to his Old World enclave, where he continues to try to sell us rarity, flying in the face of our frivolous pursuit of content and form.

The print I would like to have more than any other is Dürer's "St. Jerome in His Study." The saint sits at his desk in a fifteenth-century northern European study, his lion at his feet. Easy to see why I'd identify with this, spending my time at my computer, a dog, if ever L. and I could agree on the size of a replacement for poor Seamus, at my feet. But this print is way beyond my means. Too many people love it. I would be happy, I tell Mr. Schab, with Dürer's "St. Jerome in Penitence," if he ever comes across one in reasonable shape, not necessarily museum quality, at an affordable price. In this image, St. Jerome kneels in the wilderness, naked from the waist up, looking more like a hippie than a scholar, but his faithful lion is behind him and he exudes the sweetness of nature which Dürer seems to associate with him.

"I feel an affinity for St. Jerome," I said.

"Many artists have," said Mr. Schab. "He has been the subject of many great works. There are the Carpaccios in Venice, a Caravaggio, a Ribera."

"To say nothing of Rembrandt and Dürer," I added, mentioning the obvious.

"You know, when he arrived at Jerusalem, he showed up with two beautiful women. There was more to him than we think. Apparently he was quite the ladies' man."

Now this was just like Mr. Schab. He assumed I knew a whole lot more about everything than I did. I didn't know what St. Jerome was revered for, and Mr. Schab was telling me about little-known scandals. Arrived in Jerusalem to do what? When? From where? Like the person who is afraid of boring you by repeating what you know, Mr. Schab leaps over the essential right to the obscure.

I had to go to the library and do some research of my own to find that St. Jerome translated the Bible from the original Hebrew and Greek into Latin, a work of scholarship which made the Bible vastly more accessible. For this great work he was surprisingly controversial in his time. Some people thought the Bible shouldn't be made more accessible. Others didn't like his style, for St. Jerome preferred plain language where they thought fancy more appropriate.

Combative, unpopular, when his patron died he was driven from Rome, where he had done his early translations, and went to Jerusalem, ("Aha!") his journey financed by a wealthy Roman matron named Paula, who accompanied him to the East, along with her daughter ("Aha!"). When he was born, perhaps as early as 331, Christianity had been established for a couple of centuries. It was a time of wild asceticism, the age of the men who lived in the desert or sat on columns to remove themselves from the world. St. Jerome spent time in the great cities of the Eastern Mediterranean—Jerusalem, Constantinople, and Antioch—but he was one of the ascetics who found a life of virtue more appropriately lived in the wilderness than in cities. He established himself, according to legend, in a cave in the desert. That's where the lion comes in, a symbol of his time in the wilderness. Wherever he went, he took his library with him, a harder job then than my sending three boxes of books UPS to and from Key West every winter.

In a sense, he was the first biographer, turning out a prodigious number of saint's lives in addition to his translations, commentaries, and polemics. He lived to be a very old man—according to some accounts, ninety. He lived to see the sack of Rome in 410. He was beloved by the Renaissance humanists because he united Christian piety and classical learning, but he himself felt torn between his Christian faith and his classical culture. In a dream St. Jerome recorded, Christ the Judge asks him what kind of man he is. Jerome says, "I am a Christian." "You lie," says Christ. "You are a Ciceronian, not a Christian."

It's chronologically possible that when St. Jerome was in Antioch, learning Hebrew, he used the flat glass pilgrim flask with iridescent blue threading at the neck which L. and I bought from a Syrian dealer at the Manhattan Art and Antiques Building. I like to think he did.

When Mark and I were first married and graduate students at Harvard, we watched *The Avengers* on TV. Diana Rigg was Mrs. Emma Peel, a woman with a sense of humor and a good karate chop, dressed in what I'd call a wetsuit. She was paired with a man in a bowler hat, carrying a cane. They seemed very modern. The feel of modernity is the result of putting things together that haven't been put together before. A pretty woman, the martial arts. Her wetsuit, his bowler. Toughness, good humor. The other show we watched every week was *The Man from UNCLE*. There again, if I recall correctly, an unlikely juxtaposition: the blonde, bony intellectual-looking Russian, Ilya Kuryakin, and the fleshy, dark American, Sebastian Solo, the one partner ephebe and foreign, the other forthright and sturdy.

We had a black-and-white TV, a wedding present. We were always fussing with the antenna, trying to get better reception. There was, of course, no cable, no digital satellite system. In fact, in 1965, there were not that many TVs. Most of the other graduate students we knew did not have them. Michael B. came over to our house every week to watch *The Man from UNCLE*. After the show, Mark and Michael would play guitar and banjo, and we'd all sing folk songs. We listened to Joan Baez, Josh White, Pete Seeger, Odetta, and, despite ourselves, Peter, Paul, and Mary.

We saw the Beatles perform live on television. I started having dreams about being the only girl to join the Beatles. I later learned that such dreams were widespread among women of my age group. Closer to 1970 than 1960, the sixties got underway. There were the Beatles and the Rolling Stones. There was Bob Dylan. "Twas bliss in that fair dawn to be alive/ And to be young was very Heaven."

This fall, in the year of reading Proust, L. and I watched a TV special on the Beatles' career, with footage from the Beatles' own files and family photos. Some lawsuit amongst them had finally been settled, enabling this production along with a new musical release in which John Lennon, dead fifteen years, is electronically rejoined with the group. While the special itself may have betrayed an unseemly, desperate grasping for "product" typical of the present moment, nothing can cheapen the Beatles' story, which is to me as allegorical, as beautiful, as transcendent and compelling, as central in its way as the story of the Passion.

First, they were young. They loved their work. They loved Elvis. They loved rock. They loved their audiences. They were tickled by their own success. They feared nothing. They had nothing to lose. Every good thing that happened they appreciated. They projected fresh-faced innocent joy with no pretensions, wholehearted, high-energy joy. They sang in harmony. They spoke irreverently. They worshipped no idols. The songs themselves were not bad, but the real excitement came from the group itself.

They moved directly to perfection: *Rubber Soul* and *Revolver.* They started singing songs like no one had ever sung: "Norwegian Wood," "Eleanor Rigby," narrative songs, songs like medieval ballads that you listened to for the story, but with sounds that were entirely modern, mixing rock and Bach. They were trying things out, open to new ideas. They worked with George Martin, the producer, accepted his advice. You could feel his shaping hand, their creative energies molded by his intellect and training.

Then the moment of inspired collaboration disappeared. Their next albums were great, too, but less perfect. The discipline faltered. They included everything. They slightly overvalued their every idea, and their ideas were getting a little flaky. Eastern philosophy. Vaudeville music. They were doing drugs. They were so successful they had to escape their success. They produced prolific, magnificent, sloppy albums: *The White Album* and *Sergeant Pepper.*

The next stage is painful to think about but it's where it really gets interesting to me. They are grinding it out. The joy is gone from their music-making. It's become a business. They no longer like one another very much. The differences between them and the strains have become apparent. George and John, the kooky ones, stay in India. Ringo and Paul, the sensible ones, go home.

Paul gets the idea for "Hey, Jude" to console Julian Lennon for his parents' divorce. "Take a sad song and make it better." When he plays the song for John Lennon, he says one line needs work. "The movement you need is on your shoulder." "No," says Lennon. "Keep it like that. It's the best line in the song." You see how they worked together at their best, how Lennon provided the little bit of not making sense that lifted everything to a higher plane.

Their boyhood marriages are dissolving. New, celebrity unions are formed, more appropriate to the global figures they have become, John's with Yoko Ono, Paul's with Linda Eastman.

In footage from this period, as they're recording *Let It Be*, you see Yoko right behind John all day long. L. takes this to mean that Yoko was an overbearing woman who wouldn't leave John alone. But I sense that he needed her with him constantly to complete himself, to shore up his sense of his own identity which for some reason he had lost.

The four of them must have hated one another by then. Surrounded by mobs wherever they went, they hid in hotel rooms, isolated from normal life, normal pleasures. They were cellmates, together constantly. The recording studio had been a refuge from the insanity of their public performances, but now the studio, too, was just another place where they were locked up together.

What is the opposite of a labor of love? A labor of will? That was *Let It Be*, someone else's idea of a good idea. The idea was to follow every move the Beatles made while they recorded an album, a kind of imprisonment within their imprisonment. They realize that their career is over, played out, in the past: let it be.

It is over, but it is not over. There is still so much genius in them, so much joint creativity and goodwill that almost despite themselves they produce one more perfect album, a masterpiece, an album that's seamless and flawless from start to finish, *Abbey Road*, like a menopause baby, a last-minute child before reproduction becomes impossible, and then that's the end, the arc of their creativity is complete.

When people who are not artists meet artists, they take it as a mark of sophistication to ask, "What are you working on?" If you tell them, they are likely to follow with the only question that is worse, "How did you get that idea?" For several years now, when people ask what I'm working on I've cheerfully told them I'm burned out, retired, or goofing off. "I'm a party girl now. I'm working on absolutely nothing. Zip." I notice that many other writers perk up when I say I'm working on nothing. It could be competitiveness—"Good, she's not working and I am"—but I don't think so. I think it's, "Thank God, we don't have to get into that dreary subject." Who really cares what I'm working on? The only thing people want to know is what can feed their own work, and if it's mine, it can't be theirs.

Sometimes people assume I want consolation. "You need to restore yourself," they say. "You need to lie fallow. You need to fill up the well. When you're ready, you will write again." The true writer will be shocked, as Bob Stone was. "A writer writes," he said. Writing is health to the writer as physical activity is health to the human animal. He is as shocked that I'm not writing as I am that he drinks so much beer and gets no exercise, or that Annie keeps on smoking in spite of her vulnerable lungs. "I can't imagine a writer not writing," he said, as Annie once said, "I can't imagine not wanting to play Ping-Pong."

Ploughshares ran an interview with Ann Beattie which moved me by touching on this business of how to proceed when you're faltering, how to push a career through to its later stages. A writing career is not an obstacle course that if you do it correctly you win, Ann B. says. She wrote three hundred and fifty pages of a recent novel and then realized she had to scrap it, plot, characters, prose and all. It took her five months to recover and start again. Just writing a good sentence isn't enough, she says. She can turn them out reliably. People's surprising behavior no longer surprises her. Her success doesn't make things any easier in the public arena. If anything, the opposite. It stimulates envy and a burden of expectation. People are no nicer, she says. Rather less, says Annie D. They feel you've already gotten your share of their niceness and of the world's praise, or that you know that what you do is good without hearing it. If anything, you need taking down a peg. People feel that to take you down a peg is to perform a public service.

In the fall, *The New Yorker* ran a piece about Maria Callas. The writer said that Callas burned out early because of qualities inherent in her voice, the qualities that made it great being tied to qualities that made it unlikely to endure. It had to do with the structure of the lungs, the voice box, the abdomen, the production of sound. It had nothing to do with heartbreak over Aristotle Onassis's desertion of her for Jackie Kennedy. If she killed herself, it was because she was through as a singer and knew it, not for love. I was impressed with this piece and asked David, as an expert on opera in general and Callas in particular, what he thought. He thought that "like most biographers," this writer pushed one explanation, where maybe the others were equally true. Maybe her final despair had to do with the voice but also with heartbreak over Onassis.

David insisted that L. and I go see *The Master Class*, Terence McNally's play about Callas teaching at Juilliard, when her career was in large part over. Naturally, it being theater, the playwright relied heavily on the "love as downfall" interpretation, although one of her voice students, angrily rejecting Callas's critique, says she doesn't want to burn her voice out in ten years like Callas did. The best scene was a reverie in which Callas remembered how Onassis degraded her, how she begged him to marry her, how he made her sing him street ditties and mocked her art. "I've signed you to the most exclusive goddamned recording contract in the world." Zoë Caldwell acted them both, the profane, macho, balls-grabbing Onassis, and the lovesick, dependent Callas.

Wow! What theater! As someone who doesn't take theater seriously, I am satisfied when it is merely theatrical. But at inter-mission, we met a critic and director who was disappointed. This man takes theater seriously and wants it to be more than itself. Or perhaps he just felt that Terence McNally has had his share of praise. No one badmouths Zoë Caldwell, who has reached the age at which people say of her, "Isn't it amazing what she still can do?"

My sense of what a high-wire act any piece of creativity is can be seen in a photograph used to sell watches. The ad shows a dance troupe in impossible positions. One man balances on a fin-ger. Another is in midair bent at the waist. Another appears to be curled around himself. Each position is impossible and there are five of them. Every time I saw this photo I came close to tears. This was how good you had to be to be an artist. This was how precarious excellence was. In another second, all the perfect poise achieved in the photo would be gone. The dancers would fall. The somersault, so beautiful to see when the dancer was caught in midair, would end with a two-footed landing. The cartwheel, too, would conclude with the dancer merely upright. The whole miraculous assemblage would return to square one, the dancers at rest, less visually interesting than a random group of people reading newspapers on the subway. Burned out or lying fallow, it made no difference. There was no necessary connection between one moment and the next. Each moment was frozen. It was happening or it was not. Creativity was not part of a narrative but simply a bipolar position, on or off.

This is what my dreams are like when they are about creativity. I hear they are doing a TV show on Cavafy. I struggle to get to the studio. I fight my way into the building, up to the studio, to the stage where a woman is doing interviews. I push everyone else away and get her attention. She agrees to interview me. She holds the microphone to my mouth. I realize I have nothing to say. I make myself say something: "I love Cavafy so much that I went to a great deal of trouble to get here for this program." "Isn't that sweet," says the hostess, disgustedly.

Freud was not interested in older people. He thought psychoanalysts should take on no patients over fifty. After that age, the elasticity for change was gone, he believed, in addition to the problem that childhood material, being so far in the past, would take too long to reconstruct. It was left to Jung and his followers to pay attention to the problems of the middle-aged. Jung's experience of midlife crisis and his subsequent self-analysis convinced him that where a young person's primary task is to emancipate himself from his family and establish his own family, a middle-aged person's task is to discover and express his own uniqueness. Specializing in the treatment of the middle-aged, Jung guided his patients on a path of self-development he called "the process of individuation." Its goal he called "wholeness" or "integration." But that was a very precarious and fluid state, never finally achieved. In fact, life was a journey toward a goal that was never arrived at.

4

How We Die

"We talk of 'death' for convenience, but there are almost as many deaths as there are people. We do not possess a sense that would enable us to see, moving at full speed in every direction, these deaths, the active deaths aimed by destiny at this person or that. Often they are deaths that will not be entirely relieved of their duties until two or even three years later. They come in haste to plant a tumour in the side of a Swann, then depart to attend to other tasks, returning only when, the surgeons having performed their operations, it is time to plant the tumour there afresh."

The Captive

OVER THE SUMMER, I CAR-ried *Sodom and Gomorrah* with me on a trip out West. I didn't get much reading done. I had fallen in love. In our different ways, L. and I both had. All we wanted to think about, read about, see, and fill our minds with was the beloved, a place, the high desert country of the Colorado Plateau, the red rock canyons and Pharaonic cliffs of Arches, Canyonlands, and Capitol Reef. We hired a Jeep and driver and drove the White Rim Trail. L. sat in the back looking out, experiencing the sublime. He had found a landscape that matched his soul. "I am not a religious person, but I keep thinking of God," he said. He saw God's cities in the sandstone monuments, fins, buttes, and mesas. Jerusalem, the temples of Angkor Wat, the fortress of Carcassone, the Palace of the Popes in Avignon, the Temple of Karnak, New York City—all were there. As for me, I loved the places where people had made some mark, a Mormon settlement in Capitol Reef, where apricot orchards were planted at the base of the red sandstone cliffs; the cliff dwelling at Betatakin; even an abandoned uranium processing plant in the Moab Valley. I was seized by the desire to drive the road Mormons pioneered in 1879 to get from Escalante to Bluff, breaching the two-thousand-foot canyon of the Colorado. But we ran out of time. We had to go home.

Almost as soon as we reached New York and unpacked, I arranged to cash in our frequent-flyer miles and go back West. L. took the news with his usual Zen readiness for anything and his pleasure in my unpredictable enthusiasms. Teddy was horrified and unsettled, as the young can be when their elders do something unexpected.

"That's crazy, Mom."

"Would you say this is the craziest thing I've done in all the years you've known me?"

"Yes I would."

"Then you're lucky."

The person I was afraid to tell was my mother. Not only would she take my absence as a personal desertion, my infatuation with the West as a betrayal of our urban heritage, but she, too, would think my repeated journey crazy, a sign of lapsed discipline and sense as serious as having a second child too soon after the first. I feared her Yiddish assessments of virtue ("That's acting like a mensch!") and insanity ("What are you? A meshuggener?"). She knew me pretty well and over decades; she had not flattened me into a person who existed only in relation to her; she had had to accept some pretty hard behavior from me in the past. If *she* thought I was crazy, I'd care. I put off mentioning my second trip to her as long as I could, hoping she would forget by the time I left for Utah again that I had just been there. No such luck. Her mind is intact, and she was as outraged as I'd feared she would be.

"You were just there!"

"Yes, but I have an idea for something to write," I said, trying to make myself sound responsible, a slave of duty, not a perpetrator of whims. "I need to do research."

"Well, if you're going to write something, all I can say is, it's about time. A travel article?"

"No. It's a pretty far-out idea. It may not work out. I'd rather not try to explain it," I said, displacing the nuttiness of my travel plans onto this imaginary piece of writing.

Mother accepted it gracefully. "Please try to call as often as you can, my darling. That's all I ask."

Every time I go away, I leave a detailed itinerary with my brother, Richard, so I can be reached. I always expect to be called home for Mother. I can't count the number of emergencies she's had in recent years. Richard says he has ridden in the ambulance with her three times, my sister, Susan, has done it once, I have done it once, Claire, who comes in to make her dinner, has done it twice, I think, and the building staff has found her at least once. That makes eight. Someone told me she took her mother to the emergency room thirty times before she died. In the five years we've been spending the winter in Florida, I've been called back to New York because of Mother three times, beginning on the day L. and I arrived in Key West for the first time, when Richard called to say that Mother had taken an overdose of sleeping pills.

She later told us that she knew she had stomach cancer and didn't want to put us through what she endured eleven years before when Daddy died of cancer. But no one had diagnosed cancer, and there turned out to be none. She had an ulcer, controllable with Tagamet. The doctors characterized her suicide attempt as "a cry for help," rather than a serious effort to do away with herself. The term "cry for help," although useful for normalizing suicide attempts, cheapens a profound ritual of old age, the symbolic death. In *King Lear*, Gloucester, blinded, weak, and in despair, asks his son, Edgar, to lead him to the cliffs of Dover so that he can throw himself off. Edgar guides him to a spot he says is Dover, describes how high up they are, and allows Gloucester to jump. Of course they're nowhere near the cliffs, and when Gloucester jumps, he doesn't hurt himself at all, merely blacks out from emotion. When he awakes and sees he's still alive, he's a changed person. He accepts life, however diminished, as well as his inevitable death. As Edgar puts it, "Ripeness is all." Mother's overdose, like Gloucester's leap, was a move in the endgame, a step toward "ripeness is all."

Her doctors, I soon realized, saw my mother as a risible hypochondriac, and although this was a perception I had intermittently allowed myself, I thought they should take her ailments more seriously. So the help we got her as a result of her suicide attempt was a new set of doctors, including a younger cardiologist as her principal physician, and a kind of medical attention she would never before accept in the form of a psychiatrist.

As my father rejected alcohol on the grounds that he "didn't need it," my mother had considered psychiatry a remedy which one turned to only for raving mania and other extreme mental problems. Crazy people went to psychiatrists, and none of us was crazy. The concept of neurosis did not exist for her. Although she suffered from headaches, fatigue, and a variety of other ailments which might, conceivably, have been psychosomatic, she never once in her first fourscore years entertained the idea that she could be helped by a psychiatrist. So it was a testimony to her anguish, loneliness, and desperation that she agreed to see one.

The psychiatrist we arranged for her to see was in his forties, some years younger than me. Personable and kind as well as brilliant, he had a Ph.D. in history in addition to his medical degree and psychoanalytic training. Mother immediately saw him as a delightful child she had to herself for an hour every week, loved him like a son, and easily got the knack of therapeutic talk, which she discerned was merely a higher form of kvetching, one that produced a gratifying and unprecedented amount of praise and support from the kvetchee, instead of the usual self-justifications and disavowals of responsibility.

He put her on an antidepressant, and she became, despite her failing body, a new and wonderful person, a joy and inspiration. Where before she had sometimes been demanding and ungrateful, she now became both grateful and moderate in her demands. Where before she concentrated on what she could no longer do, now she focused on the strengths and pleasures that remained to her. It was as though a pill had been found which allowed her to see the glass half full where before she had seen it half empty. That was the beginning of what for me have been Mother's best years. She was eighty-three.

Over the years, Mother's habitat has shrunk as dramatically as that of the snow leopard or mountain gorilla. She used to be able to walk all the way to Fifth Avenue, then only to Park, to Third, then along Second five blocks in any direction, then only two, then one. Now she can hardly leave her apartment. Occasionally when the weather is fine she can walk to the entrance of the Fifty-ninth Street Bridge, which is next to her building. When we are lucky, she has the energy to get downstairs to a taxi and come to our place on Eighty-second Street for a visit, as she did last Mother's Day, when I served her eggs Beatrice, a tribute to female procreation best washed down, as it was that day, with a mimosa, whose alcoholic content Mother enjoys but ignores, calling it orange juice.

Periodically her heart falters. Sometimes this happens when she walks too far and tires herself out. Sometimes it happens when she's scared, as she was as at the thought of repeating her one visit to Key West, especially by the idea of changing planes in Miami, despite the wheelchair, the airlines attendant, and my coming up from Key West to meet her. Sometimes her heart fails because the chest cavity has filled with blood fluid the weakened heart has been unable to pump along. Leaking through the artery walls, the fluid backs up and presses on the heart, making its job of pumping even harder, beyond the capacity of the weakened organ. When this happens, she gasps for air, turns blue, or feels like she's drowning. If someone sees her, they call 911. An ambulance arrives carrying a team of emergency medical personnel. There are also two policemen and sometimes firemen as well. They slam nitroglycerine into her, slap an oxygen mask on her mouth, get her on a stretcher, into the ambulance, and rush her through the city traffic to New York Hospital ten blocks uptown and two blocks east from her apartment. She goes in through the emergency room, gets hooked up to IVs, endures various tests, and then gets sent up to a cardiac floor where they try to drain the fluid from around the heart with massive doses of a diuretic, usually Lasix. They catheterize her and make careful measurements of all the fluids that go in and come out. After three days or so she is usually well enough to go home, although exhausted by her physical ordeal and by the trauma of the hospital stay itself.

Every time my mother goes into the hospital, my brother, my sister, and I perform an elaborate stewardship dance, whose improvised moves are worked out over the telephone. Someone has to take Mother in. Someone has to take her out. Someone has to go to the apartment and get her insurance card, her checks, her bathrobe, her cane, her eyedrops, her reading glasses, her *TV Guide*, her comb and brush, her Fixodent, and clothes to come home in. Someone has to arrange for a phone and, if she's well enough, a television. Someone has to hire private duty nurses in the hospital and round-the-clock nurses for the first week or so after she gets home. I personally think that someone should be with her every possible moment in the hospital to act as her advocate. Too sick to speak up for herself, hampered, in any case, by the paralysis of a vocal chord, visually impaired, hearing impaired, she is sometimes neglected, for example, when food is left for her that she cannot even see, or when she needs painkillers she can't ask for, and often she is badgered unnecessarily by hospital routines, as when they wake her up to take her temperature. I sit for hours with my mother in the hospital, not talking, holding her hand. My brother and sister, both of whom work in offices, cannot do this. Anyway, I am best at dumb accompaniment, Susan at arranging home care, and Richard at dealing with the bureaucracies.

With a midtown office, closest to ground zero, Richard gets the brunt of the trouble. He has had to ride with her to the emergency room more than the rest of us and to take her home more often. The building calls him first if there's a problem, and, because he checks on Mother more often than Susan or me, he is often the one to uncover problems. That was what happened in August.

When he called in the morning, her line was busy. An hour later, busy still. Mother doesn't get many phone calls or talk long, so Richard thought she must have left the phone off the hook, as she often does, not seeing well enough to notice. When we suspect this, we call the front desk of her building, and the concierge calls her on the house phone. This time, the house phone went unanswered. One of the elevator men got a key from the front desk and went into Mother's apartment. He found her on the floor next to her bed.

911. Ambulance. Emergency personnel. Police. Firemen. Hospital. Congestive heart failure.

She had been watching TV when she started feeling chest pains. She went to her bed to lie down. She lay there not feeling well for quite some time. She thinks she must have tried to get up to go to the bathroom, fallen, knocked the phone off the hook. It started during *Jeopardy*, so she lay there for almost seventeen hours, unconscious.

L. and I were spending the weekend in East Hampton. By the time we got back to the city, Mother was doing pretty well. She was in a room with three other people. Across from her was a black man of about seventy, seriously ill, who made little noise, and a middle-aged white lady who moaned continually, "Eleanore, Eleanore, help me. Why are you torturing me this way? It isn't right to torture me." At night, Mother said, she never stopped. She and the man both threw off their blankets and rolled from side to side with their knees pulled up to their chests.

"It's nothing to me," Mother said. "I could care less to see their business. I can barely see anyway. But what I see, it isn't very pretty."

The doctors handling my mother's case seemed astonishingly young, probably in their twenties, and naively determined to find the cause of Mother's "episode." To me it seemed clear: she was an 88-year-old woman with a failing heart. She would have episodes like this again and again until once we wouldn't find her in time or get her to the hospital in time or her heart would have had as much as it could take. Wasn't it like the young to assume that any lapse from perfect function needed explaining?

"The tests show that your mother's medication levels are low," said pretty Dr. J., "lower than what Dr. Franklin prescribed. Is it possible that she isn't taking her meds?"

"Not possible," I said. "She's good about pills. She keeps them arranged in special boxes. But I'll ask her."

Of course she was taking her pills, Mother said, but perhaps her medication levels were low because she'd been unconscious for so long and hadn't taken her usual dose.

"That wouldn't account for the extremely low levels we found," said Dr. J. "Are you sure she is telling you the truth? Are you sure she's taking her meds?"

"Anything's possible," I said, wanting to placate her with a view toward my mother's release, like Linda Hamilton in her sanity hearing at the start of *Terminator 2*, trying to tell the examining board whatever she thinks they want to hear. No sooner did I say, "Anything's possible," however, than I realized that although Mother would never knowingly not take her medication, she could barely see and perhaps had made a mistake.

The list of medications which the nurse went over with me before they let me take Mother home was enough to defeat anyone. Capoten, 25 mgs., three times a day. Lasix, 80 mgs., once a day. Lanoxin, 0.125 of a mg. on an alternating schedule with Lanoxin, 0.250 of a mg., Synthroid once a day, Ecotrin once a day, Isordil three times a day. This was without her antidepressant (Nortriptyline, two pills in the morning, one at noon), and her sleeping pills (Terazepam, 75 mgs., as needed at bedtime) and Colace (at bedtime, as needed).

Her Lasix was crucial. This is the diuretic which drains the fluid buildup around her heart. When we got back to the apartment and Mother was resting in bed, I took down all her pill bottles and checked the labels against the protocol the nurse had given me at the hospital. The Lasix was in pills of 40 mgs. but the dosage was 80, which meant she should have been taking two a day. The print on the label was tiny and faint. Did she know the pills were 40 mgs. and she needed to take two of them?

"How many Lasix do you take, Mother?"

"One, dear. One every morning."

I felt the fury of the husband of the supposed heart sufferer in *The Good Soldier* when the valet drops the suitcase with her medication or they have to run to catch a train, causing the fragile woman anxiety that might be fatal. Why didn't the world understand how delicate she was, how easy it had to go on her? Why did everyone go out of their way to produce conditions that were damaging to her health? In this case, I felt fury against all pharmacists and printers of labels. How could they expect a woman who had no sight in one eye and very little in the other to make out the information in this pale, eight-point, dot-matrix type? I could barely read it myself. And then to expect her to master the complexities of dividing the dosage by the strength of the pills! It was too much, too difficult.

Determined to improve the labels, I wrote the name of the medications in thick black magic marker over the light type of the pharmacist's label. I wrote SYNTHROID on one and ISORDIL on the other.

"Can you see now where it says ISORDIL?" I didn't mean to test her, but I held out the wrong one, the one marked SYN-THROID.

She put her eyes against the label and spelled it out slowly: "I-SOR-DIL. Yes," she said. "I can make it out."

When I explained her mistake, Mother wept. With all her wits intact, determined to take care of herself and not to be dependent, she was losing her grip on her life. In me, the failure of her faculties inspired panic. She needed someone supervising every minute of her existence.

Mother stayed so weak for so long after this attack that I was afraid she might slip away at any time. One day I went to see her, to say good-bye.

She was sensible and unafraid about dying, said she was more than ready.

"I think about going to Washington Heights and walking around until a stray bullet gets me. Only I don't have the strength to get there."

"I don't think the bullets are whizzing around quite the way you think they are, Mother."

"Probably not. Just my luck. I only wish I could be lucky enough to die in my sleep. But I won't. God wants to get back at me for not believing in him."

She didn't die then. Who died was forty-seven-year-old Steven Lebergott, son of retired economics professor Stanley Lebergott and his wife, Ruth, who live up the street from us. For the twenty-one years I've lived on the Wesleyan campus, Stanley has walked past my house two, sometimes four times a day on the way to and from his office in the Public Affairs Center. If I'm outside, we always chat, sometimes about the flowers in my garden, sometimes about books one of us is reading, sometimes about Teddy or Steve. Stanley has the large and tolerant outlook I associate with men who contemplate economic forces, the interplay of supply and demand, the fluctuations of the markets. Once when Teddy was a toddler, I complained to Stanley about the way he was badgering me for cookies. Stanley gave me a wise man's smile. "If only you or I could be made happy so easily."

Steve Lebergott had grown up in Middletown and had stayed there as a man, working for Wesleyan as the librarian in charge of Interlibrary Loan. He had stayed unmarried for a long time but finally had married, perhaps five years before, a woman with three children. The marriage had turned out well and so had the new family. Steve took loving care of his new stepchildren and of his aging parents, whose health was jointly failing. Steve was going to drive his parents up to Maine so they could have a holiday. Instead he had a sudden massive heart attack, and, without ever going into the hospital, died.

His memorial service, in the Wesleyan chapel, lasted two and a half hours, far longer than most. An out-of-town rabbi was in charge. Affected, self-important, pompous, and *slow*, he paused lengthily between segments of the service, looking at his text and adjusting his pince-nez. His sermon was close to an hour, and although it alluded to the grief of a mother who outlives her child, it did so remotely, citing a passage in the Bible, as though to say, "Our religion has that base covered," but not so as to convey and thus help solace the pain Steve's parents must have been feeling and the pain the rest of us who had known him felt. I suspected him of misrepresenting, as rabbis often seem to do, the centrality of religion in the life of the deceased, appropriating the individual for the institution and making the funeral an occasion for proselytizing. To hear him tell it, Steven had been thinking of Judaism every minute of his life.

Eight people delivered eulogies. One was Richard Kamins, Steven's best friend, proprietor of The Bottle Shop, purveyor of spirits to many households in Middletown, including ours. He spoke more movingly than the rabbi. "Steve was a worrier," he said. "He worried about Dianna's working conditions. He worried about the library. He worried about his parents' health. I think that great heart had simply reached its capacity."

When I got home I called Mother, who was already feeling better, and put it bluntly: "Are all rabbis pompous and self-impor-tant?"

There was a silence. I thought I'd gone too far, counted too much on her secular outlook.

"I'm thinking," she said. Then, "Rabbi Levitt . . ." And another silence. I thought she was going to say that Rabbi Levitt, the rabbi of the congregation we belonged to in Woodmere when I was growing up, had been unusual. "Rabbi Levitt was certainly pompous and self-important. I think they're probably all like that."

While Mother was still in the hospital, the man who was L.'s lawyer when he lived in Paris came to New York and we took him out for dinner. He is an American from Philadelphia who grew up in a tight-knit Armenian family, went to college locally (the University of Pennsylvania) and then, thanks to some random inspiration, some vision, I think it was seeing a letter postmarked Cambridge, Massachusetts, in someone else's mailbox—a vision akin to the one I had of a woman and a small boy walking hand in hand which led me to have a child—he had the inspiration of applying to Harvard Law School, breaking with the traditions of his family and immediate circle of friends by going away, just as my father had, and his life had changed forever. After law school he went to France on a Fulbright, fell in love with the country and a particular woman, his wife Eve, and stayed, producing four children with Eve and raising also her three from an earlier marriage.

He has a warm family life and a successful practice, specializing in enterprises with American and French components, and he probably needs his success to support Eve in the very Parisian style to which she is devoted and which includes designer clothes, lots of gold jewelry, a pampered dog, spa vacations, and daily trips to the hairdresser. I suspect that Jack at some point, again like my father, promised his wife Saks Fifth Avenue's window, or the French equivalent.

But if Jack reminds me of my father in some ways, mostly he does not. He is vastly more cultivated than my father was, a man who plays Bach on the piano for hours in the evening, loves Montaigne, and writes essays himself, accounts of and meditations on current events in France from the perspective of one American lawyer of Armenian descent living in Paris which he calls his "Legal Newsletter from France," prints on yellow, three-holed paper, and circulates monthly to an incredibly diverse list of clients, friends, and acquaintances.

My admiration for his writing and the advent of e-mail have brought my friendship with Jack to a higher pitch this year. Now, when I especially like one of his pieces, I can send him off a quick note from my computer. Like a collagen cream or estrogen which restores to the skin its lost elasticity, e-mail has given me back the spontaneity I had lost to the laziness of age. I can receive Jack's newsletter at noon, read it after dinner, write him a note, and it will pop up on his computer screen when he arrives at work the next morning in Paris.

Jack is about an inch shorter than I am and quite a bit wider, and he likes to take my arm when we walk in the city. We made a noticeable threesome as we entered the restaurant, Girasole, down the street from our apartment, Jack on my arm, L. behind us. At dinner, we talked about Proust and baseball.

"Baseball has caught on all over the world because it's such a democratic game. Anyone can play. You don't have to be tall, the way you do for basketball, or lean, the way you do for tennis. It's open to all physical types."

"I cannot follow it," said L. "Nothing seems to happen. They never hit the ball, and when they do, they never run. I cannot follow football because it's too fast. And I cannot follow baseball because it's too slow."

"You have to enjoy the statistics," Jack explained. "Every time a man steps up to bat, there's a historic dimension. This might be his chance for a home-run record, or he could be about to break a personal strike-out streak going back two years."

"I never understood why guys were so fascinated with statistics," I confessed. "I thought it was a sex-linked trait, something else produced by testosterone."

"It's the nature of the game. Not quick but deep. You have time to bring history to bear."

Baseball came up because there was a lot of fuss in the news about some guy who was about to play more consecutive games than any player had ever played. Big deal, huh? But many people seemed to care a lot, proving Jack's point.

Proust came up, because I was reading him, bogged down at the moment in *Sodom and Gomorrah*, still trying to get through the Verdurins's party in Balbec.

"How would you translate *recherche* in *A la recherche du temps perdu?*" I asked Jack. I was riding my hobby horse, that *recherche* has connotations of "research," and Jack, completely bilingual and sensitive to language, seemed a good person to consult. But instead of answering, he asked what the new translation of Proust did with the title, and when I said, *"In Search of Lost Time,"* he shook his head.

"It just doesn't have any poetry, does it? It's accurate, but it sounds so clunky. I mean, compare *Remembrance of Things Past*, how beautiful that is. Do you know where it comes from?"

"I know the Shakespeare sonnet, if that's what you mean: 'When to the sessions of sweet silent thought, I summon up remembrance of things past.' "

"But do you know that when Voltaire translated Shakespeare's sonnets, he translated that phrase into French as *'à la recherche du temps perdu'*? That's where Proust got it. So when Moncrieff wanted to translate Proust's title, he went back to the Shakespeare sonnet Voltaire had been translating and came up with *Remembrance of Things Past*. The two phrases aren't literal equivalents, of course, but they have the same spirit, the same wistfulness, the same beauty."

Jack's range of interests was a marvel. Not only did he discuss with delicacy these issues of translation, he went on, fired by the two lines I had quoted, to recite some favorite Shakespeare sonnets, and, as we ate our veal cutlets Milanese, to quote Yeats.

" 'All things fall and are built again,/ And those who build them again are gay.' Do you know that? from 'Lapis Lazuli'? That is the key to happiness, as far as I'm concerned. That's why some of the happiest people you'll ever find are the ones who are forced to start their lives over again, or who choose to. Like you, my friend," he said, tapping L. on the arm.

Kathy, whom we were visiting when my mother got sick, is my oldest friend. "Oldest," she always hurries to say, in a deadpan voice which leaves people wondering what the truth is, "because we've known each other so long, not because I'm old. Actually, I'm ten years younger than Phyllis. She used to baby-sit for me in Woodmere."

Her house was around the corner from mine. As eight-year-olds (for, in fact, we were born within weeks of each other) we met after dinner to ride our bikes. When my parents went to Europe for six weeks in 1955, I stayed with Kathy and her family. We were a devoted but unlikely pair. She cared about boys and clothes. I cared about books. She was popular. I was respected. In high school, she was a cheerleader. I was valedictorian. She always jokes that she copied my papers all through grade school and high school. I'd get A's on them, and she'd get B's.

At college, she dated her childhood sweetheart, the boy she'd gone out with in high school. They married when they graduated. Soon after that, he became extremely rich. Our paths had parted in college, but by the time we saw each other again, in 1976, when I was on sabbatical in New York and having my unhappy affair with the publisher, she was leading the life of a wealthy woman in New York. She seemed to enjoy it a lot. She worked as a docent at the Met. She collected art. She had two children. It was especially lovable that she enjoyed so much being rich. When L. started making money, I took her as my role model in that respect.

By the time L. and I visited her in East Hampton, she was divorced. Her husband had remarried. The showplace on the beach in East Hampton she had shared with him had been sold. She was living in a slightly more modest house back from the water. She now worked as a real estate agent in Manhattan, specializing in high-priced properties. She loved working and didn't mind the financial sacrifices she'd had to make, which weren't very great in any case: she still wore Versace and Chanel and flew first-class. Because of her vivacity, wit, and decency she was beloved by a wide range of people, and she moved in distinguished and glamorous circles. I was fascinated by how we had started from the same point and come to such different ones. I admired her as one of the smartest and most down-to-earth of my friends. I wanted to write a book about her, an updating and Americanizing of *Mrs. Dalloway*, but when I said this to her she laughed and said, "Forget it."

We were sitting by her pool, covered in SPF 15 lotions, L. in his sexy purple European-style bikini bought in a Key West gay men's clothing store, me in my old, black, rapidly de-elasticizing Ann Cole to which I clung because its legs were not cut high, Kathy in her two-piece, cleverly draped Norma Kamali in international-high-visibility orange. She was talking on the portable phone, keeping three, sometimes four conversations in the air at a time through call waiting, now talking to a broker, a client, her daughter, now to the liquor merchant, a friend with a tennis court, her boss, apologizing, cutting off, reconnecting, switching tones and attitudes as she moved from being a mother to being a real estate agent to being a friend and back again with a click of the button.

"I saw him at the fruit stand with his new girlfriend. She's nothing. You're infinitely more attractive, sweetie."

"Hello? Yes, this is she. I need a case of Pinot Grigio Santa Margherita, half of it cold, a liter of Absolut, and a case of San Pellegrino, and can you deliver it by five-thirty?"

"I'm back. Well it's no mystery what he sees in her. His parents have money, it's true, but hers are in another category entirely. And sweetie, if that's the kind of person he is, you're really better off without him."

"Hello? Yes? No! I don't believe it. They changed their minds? It doesn't make any sense. Can I speak to them directly?"

"Stewart? You won't believe this. First they said they would vacate in January and now they say they won't. She says it will ruin their Christmas."

"Hello. Oh, Jesse. Thanks for calling back. Can we use your court at five? That's no problem. Phyllis doesn't play doubles anyway. We just thought we'd hit the ball around."

"Hello? Oh hello, Molly. What am I wearing? I'm wearing that yellow cotton Versace. Well, Molly, what can I say? We'll be twins."

"That woman," Kathy explained to me. "She's so dependent. She buys exactly the same clothes that I buy, and then she waits to see when I'm going to wear them and tells me she was going to, too. She's done this five times this summer. Usually, I say I'll wear something else. It's like I'm a free dressing service, a clothes picker. But today I'm in too bad a mood because my deal is falling through. I think I'm going to walk on the treadmill a while."

When I visit Kathy, I am, for me, very active, yet I feel like a slug, so much greater is her energy. After an hour and a half of walking on the beach, I will drag myself back to the car, legs actually aching, but she could keep going for another hour. We bike, we play tennis, we swim, we pay visits on her friends, we check out the local architecture, we buy prepared food for lunch and drinks, we slice up exotic watermelons. She still has so much energy that she has to burn it off on the treadmill, where she walks fast for forty-five minutes, tipping an Evian bottle down her throat, until the sweat is pouring off her. I see her high energy as a trait for which the new American rich, by some mysterious genetic process, naturally select. Bounciness and cheerfulness are the marks of her friends, as anxiety and intermittent depression are the marks of mine. Where my friends and I almost on principle fail to acknowledge hospitality, as though it were to risk insincerity, Kathy and her friends display an almost Heian courtesy, elaborately thanking each other for every social event, every introduction, every kind remark, every house gift, endlessly praising each other's performance in the high stakes arena of Hamptons social life.

As Mother recuperated from her August attack, L. and I spent a lot of time shopping for cars. Our Honda Accord was 100,000 miles and seven years old. I wanted a Mercedes.

I wanted three things: a dog, a haircut, a Mercedes.

"Start with the haircut," L. said.

Okay. That wasn't hard. I went back to Richard S., where I'd had my last haircut seven years before. I went back to where I'd last seen him, on Lexington in the Seventies, but walk up and down as I might, I couldn't find his salon. Finally I found a phone that worked and called his number. He'd moved to Madison. Otherwise, things were the same. There were still ladies of literary and theatrical bent having their hair cut. One was about to go to the Sundance Festival. One had just produced a play off-Broadway. One had copper-colored hair so gorgeous I wanted to trade in my blonde.

"Pretty bad, huh?" I said, as I sat down in the chair and faced myself in the mirror. My hair was pulled straight back in a ponytail. The absence of height was unflattering. My face had no frame, and it isn't sculptural enough to look good so starkly set-off.

"You're an intellectual," said Richard tolerantly. "You don't have time to think about your hair."

He cut off two or three inches, taking up a small clump of hair at a time, flattening it, and cutting at an angle. Then he ran his fingers many times from the base of my neck up to the top of my head, raking the hair. Each hair seemed individually coddled. My face, which had looked like a Franz Hals stuck in modern aluminum metal section box, now had a baroque-carved golden frame more appropriate for it.

"Don't even blow it. Just run your fingers through it like that."

"*Your* fingers, you mean."

That was the haircut.

The dog was an impasse. I wanted a small one, a little white lap dog, a bichon frisé or a maltese. L. wanted something more like Seamus, our sainted springer, something at least the size of a cocker. Teddy, of course, wanted a Lab and promised to walk him whenever we had him in the city. I went into Karen for Pets + People and asked what dogs they recommended. They said, "Not a white dog. You can't imagine how dirty they get in the city. And we're not cheap. I mean, how often do you want to spend seventy-five dollars to get your dog washed? Think about that."

I got interested in pugs. They were small enough to suit me, but masculine enough to suit L. and Teddy. A man does not look foolish walking a pug, as he would walking a Maltese or Shih tzu. Similar reasoning, I was to suspect, had made the pug the gay man's dog of choice. There was something of a boom in pugs. Cruising the Net, mooning about dogs, I found my way to the Pug Dog Home Page. I got to read many pug owners' encomiums to their pets. I could even see their pictures. I learned when the Pug Dog Owners' Group met in Central Park. I got the names of pug rescue organizations all over the country, including Cromwell, Connecticut, where I could adopt pugs that had been abandoned. I read about the gathering of pug fans in which contests were held for the best-dressed pug in various categories, including matching outfits for pug and owner. None of this information satisfied my mental cravings, which is typical of my relations with the Internet. There's a lot out there, but not much you really want.

As it happened, pugs were featured in that month's issue of *Dog World*. There was a pug centerfold, which I tore out and tacked on our bulletin board. Now, whenever I walked into the kitchen, I could look into the dark and loving eyes of the most perfect, adorable pug I had ever seen. This was more like it. When I got around to reading the accompanying article, an interview with a leading breeder of pugs, I learned that pugs were playful, loyal, fierce in defense of their owners, excellent guard dogs, capable of keeping their own counsel, resourceful, and gratifyingly affectionate. Any problems? "They shed like buffaloes. You wouldn't think it to look at them. But they do."

Soon after that, L. and I, walking in Central Park, saw a good-looking man of about forty walking a pug.

"Are you happy with your pug?" I said, as we approached him. "We're thinking of getting one."

"This is my third," he said, stopping so I could pet the dog. "They're great dogs. I wouldn't have anything else. Go for the fawn-colored, not the black. Only if you want to have a life apart from your dog, I wouldn't recommend them. They're very demanding. They won't stand being left alone. I have to take Fifi to the office with me. I can hardly go out to the movies. She's very demanding, aren't you, Fifi? Yes, you are, you demanding little girl!"

Fifi really was cute and good to the touch. I asked if I could pick her up and liked the way she felt in my arms, too. When I put her back, I asked the man if he could recommend a breeder.

"I don't think highly of American pugs," he answered, severely and with a certain amount of self-satisfaction. "I went to France for this one."

"I understand. Thanks," I said, taking L.'s arm and waving good-bye, my clothes covered with fawn-colored hairs.

That was the dog.

The car took even more time. The Mercedes alone meant two trips to New Haven for test drives. Then a trip to Hartford for the BMW, and about five trips to Wallingford before we bought the Saab. It was a reasonable choice, but I never imaginatively engaged with it, and a car, as everyone in America knows, is not a machine to convey you from place to place but a fantasy object, inherently frivolous. I was ready to go all the way and buy the top-of-the-line fantasy, but top of the line meant different things to L. and to me, as did "Mercedes." For him, the Mercedes was a bourgeois car, reeking of conspicuous consumption, the choice of executives and fat cats. For me, the Mercedes was the car of artists and intellectuals, people who appreciated classics, who considered every seven years too often to buy a new car, who wanted a car to last a lifetime, who wore vintage clothing, who read Jane Austen and Thackeray, who watched *Casablanca*. However, we both like driving, and we discovered to our dismay that, in the United States, Mercedes no longer sells cars with standard transmission; try as we might we couldn't get to like the way the automatic transmission felt. With the BMW, I liked the way it drove but L. didn't, and he didn't mind its yuppie image, but I did. So that was out. I'm radically flattening the amount of discussion involved in all this. This was hours, days, phone conversations with friends and relations, discussions with salesmen. Fortunately, car buying has changed since the last time we did it, and car salesmen are now prepared to tell you a price. Last time, at a VW dealer, when I asked the price of the car I liked, the salesman replied, in a tone of offended propriety, as though I had asked him about his sexual prowess, "Are you prepared to buy this afternoon?" I said no. I just wanted to know how much it cost, and he became even prissier, more censorious. "We don't do business that way," he said.

We bought the Saab, with a ten-disc CD player and a good sound system as a sop to me. Nothing marks the distance I've traveled from my upbringing more than this willingness to care about "options," which my parents brought me up to believe, as an article of faith, were sucker bait, something only immigrants and idiots would be dumb enough to pay for. Options alone could reconcile me to this sturdy, well-built, quietly luxurious car, which had sold, according to an article I read in a car magazine, only a few thousand in the whole United States. It took, apparently, exceptional character to appreciate its engineering and surmount its absence of allure. More than I had. We called this no-nonsense vehicle "Silver," so I could say, "Hi ho, Silver, and away!" But the name didn't stick and, in an effort to give it some glamour, we changed it to Greta Garbo.

As the Mercedes slipped away, a certain persona slipped away also. For awhile, we had had money, and I came to look it. I could afford designer clothes. I wore my hair sleeked back, in a soignée twist. I wore gray and silver clothing, Mercedes colors. I was thin. Now menopause started kicking in. My weight went up, though I ate no more. I wasn't fat, just loose around the edges, rounder, softer. My hair in its new styling billowed out, crinkly, around my face. The clothes I bought were less tailored. Even with the money down to a trickle, I had saved enough, cautious as I am, to buy the Mercedes. But I wouldn't have looked right in a Mercedes anymore.

On a cold night in early December, L. and I went to the opening of a show of Nadia G.'s paintings at a new arts center just north of Houston Street at First Street. It was called The Synogogue Space, and I almost called my mother from the opening to tell her about it. I thought she would be amused to hear that the synogogues of the Lower East Side were being turned into art galleries and performance spaces.

Afterward, we walked around looking for a restaurant, turned away from several places because they were full and from Il Buco on Bond Street because it was booked for a private party, enjoying the walk for awhile but then getting cold, tired, and hungry. At Il Cantinori on Tenth Street, they said there would be a forty-minute wait for a table. We sat at the bar and drank Pinot Grigio. I asked the bartender whether martinis were making a comeback. Everyone around us seemed to be drinking them. He said, "About like usual," but seemed to take the question as a friendly gesture because he filled our glasses up again for free. I was enjoying everything: the huge lily, eucalyptus, and ivy arrangement on the bar; the prospect of a splendid dinner; L.'s company; the memory of the synogogue turned gallery; the presence of Richard Gere two tables away in a lumberman's red-check shirt.

When we got home, there were several messages on the machine, including two from Susan. The first said she was at Mother's apartment; Mother was in bad shape, and Susan didn't know what to do. The second said she had called 911, she was now at the Emergency Room, Dr. Franklin was there, and it didn't look good.

This was Susan's virgin journey in the ambulance. By the time we got to the emergency room, it seemed that Mother would live, and Susan was experiencing the exhilaration of someone who has been present at a disaster and behaved creditably. She went back over every minute of the crisis in appreciative detail: how she had returned from dinner and found Mother gasping for air, how she had called me and I wasn't there and Richard was away for the weekend, how hard it had been to bring herself to call 911 because Mother had said not to, but how she'd finally done it, how six people had arrived, how nice they'd been, how they'd rushed her to the ER, which was better than the TV show, how they didn't need the insurance card, although she'd remembered to bring it, how she'd presented Mother's living will, which the ER staff said had to be updated every three months and was no longer valid, how Dr. Franklin had arrived and said Mother might not pull through, how she'd called me and I was still out, how Dr. Franklin had said things were turning a corner, how surprised she was to see us.

When Dr. Franklin said Mother might live, Susan understood that there was nothing further to worry about and went home, relieved. We went home, too. But when I went to visit Mother the next day on the cardiac ward, I had never seen her sicker. She had no color in her face and no life in her eyes. Since she had already been ready for bed when she had her attack, her teeth were out and no one had brought them to the hospital. I'd never seen her without them. Her face looked vacuumed from within, a collapsed mask of what it had been before, the face of a befuddled, pathetic, ancient crone. She had no strength and could barely speak, but when she half-gasped, half-whispered a few words, they were, "Is this never going to end?"

I sat by the bed and held her hand. "The pain," she said. "Thirsty. Water." Then something it took a huge effort to articulate and which I finally deciphered as, "Susan's pearls. Top drawer under pajamas." As soon as she sipped some water through a straw from the cup I held to her lips, she threw up, greenish slimy vomit that looked like she was vomiting up her innards rather than food. She wept and said, "So tired. So tired."

I went to the nursing station. "My mother is very sick. Can you do something?"

A nurse cleaned up the vomit and patted her pillow.

"Can you give her something for the pain?"

"She's on a morphine drip."

"What about the nausea?"

"I'll see if I can get the doctor to order some Compazine."

"Food," said Mother. "Hungry."

I peeled her an orange and put a section into her mouth. She seemed to enjoy it, and then she threw up again.

"Please," I said to the nurse. "Can you get the Compazine?"

"Here's the doctor."

The doctor was a very young woman. She took in the situation and ordered Compazine. I said, "What's going on?"

"Your mother's condition is very, very serious. It's unlikely she will pull out of this."

"My God. Are you saying she's going to die? How long does she have?"

"I can't tell you that," said the resident. "You should speak to the attending physician."

"Is the attending physician around? How do I find him?" Hospital hierarchy was obscure to me.

She looked at me as though I was an idiot. "The attending physician. The person in charge of her care."

"Oh, you mean her doctor, her cardiologist, Dr. Franklin. Yes, of course I'll speak to him. But in the meantime, can you give her something to help her sleep? She's exhausted. She didn't sleep at all last night."

"There's a tranquilizer in the Compazine. That should help."

I sat next to Mother for hours more, holding her hand, glad now she couldn't see me because I kept weeping. But as it approached three in the afternoon and I'd been there since ten, I had a problem. I had an appointment to have my hair cut at three. Should I keep it? Ever since John F. Kennedy was assassinated and I had to decide whether or not to eat a hamburger I had ordered before I'd heard the news, this problem kept recurring, whether a moral or an aesthetic problem I could not say, of how to reconcile large-scale and small-scale events, and I could find no principle to apply better than immediate necessity and never to feign that grief was incapacitating when it was not. I had not been hungry in 1963, but I could not afford to let a paid-for hamburger go uneaten. I had eaten it. I wanted my hair done. I decided to go.

"Mother, I'm going to get my hair cut. I'll be back in two and a half or three hours."

"Go, my darling. I'll be here. Bring my teeth."

Richard S. never gave me a better cut, seeing how upset I was. He is a tenderhearted man, and I think he kept my face hidden by a veil of wet hair as he worked so he wouldn't have to see my tears. He was so concerned he kept working away and ended up cutting more than usual. He ran his fingers from my neck up to my crown. He used the blower while twirling hair around a brush, and soon I looked good enough to go on television, which made me feel good enough to face the hospital again, stopping at Mother's apartment for her teeth and Fixodent and to reach Dr. Franklin. He said, "She is a very old woman with a very bad heart. There's no good way out of this. But I wouldn't say she's in any immediate danger. The resident must have been referring to the overall gravity of the situation."

The resident, in other words, when she scared me by saying that mother wouldn't pull out of this, wasn't saying anything I didn't already know. She meant that Mother was failing faster and more irreversibly than she, the resident, was prepared for, whereas Dr. Franklin and I, who had long ago accepted the fact that Mother would never again walk to Fifth Avenue and that she was headed inexorably toward death, saw this episode as part of the process of dying, but probably not the last. As Winston Churchill said of the Normandy landings, "This is not the end. It is not even the beginning of the end. But it may be the end of the beginning."

With her teeth restored, Mother regained some of her dignity but no strength. I sat beside her listening to the conversations of her roommates, who seemed insultingly hale. One was a landlord, concerned about a building he owned. "I know exactly how many windows there are in the building. There are one hundred and thirty-eight windows. You don't have to tell me!" Another had just had a balloon angioplasty with a Stant device inserted to keep the artery open. He was trying to explain it to his daughter. "Yes, it does stay inside. Well, it's stainless steel. Don't worry. They know what they're doing."

"If only I could get some sleep," said Mother.

The next day Richard got back from his business trip, and Mother had a fight with him. She asked him to bring her sleeping pills from her apartment to the hospital, and he refused. He said it was probably illegal and certainly inadvisable to add sleeping pills to her already carefully controlled hospital regime. She said, "You're so mean! I can't sleep without them! Who are you going to listen to, your own mother or some twenty-year-old intern?" She accused him of cowardice, spinelessness, cruelty, and slavish obedience to authority. She hung up on him. One way to take this was that she was getting better.

Teddy came with me to see her the next day. I thought she was so weak that he might never see her again if he didn't take this opportunity. Also, in my ongoing effort to educate him in the grim realities I myself had been spared, I wanted him to witness the awfulness of the hospital, to know the smell of four unemptied bedpans, to see the shrunken face of a dying person he'd loved. We arrived to find my mother moved into a clean, bright room, with only one roommate, a lady with a nice voice, not too sick. Mother was propped up, had her glasses on and her teeth in, looked cheerful, and sounded positively giggly. "I've been having the most marvelous hallucinations," she said. "I was staying at the Waldorf-Astoria with Daddy, and someone sent the most beautiful flower arrangement. I had a visit from Cary Grant, and who else? yes, it was Audrey Hepburn! We all listened to music and danced. We took the Staten Island ferry. We went out to Far Rockaway in Uncle Davey's car. We stayed at the Meurice in Paris. The plane got fogged in and we had to land in Morocco. We stayed at the Mamounia. We went for a camel ride. We flew on the Concorde." She smiled at us happily. "I feel like the queen of England."

Teddy and I looked at each other with comic-book expressions of amazement. What's she on?

I went into the hallway and found a nurse. "What's she on?" I asked. "She seems pretty happy."

"It may be the morphine finally kicking in."

Susan came to visit that day and couldn't understand why I'd been so upset the day before. I think she suspected me of exaggerating the seriousness of the portion of mother's illness I had had to deal with. Although the three of us siblings loved one another dearly and were remarkably harmonious, each of us no doubt thought himself or herself the golden mean between underreaction and overreaction, between hysteria and coldness.

Teddy on Key West: "The only trouble with it is, you have to go through Florida to get there."

He arrived at the little Key West airport at 8:30 Friday night. By noon the next day, he was on his way back to New York. At about the time his flight was taking off from Miami, Mark had called to say that his father, Sydney Rose, had had a stroke and died. Every death makes a novel out of the inchoate family dramas that have preceded them, giving them irony, direction, and most of all resolution. I won't get into the drama of Sydney Rose, except to say that he hadn't lived much for twenty years, not since he got diabetes and had to have one leg amputated, long before he lost the other as well, long before my beloved mother-in-law Rose Rose died of Alzheimer's, her haphazard charm having turned into a horrible parody of itself, long after Syd's bitterness had distressed his children unto the second generation.

Still, Teddy had to go back for the funeral, and I, as things go, had to pay the bill, $300 for fourteen hours of his company. The airlines offered to give him a percentage off the full coach fare in token of his bereavement, but that meant he (I) still had to pay a penalty of $500 for going back early.

"I'm sorry, but you're no longer eligible for your special fare because you aren't staying over on a Saturday night."

"Gee, my grandfather didn't think of that when he died. What kind of bereavement fare makes you have to wait until Saturday is over before you go home for the funeral? Anyway, the plane arrives at one minute after midnight. You're saying if it comes in two minutes early, I wouldn't have to pay five hundred dollars extra?" Bless the child. He really knows how to talk.

The reservations clerk told him if he went standby, there would be no additional charge.

We ate shrimp. He swam. He left. He got out of Florida just before the first enormous blizzard of 1996. By the time of the funeral next morning, it was snowing so hard that fewer people than would have came. Teddy and his father, aunt, uncle, and cousins were snowed in in the house in which Mark and his sister had grown up, the irony level almost unsupportable as these clever people pondered how the death of the patriarch had provoked a storm of biblical proportions. They were snowed in for two days. The streets were unplowed. The cars were buried. The snow was up to the windows. Fortunately, they had plenty of lox and cold cuts to eat, ordered for the funeral guests. "Thrift, thrift, Horatio!" Bob Stone quoted without missing a beat, upon being told this story. "The funeral meats do coldly furnish forth the wedding feast!"

I went to have my hair color touched up by Gabriela, who, since I'd seen her last year, had gotten divorced, changed salons, had a radical mastectomy and two operations on her uterus. She's a beautiful woman, with red hair, always elegantly arranged, spilling down the back of her head, white-skinned, luminous, perfectly made up. She can wear white pants and tropical-print blouses to work in and never get a spot on herself. She has lived in Key West all her life and can remember picking conch up from the ocean when they wanted some for dinner. Now all conch has to come from the Bahamas. The only "conchs" around here are native Key Westers, like Gabriela, and even they are almost an endangered species.

Gabriela has many elderly clients whom she treats with great courtesy, calling them Miss Louie or Miss Clarisse in the Southern fashion. She always asks me how my mother is, how my son is, and I ask in return, "How are your boys, Gabriela?" She has two, the youngest twelve, the oldest at college. Her parents both died young and she was raised by her grandmother. They were Cuban-descended and spoke Spanish at home. The mirror at her work station is covered with family photos, also a picture of the pope, a badge saying "World's Best Mom" and inspirational messages, like "Let me have the courage to change the things I can, the patience to bear the ones I can't, and the wisdom to know the difference." She used to bring her little dog, Lady, to work with her, but in this new salon (her ex-father-in-law ran the other one) she doesn't feel she can do that.

"How is your son? your mother? your husband?" she asked, as she wrapped a towel and cape around my neck.

"And how are you, Gabriela? You look beautiful."

"Not too bad. Tired. I work every day until seven. I'd like to get home earlier, make dinner for the boys, but most of my customers you know they work, Miss Phyllis, and they can't come in until five. I take in fifty, a hundred dollars a day after five. So I can't leave until seven. Then I make dinner, get food on the table by nine or ten. I'm in bed by midnight, up at six, set the table for the boys for breakfast before school, do the laundry, come in to work. My boyfriend's getting divorced. It's very bitter. His wife wants to leave him ruined. I don't know if I have the strength to go through it. I've had so much else to get through this year."

"Your divorce. Was it hard, Gabriela?"

"It was hard but not like my boyfriend's. We didn't fight because I didn't ask for anything."

"Not even child support?"

"No, I suppose when he gets out of prison I'll have to take him to court for that, but it's not worth the trouble now. After all I did for him, to have him turn against me when I got sick, it was too much. I'm Catholic, but I just said to myself, 'What for?' My boyfriend was great with the surgery, the bandages. I'm vain. He doesn't mind."

"God, Gabriela. You're gorgeous. He's getting a really good deal."

"Well, yes. But you know, Miss Phyllis, I don't think I want to get married again. My friends don't understand. They think that marriage is what it's all about. They are shocked. But I've never gotten anything out of marriage. It's always me does everything. This man, I've known him for twenty years. We weren't always as close as we are now, if you know what I mean. He's a nice guy. He saw me through the surgery. But as soon as I marry them, it all goes wrong. The kids understand, but my girlfriends don't. I'm really close to my girlfriends. They're like my parents. I never really had parents. But I have my friends. We grew up together. They were always there. They treat me like a child, even though I'm thirty-nine. They say, 'What are we going to tell the kids if you just live with him?' I say, 'Tell the truth. That's what I tell my kids. I tell them the truth.'"

"My God, Gabriela, it's 1996."

"Yes, that's what I tell them. But they're shocked. They fuss over me like a little girl. If I drive Kevin to a baseball tournament and stop in Miami, my friend says, 'I'll drive him the rest of the way, it's too much for you, Gabriela.' Here, look at these pictures. This is Kevin. This is Grant. Look at Lady. Isn't she precious? Look at the twins. They're my niece's daughters, one year old. Aren't they adorable? Cute as two buttons. Here's another one of Kevin and Lady."

"Kevin has gotten big. He must be taller than you, Gabriela."

"Yes he is. He's twelve now and taller than me. This is my grandmother. And here's my grandmother with her sister. Did your son get down this year?"

"Yes he did, but his grandfather died and he had to go right back after fourteen hours. We hoped his father would pay for him to come back."

"Yeah, right!" said Gabriela.

"We were lucky not to have to pay five hundred dollars extra to get him home. That bereavement fare doesn't mean a thing."

"No, Miss Phyllis. They make money from it. Every day. They make money from people's misery. Isn't that the way of the world?"

The doctors want to do a mastectomy on her eighty-seven-year-old grandmother, she told me, and she is the only one in the family against it.

"What kind of world performs a mastectomy on an eighty-seven-year-old woman? My family says, 'Doesn't she deserve a chance?' 'A chance for what?' I say. 'What she's going to get is horrible pain, and then what?' They did this to my other grand-mother. She was ninety. They took her in. They did a biopsy when I wasn't there. They said it was an emergency. I said, 'A biopsy is not an emergency procedure.' Then they wanted to cut more. I said, 'Grandma, I'm going to take you to the oncology wing and let you look at these people after surgery. Then you decide if you want them to do that to you.' But she didn't make it. The biopsy took everything out of her. She tried to hold on. She fought and fought. Her skin was cracking open from the edema. The fluid was running out. I said to the nurse, 'Give her mor-phine.' She said, 'The doctor has to order it.' I said, 'Get the doc-tor.' She said, 'I can't bother him now. It's the middle of the night.' I said, 'Get the doctor or I'm going to tear down this hospital.' She said, 'Am I going to have to call security for you?' I said, 'Yes, security for me and an ambulance for you.' So she finally called the doctor, and I said, 'Why don't you give my grandmother mor-phine? She's suffering.' 'If we give her morphine, it will weaken her heart and shorten her life.' 'Shorten her life! My God, she's a ninety-year-old woman in terrible pain! What kind of doctor are you! What kind of compassion do you have? What kind of ethics are those! Give her the goddamned morphine.' And finally he did. But that's what you have to do to get compassionate care in a hos-pital. She lay there for days. She couldn't talk. I came in one day and I lay down next to her and I said into her ear, because she could hardly hear, 'It's okay, Grandma. It's time for you to go. You don't have to fight anymore.' And we said the Lord's Prayer together and Hail Mary and then her line went flat. Nobody had ever told her it was okay to die. Now they're doing it again with my other grandmother. I know what that pain is like. I had that operation. I couldn't breathe. I wanted to die, it hurt so much. I couldn't move because the muscles were gone. And to do this to an eighty-seven-year-old woman? They say, 'How can you not give her a chance, Gabriela?' and I say, 'How can you want her to endure this?' They say, 'What kind of person are you?' And I say,

'I'm a person who cares about life.' I'll tell you, Miss Phyllis, I'm a good Catholic, but I could be like that doctor, that Dr. Kevorkian. I don't see the point of just hanging on. I know what life can be and that's not life."

There's not much to read when someone is dying. Almost everything seems frivolous, an insult to one's grief. Any satisfaction on the author's part with his or her performance, any mere literary pirouetting, stands out. When my father was dying, the only book I could tolerate was Tolstoy's *The Death of Ivan Ilyich*, which describes the dying patriarch's alienation from his bourgeois, sentimental family, his ability to stand the company only of his servants, whose treatment of his dying was matter-of-fact, oriented toward the physical. I remember the scene in which his valet bathes his feet, and he experiences a kind of peace. I have tried to provide that kind of physical comfort for my mother. That's why I like best to cook for her or simply to hold her hand. That's what I got from Tolstoy. That, and to know that when someone is in their final moments they often pick at the bed clothes, then at themselves, as though their own skin has become an encumbrance. When I saw my father do it, I knew what it meant, because I'd read *The Death of Ivan Ilyich*.

Now I have *How We Die*, which I turn to periodically to understand what is happening to Mother, or what has happened to all the other people who've passed into the realm of death while I've been reading Proust. The author of *How We Die*, Sherwin Nuland, teaches surgery and the history of medicine at Yale. He describes death by cardiac failure, death from stroke, death from AIDS, death from cancer. I use his book as a guidebook to death, a kind of Fodor's or Frommer's. It is also a very elegant polemic, in favor, like my Key West hairdresser Gabriela, of letting people die. He points out the disinclination of medical authorities to accept death as anything but an exceptional event. Never do they allow a physician to give "old age" as the cause of death. He describes, most movingly, the death at the age of ninety-seven of the grandmother who raised him. The stroke that killed her was a "terminal event," Nuland insists, not a "cause of death," and the difference between the two is huge. She died of having lived. If every death is caused by disease, death is unnatural. If it's unnatural, we must fight it. We certainly can't allow assisted suicides. But death is a normal part of life.

It's hard for me to read more than a few pages of *How We Die* at a time. After a few pages, all the deaths start swimming together. Life seems a dance of death. All of us seem to be dying. I think that is how Nuland sees us, all dying from the age of fifty on, our hearts beating ten beats less every minute every year, our bladders shrinking, our arteries filling up, our brain cells disappearing. We are all dying, the only difference is how fast, how slow, how close we are to our "terminal event." I read Nuland's cool and rational words, and in the back of my mind I hear the bombastic narrator of *Bleak House*, intoning, "Dead, your Majesty! Dead, my Lords and gentlemen! And dying thus around us every day!"

5

Estrogen

"One is no more distressed at having become another person, after a lapse of years and in the natural sequence of time, than one is at any given moment by the fact of being, one after another, the incompatible persons, malicious, sensitive, refined, caddish, disinterested, ambitious which one can be, in turn, every day of one's life. And the reason why one is not distressed is the same, namely that the self which has been eclipsed . . . is not there to deplore the other, the other which is for the moment, or from then onwards, one's whole self."

The Fugitive

My favorite time for sleeping has gotten to be the half hour or forty-five minutes after L. gets up. He goes downstairs and makes coffee. He enjoys making his breakfast—coffee, and a toasted bagel with cream cheese—and eating it by himself. I enjoy the smell of coffee and having the bed to myself. Proust compares the pleasure of having someone next to him in bed asleep to the soothing sounds of nature, like falling water or birds in the trees. I do not feel that way. A hardcore fan of autonomy, I think, like Goldilocks, "There is someone in my bed." Sometimes it shifts its weight. Sometimes I hear it breathe, even snore. Often it tosses and turns, which creates a seismic movement in the mattress and makes me roll down my side as though down the side of a hill. I am always aware of that other person, whose independent being, however loving, however loved, is a kind of assault.

Often I fall back to dreaming in that postlude of sleep after L. has left the bed, and I dream intensely. A fluid world exists in which what's done is undone and what's undone is done, and in that half hour with the bed to myself I throw myself into it. Yesterday I dreamed about Teddy. He needed me. I had left him alone. He was a baby and I couldn't remember, couldn't remember who was taking care of him. I went down the list of baby-sitters in my mind; it was none of them. On the outer edge of sleep, waking up, between dream and breakfast, I solved the problem. Teddy wasn't a baby. He was twenty-three and living on his own. He had a job. He was a grown-up. I didn't need to find a sitter for him anymore! The guilt, the sense of responsibility, the horror of having let my child down dropped away from me like a suffocating plastic poncho one throws off after the rain, and I woke up refreshed and happy.

This morning, in that same fluid period of dream, I was daughter, not mother. With my mother and father, I was going to the movies in a snowstorm. No tickets were available, however, and we had to leave. We had to climb down from the theater as though down a cliff face, from one foothold and handhold to another. I was worried about my father who was overweight. "Put your foot here, Daddy. Now put it there." I talked him down. Even dreaming, I knew how happy I was to have him back from the dead. This time when I woke up, I didn't feel refreshed and relaxed. I realized my father wasn't taking me to the movies, however ineptly. He was in the ground on the border between Queens and Brooklyn, with all the other dead New Yorkers.

I was in the English Department reading room at the top of Harvard's Widener Library, a senior in college studying for an exam, my large volume of Chaucer on the table before me, when a young man asked me what line we were up to. It was a good opening gambit. Professor Whiting proceeded through Chaucer's poetry line by line, annotating, explicating, and providing a commentary on the Middle English. Anyone who asked what line we were up to knew how the course worked. He was either an English major or a graduate student in English, therefore trustworthy. But it was patently a line. No one really cared where we were in class. A close reading of the footnotes told you almost as much as Professor Whiting, albeit without his Yankee wit.

My first glance at my questioner revealed that he was cute, blue-eyed, preppy in type. The weak chin he would one day seek to cover up with beard and goatee I found adorable. I was attracted by the thick tortoise-shell glasses which would, in the fullness of time and to my sorrow, be replaced by contact lenses and a squint. I allowed myself to be drawn into conversation. We moved quickly from Chaucer to Whiting to D. W. Robertson, the Chaucer scholar who taught at Princeton, to the fact that the young man I was talking to had gone to Princeton and was now doing graduate work in English at Harvard.

We decided to go out into the hall to continue our conversation.

His glamour, as he laid the basic facts of his life on me at our initial conversation in the hallway, seemed considerable. Not only had he gone to Princeton, which from the perspective of Harvard seemed like four years of elegant romping in the manner of F. Scott Fitzgerald, he had also spent two years at Oxford. He had written his undergraduate thesis on Thomas Hardy and it had won a prize. He had fought with the authorities at Oxford, because he wanted to continue working on Hardy, but they recognized no novelist more recent than Dickens. He was a fiction writer. His short stories had been widely admired at Princeton. He was going to get a Ph.D. in English and teach at a university, but his real life was going to be writing novels. He had studied with Kingsley Amis, when Amis was a visiting professor at Princeton, and then continued to be his friend in England. He had driven him around to assignations. He had firm opinions on Iris Murdoch, Evelyn Waugh, T. S. Eliot, and William Empson. He affected a Kingsley Amis–style cantankerousness I found irresistible—Antonioni's movies were "fuckin' phony foreign films." I liked him more than anyone I'd ever met. Then he told me his name.

That summer I had spent some time with a young man in my

class at Harvard who had grown up in Bayonne, New Jersey. He was a journalist, and our temperaments were perpetually at odds. One day in exasperation with me he said, "I know someone you would really get along with. The two of you are exactly alike. He grew up in Bayonne and went to Princeton. His name is Mark Rose."

Mark Rose! I liked everything about the name, its lack of ethnicity, its monosyllabic simplicity, its efficiency, the way it combined a maximum of identification with a minimum of letters. It struck me at the time that it was bizarre of the journalist to mention it, because what were the odds of my meeting this person, this Mark Rose, I was made for? Why bother to tell me his name? But now, outside the English Department reading room, the person I liked offered "Mark Rose" as his name.

"Not Mark Rose from Bayonne, New Jersey?" I said, taking in the enormity, the fatedness, the conclusiveness of this meeting.

It was November, 1963. I had just turned twenty-one. I was now old enough to drink in Massachusetts, to vote, and, I had decided, to lose my virginity. Mark's arrival in my life was providential. He had an apartment right across from Widener, at the corner of Plimpton Street and Massachusetts Avenue. He was on the fourth floor, and from his window you could see the river. A glance around the apartment—at the prints on the walls, his two fine guitars and excellent banjo—suggested that he came from a family of sufficient means that if I got pregnant he could pay for an abortion. I decided to let myself go.

We were having lamb chops for dinner at his apartment. We had spent almost every minute of the previous two days together. The Chaucer exam was still one day away. He hadn't yet kissed me. I knew that when he did, a man of his sophistication, unlike the boys I had been dating, could not be expected to stop there. I could hardly make rational conversation, I was so keyed up. At the same time I was keenly interested in the cooking of the lamb chops. I had never realized that food could be cooked, that if you exposed raw meat to a flame for five minutes and then turned it to the other side and did the same, sprinkled on salt and pepper, you could have deliciously prepared food that would satisfy hunger. I never realized you could do this for yourself. You didn't have to have your mother or a cook or someone in a restaurant do it for you. I was impressed that Mark knew all this. After dinner, I got up to put some water on to boil for instant coffee, which was something I did know how to do. He grabbed my hand and pulled me back, saying, "Kiss me first."

And so, somewhat belatedly, I got the point of the flashlight jokes of my childhood. I finally understood some mysterious sensations I'd experienced in my nether regions at odd moments from high school on and why they pleased me, and I appreciated the elegance, from an engineering point of view, of male anatomy. I was amused and excited to realize that every man walking down the street, every nerdy undergraduate male, had such an interesting capacity. Still, I didn't regret I hadn't started all this sooner. As my mother had always delicately suggested, through parable and sermon, it wasn't worth throwing one's life away for.

Nine days later, I was sitting at Mr. Bartley's Burger Cottage having lunch. I ate there every day, every meal: a boiled egg for breakfast, a hamburger without a roll for lunch, a hamburger without a roll for dinner. I hated going all the way to the Radcliffe Quad to the dormitory where I was supposed to take my meals, so I stayed in Harvard Square between classes and ate sparingly at Mr. Bartley's. I liked his hamburgers, and eating the same thing every day saved me having to think about it. Twenty years later, long after my Harvard professors had forgotten me, I could still walk into the Burger Cottage and Mr. Bartley would say, "Rare bun, hold the roll, right?"

I had given my order and was waiting for the food when I noticed the radio was on, turned to the news, louder than usual, a sign that something was up. The last time they had played the news loud at the Burger Cottage was for the Cuban missile crisis. What now? Something about the President. He was in Dallas. He'd been shot, was dying, was dead.

Within minutes a sense of exemption many of us had grown up with was gone. Raised in peace and plenty, we assumed nothing bad could happen to us—only to other people, the old, the unfortunate, the losers. But now it seemed that even a young, successful, handsome, rich, and democratically elected human being could be obliterated, despite all the protection in the world. Hard as it was to take in the news that the President had been shot and was dead, it was fractionally easier than to take in the news that young Jack Kennedy, husband of Jackie, father of two little children, was shot, was murdered, was dead. For the death of the President was an event in American history, and although it was shocking and horrifying that the President could be killed, it took only a moment to realize that Lincoln's countrymen had felt the same way, that although one had to go far back in American history to encounter similar events, there were similar events. It was shocking to have such a thing happen in one's time, but it meant one's time was historic. Into the next century, as long as we lived, we would all remember where we were and what we were doing when we heard the news of Kennedy's assassination.

It was just then that the waitress set before me, horrified, bewildered, and grief-stricken as I was, the rare hamburger without a roll which in my naive reliance on day-to-day continuity and uneventfulness I had embarrassingly ordered. It came to me from another world, a world in which people ordered lunch and lived to eat it, made appointments with the dentist and kept them, had children and raised them, a world in which tragedy didn't figure, and to eat it, I would have to return, however briefly, to that other world.

I ate, paid, and went outside to mourn. The bells of the Harvard churches tolled slowly. People stood, not even in groups, but alone, all around Harvard Yard, with their heads bowed from the weight of grief. I stood like them, head bowed.

After a while I wanted not to be alone anymore and went over to Mark's. We hugged each other in tears and then sat on the sofa to listen to the radio. Responses had already started coming in. Lord Carnarvon quoted Aeschylus: "Slowly drop by drop pain falls upon the heart." Whenever they mentioned Kennedy's age or his children, I started crying.

We wanted it all to make some sense but it didn't. Later we would try out explanations. Perhaps his death was caused by "forces" at large in America. Perhaps the new energies of the time which bordered on lawlessness. This was how I understood Jackie's remark in refusing to change her bloody clothing: "Let them see what they've done."

In the course of that afternoon, the idea I worked my way toward was simpleminded but it represented quite a step for me, who had never suffered so much as a death in the family, except for that of my grandfather in his nineties. My idea was that Kennedy was dead and it must be accepted. I couldn't undo his death by wanting it not to have happened. It was a tragedy which caused me pain that only time and forgetfulness could ease. I've never gotten any further in my thinking about death.

Perhaps it was to convince ourselves that all life was not over, that life was not over, at least, for us, that we made love. I remember it seeming a completely natural thing to do and not at all unfeeling. Out of the same inner necessity we worked our way by the late afternoon to a kind of giddy excitement and found ourselves on Mass Ave. holding hands and laughing, to the horror of passersby. It was part of the same biological response to grief, despair, and fear that led people to make love in the cattle cars on the way to Auschwitz, and I never felt guilty about it although many years later I met someone who admitted that he had never wanted to be my friend because he'd seen me laughing on the day that Kennedy was shot.

That was my sexual initiation. The rest was maneuvering. I had no doubt but that I wanted to marry Mark. He made me feel that things could be done—and by me. Lamb chops could be cooked, love could be made, music could be played and sung, art could be collected, books could be written, grief could be lived with. To secure this competence and optimism for life, I had to go far enough away to graduate school so Mark could not take me for granted but not so far that he would forget me. That ruled out England, where I would have liked otherwise to have gone. It also ruled out Stanford or Berkeley. I settled on Yale, as just far enough away to make me desirable, but not so far as to make me unobtainable. It also happened to be considered the best graduate program in English in the country. But that was much less important to me. In fact, I went out of my way not to take classes from the most renowned instructors, like Wimsatt, Hartman, Bloom, and Berger. I didn't want to become a disciple. I had my own agenda. Mark and I were engaged by Halloween and married that June.

Until just before I met Mark in the fall of my last year of college, I had been planning to be a doctor, a career choice largely informed by novels of Walker Percy and Saul Bellow in which the protagonist solves all his problems by becoming a physician and by undergraduate wisdom which held that one should not make one's living at the activity one held most dear. Since what I loved most was literature, by no means should I make that the center of my life. Besides, medicine served as a trump card in the endless discussions we all had of what to do with ourselves. If I said I was going to be a doctor, no one asked me any more questions.

I had taken premed courses and planned to take more. I had taken the MCATs. I had applied to Columbia and Harvard Medical Schools, and Harvard had already asked me to be interviewed by a member of the Admissions Committee. My interviewer was a Cambridge physician, a woman, Dr. Elizabeth Z. She was a psychiatrist.

I don't want to make it sound as though Dr. Z. was wholly responsible for my not becoming a doctor. The cracks in that particular structure of intent were already beginning to show. More than once I cried in my science classes. I was depressed when I thought about a future spent in hospitals. But it was also true that no one in my family had ever talked to a psychiatrist before my med school interview with Dr. Z., and the understanding I had been given was that psychiatrists had a kind of X-ray vision into one's deepest thoughts and feelings. So when Dr. Z. questioned my commitment to medicine, I thought she knew something about me that I didn't know.

"Do you plan on having children?" she asked.

"Some day," I said. It was the furthest thing from my ambitious mind, but I didn't want to sound too negative, lest I come across with a ruthlessness unbefitting a healer.

"Do you know how old you will be before you can have children, if you undertake medical training?"

I did some rapid calculations. "Twenty-eight?"

"About that. Do you really think you can postpone it till then?"

"I don't really think I'll want children before then."

"Hm," she said, shattering my confidence.

I withdrew my applications to medical school, applying to graduate programs in English instead, and for many years I told this story to show how an older generation of feminists had thwarted my own. But now I think that Dr. Z. was a sibyl and my benefactor. I am glad not to be a doctor. She was wrong, however, about the maternal urge. It did not claim me until I was twenty-eight.

Like most creative acts, it started with a vision. I saw, as though irradiated, italicized, printed in bold face, surmounted by cherubs, a halo, and a dusting of stars, an apparently simple and ordinary sight which was charged for me with meaning—a young woman walking down the street holding the hand of a little boy. Looking at this woman and this child, I experienced an inner melting, balm for a loneliness I hadn't been aware of. I felt like a goal was in sight, when I hadn't known I needed one. An abrupt certainty seized me, which, translated into colloquial speech would be something like, "That's it. That's what I want."

Thereafter certain sights would make me instantly cry, out of a sense of loss and loneliness. They were images of innocent enjoyment, often but not always involving children. They were stimulated in me by the sight of total concentration on some sweet, nonintellectual act. Once, driving to work, I saw a baton twirler practicing in the yard of a high school near the parkway and burst into tears so consuming that I had to pull off the road. Another time, it was a parade. I wanted to participate in human life at its uncomplicated core, the passing on of life from one generation to another.

I wanted to be a mother. So used to checking on my own pleasure and displeasure, so demanding, so critical, so self-aware, I wanted to take care of someone wholly dependent on me. I wanted to expend myself on someone else. For some women, love and marriage might satisfy these desires, but they did not for me. A husband could not be as dependent as I needed him to be to touch my emotional core. Weakness engaged me in a way that strength did not. Helplessness authorized me to be strong on its behalf. There were parts of me I felt were unused, people within me I wanted to be, as in those recurring dreams in which you find a closet full of clothes you haven't worn, or discover, in a house you've lived in for years, rooms you never knew were there.

It took two years of increasingly dedicated effort for me to get pregnant. I was convinced that teaching, which kept me anxious and wrought-up, was preventing some smooth internal functioning. My first year of teaching (and the first year I tried to get pregnant) was the year of our bombing of Cambodia, of the killings at Kent State, of student protests and strikes at colleges all across the country. I was just out of school myself, but my students treated me as part of the structure of authority they wanted to reject. Since I scarcely believed in my authority myself, it was a bad time to have it questioned, a bad time to start a career as a teacher. If you add to that a massive lack of self-confidence, perhaps innate, but more probably the result of my sex and upbringing at a historical moment, you may see why teaching was making me anxious and wrought-up, I think quite literally tying my insides up in knots and making the smooth union of egg and sperm an impossibility.

I finally got pregnant in May of 1971, in my second year of teaching, probably the week after classes ended. When Teddy was born, I was thirty. Now, when even postmenopausal women can give birth and professional women routinely postpone childbearing to their late thirties, thirty does not seem old to be having a first baby, but in 1972 I was considered an aged primipara and was young enough to be tickled by the term. My sister had had her first child at twenty-one, which was much closer to the norm.

I was thirty, and I was a high-strung young woman, resentful of the ways in which I was unprepared for my bodily existence. So when the obstetrician asked me on the phone if I was in labor, I answered indignantly, "How should I know? I've never had a baby before."

He asked me to describe what I was feeling, but what I was feeling was not something I could easily bring myself to say to this genteel, white-haired man. "There's a sensation at the base of my spine, not exactly a pain. But I'm aware of it. I feel like I have to go to the bathroom."

"That's it," he said. "It's starting. Today's the day. Call me back when the contractions are twenty minutes apart."

"What's a contraction like? How will I know when I'm having a contraction?"

"You'll know."

I hated this phrase, which people offered in reply to so many important questions. What was it like to be in love? What was it like to have an orgasm? "You'll know." For a person of my cautious temperament, who always wanted to exactly know what she was getting into, "You'll know" was a major source of frustration. I was not one to throw myself into experience. Given a choice, I would have spent every minute in rehearsal for the next, sacrificed the present so as not to be hit unawares by the future. I couldn't ski because it required, as I saw it, hurling myself recklessly into the unknown. Skiing with the brakes on, I never got up enough speed to have control. And without control I couldn't live.

Now I was doing something for which there was no rehearsal and over which I had no control. I had gone to childbirth preparation classes, learned all the breathing routines, seen movies of lovely Scandanavian women giving birth, but I knew that this would be little help to me. I would not go through this ordeal like those serene women who accepted life and gave themselves up to it. I would greet childbirth with outrage, as a violation. I would never feel it as natural and coming from within.

Like me, my husband was more a fan of art than nature. In preparation for childbirth, he had chosen some short stories to read to me while I was in labor: "The Pit and the Pendulum" and "The Masque of the Red Death." I concurred with him in thinking Edgar Allan Poe a stylish choice. Both of us approved of the image we imagined ourselves cutting—a literate young couple in the hospital, facing the pain of childbirth and the trauma of new beginnings with witty denial and panache. He was an assistant professor of English at Yale, while I—in tandem—was an assistant professor of English at nearby Wesleyan. We had been together for eight years, married for six and a half. I think it's fair to say that we married because each thought the other an appropriate mate.

That day, the first of my adult life, fat snowflakes were falling thickly, covering the streets with drifts of snow. Since it was Sunday, the snow stayed unploughed. I feared we'd be cut off from the hospital and insisted Mark take me there early, just after noon. The contractions weren't coming nearly as quickly as the doctor had said they should be before I went in, and I wasn't even sure they were contractions, but I wanted to proceed with the momentous event. At the hospital they examined me, said I was not in labor, and told me to go home. I refused, afraid that the snow would keep me from ever getting back. I already considered the pain I was in to be intolerable. The doctor ordered me given an injection—he said it was Demerol to ease the pain—and from then on I felt terrific.

I was lying in a labor room. My head floated up and sat on a cloud and looked down at my gown-clad body on the gurney. A pain started. I knew it was a pain, but it didn't feel like pain. It felt like an opportunity. Here is a great big wonderful wave, I thought, and I am surfing. *Whee!* Up and over, lifted from underneath the way I was as a little girl swimming at Atlantic Beach. I felt the lofting loss of weight, the buoyancy, and then the gentle return to solid ground. This was fun. This felt good. I liked this. I could imagine doing it again, even if I wasn't about to have a baby.

About to have a baby! The thought brought me back to earth from the clouds, the surf, and the wafting of my spirit on the gentle waves of pain perceived as pleasure. I had learned in my prenatal classes that certain drugs were not good for women about to give birth or for the babies they were about to have. I strongly suspected that this pleasant drug I was on was one of them. It was too good to be Demerol. In my heart I knew it was morphine.

As soon as I stopped surfing and struggled to be conscious, to protest, to argue, to stand up for myself and my baby, I was in nothing but pain. I felt torn in two directions. The drug would hurt the baby. I didn't want to be on it. But the more I cried and carried on, the more the doctors thought I was hysterical and pumped in morphine to calm me down. They kept saying I wasn't in labor, only hysterical. Mark came in with another doctor and said, "As you see, she is hysterical."

They had no idea. Now I was being crucified. I knew I had to teach *The Ambassadors* on Wednesday. If I wasn't in labor, I ought to be home preparing my class. Lambert Strether and Madame de Vionnet pulled me in one direction. My husband and the doctors pulled me in another. My arms were stretched out horizontally, my legs were pulled down from my body. If I wasn't being crucified, I was being drawn and quartered. This was my state when Mark decided to calm me down by reading me "The Pit and the Pendulum."

"No," I wimpered. "Read something else." But I was already too weak, it seemed, for him to hear me.

I moaned as he read to the end of the story. It took quite awhile, longer than he'd thought, so fortunately he decided to forego "The Masque of the Red Death." The doctors still said I wasn't anywhere near giving birth, and he had his own classes to prepare, to say nothing of sleep. It was nighttime now, and I begged him to leave me alone. By myself, I thought I'd be able to give myself over to my misery, with no distractions, and without having to worry about the unattractive spectacle I was making of myself.

As soon as he left, my moaning turned to screams. A nurse came into the room, I thought to help. Instead she yelled at me.

"You're as bad as the woman next door," she said.

"What's her name? Do I know her?" I was sure she was someone from my prenatal class, and I really needed a friend.

"Believe me, you don't know her," the nurse said. She stood there looking disgusted as I moaned and screamed some more. I felt like a huge building had collapsed on top of me, and all the stones and bricks were lying on my chest. Then a giant with a nutcracker had me in his grip and was squeezing me from both sides to get out what I had inside. I would split open in another minute. I couldn't breathe, and partly my screaming was from pain, partly from terror, because I thought each breath was the last I could manage.

"Pull yourself together!" the nurse said. "Half the people in the world are women, and half of them go through this! What makes you think you're special?"

"Why are you yelling at me?" I managed to ask, and with a little shake of self-awareness, she stopped and went to get the anaesthesiologist.

My son was born at four in the morning, about six hours after they artificially induced labor. If I had it to do over again, I would live out the joke about the Jewish princess's idea of childbirth: get anaesthesia at the first pain and wake up at the hairdresser's. All I wanted was the baby, not the experience of giving birth. That would have been perfectly understandable to my mother's generation but not to mine. The mythologizing of childbirth as a binding, beautiful family event was just taking hold, and Yale–New Haven Hospital was in the forefront, encouraging husbands to accompany their wives into the delivery room.

Because of the morphine, the baby was born breathing sluggishly. He was also small, under five and a half pounds. The pediatricians rushed him off to intensive care. He was wrapped in a white receiving blanket, and one of the doctors had him under his arm like the rolled-up towel of a swimmer on his way to the beach. I was in pain. A nurse was pushing on my stomach to expel the placenta. I looked over for my husband and saw him fawning—yes, fawning was how I saw it—on one of the pediatricians. He said something, something clever from the look on his own face, and peered into the pediatrician's eyes to see if his remark was appreciated. He was trying to say (I saw it clearly), "We understand and appreciate each other. We are both educated men." It was an epiphany. My husband had room in his soul at that moment for vanity, wanted the doctors to think well of him, was as concerned about that, I thought, as he was about me and our son. An objectivity about him frighteningly close to dislike was born in that hour along with the baby.

The dean of New Haven obstetricians approached. My legs were still spread, my feet in stirrups. There was still a mirror placed in front of me, angled so I could see the actual birth, although I had taken one look many minutes before, seen what I described, when asked, as "a bloody mess," and stopped looking. I had made the doctor promise he would deliver the baby himself and he had promised, but of course he did not. He allowed one of his students to do it. Now, however, he stepped forward to sew up the incision the student had made to prevent tearing as the baby emerged. Since they had given me a local anaesthetic, I felt the stitches merely as unpleasant tugs.

"There," the obstetrician said. "Good as new." And then he looked at my husband with just the look of complicity my husband had sought from the pediatrician. "Better than new."

I heard it, but I put off thinking about what it meant until some other time, when I was less exhausted. Surely it couldn't mean what it seemed to, that he had sewed me up tighter than I'd been before as a kind of gift to my husband.

The next hours were a blur. I threw up. I had a fever. I was catheterized. I think I would have been one of those women who died in childbirth in the nineteenth century, so I suppose I should be grateful for all the modern medical care which in fact I found barbaric. When I came back to myself and had my son in my arms, I asked about the woman who had been in labor in the room next to me. She was black, unmarried. That was what the nurse meant when she said I wouldn't know her. Had her baby been born?

Yes, indeed, my husband said. He'd been in the waiting room with the father, or the man who hoped he was the father. For it seemed if the baby was born in January, the father was one man, whereas if he was born in February, it was someone else. The January father was in the waiting room. It was February 7, but he wouldn't concede. He said it wasn't far enough into February to know for sure. They were fighting about it on the pay phone outside the waiting room. My own sudden wish that my husband would duke it out with someone else over my son's paternity was of course irrational, brought on by some postpuerperal hormone surge. My husband was just fine. He brought me a lovely bouquet of mimosa.

I left the hospital, as insurance regulations require, seated in a wheelchair. They handed the baby to me wrapped in a blanket. I burst into tears. The nurses were moved by my joy. They patted my arms and hugged my shoulders. Some of it was joy, but not all. Does a mother lion feel joy when she looks at her cub? Maybe she feels devotion, maybe the enormity of the task of defense. Maybe she feels that the boundaries of her identity have permanently altered, so that she is no longer a single being but one and a half if not two. That is more like what I was feeling. I wouldn't call it joy.

Mark would say in the next weeks and months that I didn't want the baby to touch me. He pointed out that I screamed when the baby pulled my hair. He said I had a "Noli Me Tangere" complex. He said I had suffered so much in childbirth because I didn't really want to be a mother.

"Stop psychologizing," said the marital therapist we consulted after a year of this.

I was bewildered by Mark's accusations. I loved being a mother. I found the relationship with the baby more satisfying than any relationship in my life had been. Now I believe that in complaining about my treatment of the baby Mark was really complaining about my treatment of him. He was right to do so. From the moment my son was born, I found someone I preferred to all other men, someone who satisfied me as I could scarcely allow myself to be satisfied by a man my own age. I loved the baby's little hands on me and mine on him. It was Mark I didn't want to touch or be touched by. Of Teddy I approved without reservation. I loved his self-sufficiency as it grew, and I loved whatever lingered of his dependency. His maleness was my own.

At the end of my estrogen, in the year of reading Proust, I was told by my doctor that my breast should be biopsied. A mammogram showed tiny spots of calcification in the right breast that hadn't been there before. Although they weren't necessarily cancerous, or even precancerous, the recommended procedure was to take them out. The odds were one in five they were malignant.

The doctor urged immediate action. I was about to leave for

Key West for the winter. I thought the biopsy could wait for three months, until I got back. With odds of one in five the danger didn't seem to me great. I thought that all the urgency had more to do with the way that medicine is practiced in America, hypercautious, liability-driven, than with my particular case.

This proved to be an unpopular position. People said I was "in denial." The closer my friends, the harder they were on me. Some got quite cold: I was irresponsible. As time went by and I agreed to have the biopsy sooner rather than later, the situation with my friends did not improve. Now they accused me of being flippant. They didn't like my attitude. I wasn't taking the problem seriously enough.

To cling to any personal preference, to value personal convenience in the face of a threat of cancer is to defy a cultural style so widely approved that it has the force of wisdom and responsible practice. Also, once the god has touched you, people treat you with respect and solemnity, and they expect solemnity from you. Committed to having the biopsy, nevertheless I talked about it with a studied levity which to me signaled equanimity and mastery of my fate, but which to many of my friends bespoke shallowness, until, one day, talking to a good friend, I was reduced to tears and bewildered questions: "What am I doing wrong? What do you want me to do?" That varied. Some people wanted me to have the biopsy done in New York or Boston instead of in Middletown, where it would be covered by insurance. Some wanted me to consult specialists, although one considered an excisional biopsy a fairly routine procedure, "a step up from dentistry," and nothing to bother experts about. My telephone pad was filled with names and numbers. Every friend had a friend who had had a biopsy, and all of them had to be called.

I left Key West and went back to Connecticut for the biopsy. L. came with me to our local outpatient surgical center, where I had already taken him once this year for one unpleasant procedure and would do so twice again before the year was out. I changed from jeans and a T-shirt into a hospital gown, got hooked up to an IV, and presto change-o, I was a patient.

Because the spots they're after are microscopic, they cannot be located by cutting you open and peering inside. They can only be seen on X-rays, and not even reliably then. So, in the mammography room, I underwent an improbable procedure called wire localization, which precedes the actual surgery. The radiologist, whose skill is more important than I ever imagined, locates the approximate range of the spots and works a wire into the breast to mark them. Then she takes another X-ray to see how close she's come and keeps moving the wire until it just about touches the suspicious spot. The wire is left in to guide the surgeon, who follows it down into the flesh and removes an area at the end of it as large or small as the radiologist decides. The breast is numbed with novocaine, but all this poking and prodding can be more or less unpleasant for the patient, depending on how she's built and the number and location of the suspicious areas.

In my case it wasn't bad. People with bigger breasts, deeper areas to be biopsied would have a harder time. They tried to keep me talking as a way of monitoring my state, but I felt fine, given that my right breast was crushed between the platform and the glass plate of the X-ray machine and my head turned awkwardly in the other direction. Once I tried to look at the breast, and the nurse grabbed my head to turn it away again. The sight of wires sticking out of your body does not, apparently, sit well with many patients, some of whom faint. They entertained me with stories about some who fainted: a hefty woman who was a nurse herself and who collapsed onto the radiologist when there was no one else in the room, pinning her to the floor.

We were all women—the radiologist, the technician, and the nurse. The surgeon, too. So at least they knew what was involved when they squeezed my breast like a pastry bag and slapped it onto the X-ray platform or stuck pins in it or cut it open. In times gone by, they told me, not all that long ago, when men were in control of this procedure, it was not routine to give novocaine for the wire implants, on the theory—also applied to the withholding of anaesthesia from infants—that it could not hurt.

They all joined in to explain to me enthusiastically the difficulties of locating anything within the breast. Imagine, they said, a plastic baggie filled with Jell-O. Then imagine trying to tell the surgeon where something is inside it when it keeps moving, depending on how you push the Jell-O around and the degree of compression you exert. They told me that the procedure I was undergoing would probably soon be obselete and (no one had told me this beforehand) that this very hospital was about to get a new machine which would radically change the practice of breast biopsies.

The patient who had preceded me was a professor of art history, and she had wowed the radiology staff with a lecture on Thomas Eakins. The technician repeated some of what she'd learned. "He painted two versions of the same scene fifteen years apart. In the first one, the surgeon and his assistants are wearing business suits in the O.R., but in the second one they're wearing white scrub clothes, and that shows you how much surgery changed just in fifteen years a hundred years ago."

I was filled with admiration for the art historian. Had she, I asked them, told them all that stuff about Eakins with her breast squeezed in the X-ray machine (I couldn't bring myself to say tit in the wringer)? She had. Wanting to match her, yet unable to come up with an equivalent in the history of literature to Eakins's *The Gross Clinic*, I mentioned a dream I'd had, which I thought was about the biopsy: men were in a longboat, harpooner at the bow with barbed pole poised to hurl. Suddenly, the harpooner dove, weapon and all, into the water and, instead of throwing the barb, planted it directly in the whale.

"What a dream!" the radiologist said, excited. "Wait til you see the X-ray!" She held up the film to show me the soft-edged murkiness of an X-rayed breast (the whale) onto which was superimposed a hard-edged something that looked exactly like a fish hook. She was so impressed with my prophetic powers that I couldn't bring myself to tell her that, thanks to *Dr. Susan Love's Breast Book*, I had known something of what the procedure was like beforehand. None of us knew in January that in April the CIA would announce that secret technology used to locate military targets would be made available for locating tumors in the breast, another advance on harpoons.

Before I left the mammography room, the radiologist told me

in a spirit of reassurance that I probably didn't need the procedure I was about to undergo. There seemed very little likelihood that the spots were cancerous. "Now that I take a good look at the X-rays," she said. I had an impulse, so fleeting it could not really even be said to have been there, to rise out of my wheelchair, tear out my IV, and walk back to my blue jeans and T-shirt, but, with the reluctance I have to interrupt anything that makes me watch many a bad film to the end and with the tendency others share, I imagine, to believe that whatever is painful is somehow good for us, I decided to put off thinking about what the radiologist had said until later, after the biopsy.

They wheeled me from mammography to the door of the operating room. From there, I had to walk unassisted and lay myself out on the operating table, which had supports for both arms and looked unnervingly like a crucifix. The room was very cold. I lay on the table and shivered. New age music was playing. The nurses were setting up instruments. No one paid attention to me until the anesthesiologist came in and said she'd be giving me a sedative. The IV was still in my arm, so all she had to do was open a tap. "Wow!" I said, "I feel that!" and that was all I knew until, after the most delicious sleep I've ever had, dreamless but happy, I woke up in the recovery room, feeling great, to find my chest splendidly wrapped in an Ace bandage.

Eventually I found the text I should have lectured about in the radiology room: a letter written by Fanny Burney, the eighteenth-century novelist, describing her mastectomy without anaesthesia. It's an amazing document in the annals of surgery, one of three descriptions of mastectomies before 1850 and the only one written by the patient herself.

Fanny Burney, who had been Samuel Johnson's friend in London, was married to a Frenchman and living in Paris, her son eighteen years old, when a tumor was discovered in her breast. It was 1811, and her surgeon, Baron de Larrey, had developed his skills on Napoleonic battlefields, doing as many as two hundred amputations in one day. He became Napoleon's personal surgeon, and Fanny Burney was lucky her tumor was not discovered slightly later, because by the spring of 1812, Larrey and most of the six men who assisted him at her operation were on the way to Moscow with the emperor.

Burney's description of the events leading up to the mastectomy and of the operation itself, in a letter to her sister in London, is harrowing. You cannot read it without feeling moved by terror, pity, and admiration for this extraordinary woman. At one point, her face covered by a handkerchief (the only mitigation of the horror she was about to undergo except a glass of wine cordial), she heard the surgeon ask of his assistants, "Who will hold this breast for me?" and offered to hold it herself. Ellen Lambert, in whose book *The Face of Love* I found Burney's letter, sees in this moment evidence and symbol of Burney's palliative consent. Her desire to protect her husband, who was not even told about the operation until it was over, her trust in and rapport with her surgeon, and her belief that by allowing her breast to be cut off she would save her own life helped Burney to participate in what might otherwise have seemed to her an unbearable act of torture and mutilation. She survived the operation to live another thirty years, but there's speculation that the surgery may not have been necessary. Some experts think that if she really had had cancer, she would not have survived, even with the breast removed.

Back in Key West, I reached the end of the four weeks in which I had to restrict my activity to keep my biopsy scar from stretching. For four weeks I had to forego swimming, tennis, and workouts, and I wore a sports bra twenty-four hours a day. Just when the end was in sight, I sliced my fingertip while cutting a bagel. Now I could not swim because the wound might get infected. I could not work out because I couldn't grip the weights or bars. Bandages swaddled my finger. I'm sure the two events—the biopsy and the bagel cut—were connected, there being a law of the unconscious which impels us to do things to ourselves that have been done to us against our will, to prove to ourselves our freedom and consent in matters where we did not consent and had no freedom.

My scar healed well before the year was up, although there was a period, about six months after the operation, when it suddenly started hurting and I couldn't find a comfortable position to sleep in. I slept with my head on one pillow and my breast on another. But as things go, I was lucky. D. had the same procedure and the scar healed badly. E. had the same thing and they found cancer, requiring more surgery and a year of radiation. C. had to have her breast removed and undergo a year of chemotherapy as well as radiation.

This is my age group. Judith B., Judith C., and at least five other women I know, had biopsies about when I did and were also okay. Just as we all got our periods at the same time, now we have reached the age of menopause and breast cancer, comparing notes, sharing an occasional laugh, somewhat comforted to know that what is happening to each of us individually is happening to others as well.

Last week I had another dream that stayed with me after I woke up. I went to a brothel and was going to make love with a woman. I was me, Phyllis, a woman. We were lying facing each other on a bed, she had started making seductive moves, and it was very pleasant. Then her dress rose above her waist and I could see it was a man. This disgusted me. I went to the pimp to complain and ask for my money back. I began casually. "How ya doin'?" I asked. Eventually I got around to asking for my money back. Not only would the pimp not give it to me, he demanded five hundred dollars more. I was in a bad part of town. There were no taxis. The situation was dangerous.

I was totally mystified by this dream when I awoke. By breakfast I had forgotten it. Then I sat down to work, had computer problems, and Alison called.

"Am I interrupting you?"

"No, my computer's driving me crazy. I can't get his screen to sit still. The icons are wandering."

"So, your computer is male?"

"Sometimes male. Sometimes female. It's like an Ursula LeGuin character who changes sex according to the circumstances."

That mention of gender ambiguity made me remember my

dream, and I blurted it out to Alison, who, like all students of human character, takes an interest in dreams.

"I have a method for getting at their meaning," she said. "You ask yourself, which parts of it made me feel good, and which parts made me feel bad?"

"I was glad to be in the brothel. I never thought I'd see one. I never thought I'd get to make love to a woman. That was pleasant, too. It was a bummer that she turned out to be a man. Where does that take us?"

It took us to the name of the prostitute, Sonia, which suddenly appeared in my mind, along with the recollection that Sonia was the name of the daughter in the Jim Harrison novella I had recently finished, taking a break from Proust, *The Man Who Gave Up His Name*.

"It's a dream about prose style," I said to Alison. "It's about liking Jim Harrison's work and wanting to write like a man."

I was the prostitute, I explained to her, a man disguised as a woman. I was also the john (or jane). I knew it was wimpy to pay the pimp the five hundred dollars he wanted, but I would do it. A Jim Harrison hero wouldn't. He would most likely kill the guy. I was pleased in the dream that I had the cool to begin my conversation with him, "How ya doin'?" That's what a Harrison character would do: if he wasn't going to kill the enemy, he would talk to him like a man and work things out. The dream told me that I envied the toughness of Harrison's stories and would rather write *Revenge* or *The Man Who Gave Up His Name* or *Ninety-Two in the Shade*, to mention another macho novel I've been reading, than any book I could write. Which may just be another way of saying—it wouldn't have been the first dream to tell me this—that I'm a woman who, however much she's enjoyed her life as a woman, has often regretted she wasn't a man.

6

Skinned Alive

"Perhaps people must be capable of making us suffer intensely before they can procure for us, in the hours of remission, the same soothing calm as nature does."   *The Captive*

"The talent of a great writer . . . is simply an instinct religiously listened to in the midst of a silence imposed upon all other voices."
                                                        Time Regained

MOST OF PROUST'S INSIGHTS and assumptions haven't dated, whereas those of his biographer, George Painter, who wrote in the late 1950s and early 1960s, seem like exhibits in an ideology museum. Painter says that Proust's mother made him a member of two despised groups: Jews, because of her lineage, and what he insists on euphemizing as "the Cities of the Plain," because of her excessive love. Do people still think that mothers cause their sons' homosexuality by excessive love? Do they still think of homosexuality as a sickness with a pathology?

Or check this, about the end of Proust's childhood infatuation with little Marie de Bernardaky, said to be a model for Gilberte: "His first attempt to love and be loved by someone other than his mother—to escape, that is, from incest—had failed. Ability to love a person of the opposite sex, and of one's own age, is the only valid escape from the prison of the family (?!); and that way was now barred. If he were to risk loving another young girl his suffering, his humiliation and his mother's displeasure would only be repeated (?!). No doubt he was doomed (?!) even before he met Marie de Bernardaky—if not by some antenatal predisposition, then by tensions whose work was done for ever in his early child-hood (?)—to lifelong homosexuality. Perhaps, too, as not infre-quently happens in the puberty of a future homosexual, his unconscious mind had deliberately made a heterosexual choice which was certain to fail, in order to set itself free for its true desire. In every homosexual, perhaps (!), there is a heterosexual double, uppermost at first, who must be imprisoned and made powerless before his stronger brother can come to life (?!). Marcel had tried to be 'normal': if he had failed, it was Marie's fault for rejecting him, and his mother wished it, and was therefore partly to blame. He was absolved." (p. 49)

Thank goodness this kind of biographical criticism is out of fashion, but like a flooded river receding, it leaves a line of garbage behind.

Why did Proust break with Marie de Bernardaky? Painter can only tell us that in *Jean Santeuil*, Proust's dry run for *Lost Time*, it's because his parents make him do it, concerned about his health, and in *Lost Time*, it's because of his own despair at ever winning the girl's love. ("Despair" is a flattening of Proust's complex depic-tion of Marcel's gradual, partly self-protective loss of interest in Gilberte.) In other words, Painter's biographical "facts" are derived from the novels themselves, which he barely distinguishes from autobiography. Then he uses them as fodder for punitive, Freudian speculation.

They handle these matters much differently now. "Proust in the Tearoom," an article in the October 1995 issue of the *Publica-tions of the Modern Language Association*, once the stodgiest of all the professional journals for literary criticism, shows what's hot, hip, and happening in Proust studies. We learn that "to take tea" meant to have homosexual sex in slang contemporary to Proust, with "teapot" and "teacup" both referring to public urinals, popu-lar sites for "homosex." This knowledge adds to the interest of some passages, notably one in which the butler, observing how long Monsieur de Charlus remains in the urinal, assumes it's because he's gotten the clap from womanizing, and the ambiguity of others, even the famous passage describing the taking of tea with the madeleine that sends Marcel in pursuit of his past. Could this description be coded? The author cites slang sources with intriguing things to say about dunking one's cookie.

"Something Queer About the Nation: Sexual Subversions of National Identity in Maghrebian Literature of French Expression" is the title of the Ph.D. thesis upon which the author of "Proust in the Tearoom," Jarrod Hayes, is at work. The title is a tip-off that he marches beneath the banner of queer theory, an in-your-face gay subdivision of the extremely lively academic area of Gender Studies. Queer theory has provided a congenial home to, among others, my colleague Henry A., once an unprized member of the History Department at Wesleyan, then a treasured, tenured member of our English Department, now a star of the new field, having published (among other things) an article proving from a close reading of *Walden* that Henry David Thoreau was probably gay. Currently spending the semester at Princeton's Center for Advanced Studies, our Henry has risen to respectability with as much improbable speed as one of Proust's courtesans. Because of him, and others like him, students chalk the sidewalk in front of the English Department with messages like, "This is where queer professors work, and we love you," or, most recently, "Oscar Wilde did it—shouldn't you?"

After its revelations about tea, "Proust in the Tearoom" peters out (?!) into standard stuff about de Manian allegory and epistemological doubt. There's some debate about the outing of Proust's narrator. Is it better to think of him, as has been traditional (?!), as a closeted homosexual and transpose genders as needed, so that Albertine is understood to be a man? Or does Marcel enact the instability of heterosexual masculine identity?

Still, it's a treat to read such outrageous stuff in the *PMLA*. Toto, we're not in Widener Library anymore!

•   •   •

When I was thirty-one and in the tenth year of my marriage to Mark, my discontent with him and my general despair over my private life expressed themselves as an interest in, then an enthusiasm for, then a passionate infatuation with another man, a man in almost every way his opposite. David was three years my junior and looked like Pushkin, or Pan, with brown eyes, curly black hair, and a beard. People from Southern or Eastern Europe placed him as coming from one country farther east. In fact, his ancestry was Hungarian.

David was in the Art Department of Wesleyan, and between classes, meetings, office hours, and lunches we had time to play. Like kids, we went to the Army-Navy store and tried on fatigues, spats, and goggles. We put on Motown records and danced in the afternoon. It was his capacity for play, above all, that set him apart from my husband, who seemed to me at that time grimly bent on advancing his career.

At first, David told me that he was bisexual, but as we spent more and more time together, as we fell in love, he changed that to homosexual. He had had sexual relationships with women in the past, but always felt put upon. However keenly he appreciated certain women—and he really did like women—his sexual excitement was aroused only by men. He wanted to be quite clear that he had no intention ever of making love to me, and that, whatever happened between us, sex was not a possibility. He needed me to reassure him that that didn't matter.

It didn't matter. Perhaps unusually naive, I was not accustomed to expressing my attractions to people through sexual activity. My husband was the only man I'd been to bed with, and sex with him had evolved into the typical battleground of late-stage marriage, with my refusal to be aroused my greatest weapon against him.

I wanted affection. I wanted diversion. I wanted a secret life, perhaps, and excitement. But I didn't especially want sex. A homosexual lover was from many points of view a perfection I could not have invented for myself. Whenever my husband was especially loving, it seemed to turn out to be an early move in a sexual campaign. What a pleasant change not to have every affectionate gesture, every moment of intimacy, serve as a prelude to having sex.

What David and I shared seemed more fun. We shared music, poetry, art, clothing, antiques, jokes, and gossip. One day we went to New York together on some quickly accomplished business whose nature I no longer recall. The city was just another playground. On the streets, he noticed everything. "That man was attracted to you," he'd say, or "That man noticed us both." In the stores, he went through racks of clothes saying decisively, "This is good for you," or "That's impossible."

He enjoyed dressing me and seeing me play different parts. It was part of the theatricality of his approach to life. Whatever we did, we not only did it, we observed ourselves doing it, so that having a hamburger and a Bloody Mary for lunch, running into an old friend from college, became the stuff of Noël Coward comedy in the instant replay that was our conversation. All this contrasted favorably with the way my husband and I discussed our daily life. Our discourse tended to be analytic, drearily searching for motives and assessing effects, hopelessly bound to reality. On the one hand I had someone who rebuked me for failing to record checks in the checkbook or for spending too much on a lipstick; on the other I had someone who would calculate delightedly that his printing press cost the same as corned beef, $3.50 a pound.

On the drive back from the city on the day I remember, David and I sang songs. We loved to sing while driving. We specialized in lyrics from Broadway musicals of the 1950s and got a special pleasure from recalling all the words to introductions, like that of "Shall We Dance." The recitative of the intro, a kind of pathless waste we had to negotiate, prepared for the grand, melodic outburst of the song itself, fulfillment after suspense. In the car, singing, we had intimacy with no possibility of sexual demand. There were words in our minds that overlapped exquisitely.

Back in New Haven, after dinner, David seemed unusually anxious to be on his way again. He did not tell me until days later that he had a party—for men only—to go to in New York that night. He had not left me in New York and let me drive back to New Haven alone, the sensible thing to do, because the day would have seemed incomplete. He had not even told me about the party because he did not want to spoil a day of perfect intimacy by mentioning something that did not include me. For that delicacy, he did an extra round trip from New Haven to New York, three hours of driving.

Details of the party, when they came, were as fascinating to me as a firsthand report on the behavior of Martians somehow found living happily in Brooklyn. What did I know about homosexuals? As far as I was aware, there had been none at my high school in the later 1950s and none at college in the early 1960s. At college, no one I knew admitted to being sexually active at all, to say nothing of indulging in the sophisticated refinement of sex that homosexuality seemed to me to be.

David told me that the host at the party that night was an old friend of his named Thomas who had changed his name to Aubrey. At midnight at Thomas-Aubrey's, about the time that I was going to sleep, the party became an orgy. Many people left, but the rest began coupling up and retiring into bedrooms. They would make love, emerge, find a new partner, make love some more. The host wandered from bedroom to bedroom offering orange juice. At three o'clock he rang a bell and summoned everyone from the bedrooms to eat masses of Chinese food which had been brought in. David had gone to the party with Tony, but no, he said, of course they didn't make love with each other at a party like that. They can do that any time. And what would they have had to talk about on the drive home?

From my point of view, David changed my relationship with my husband in good ways. For one thing, as a connoisseur of men, he enjoyed my husband's company and admired his looks: I found my husband more attractive by seeing him through David's eyes. For another, my demands on him eased as David provided more and more of the laughter and joy in my life. I was no longer so resentful and disappointed.

But my husband had not signed on for a ménage à trois. Although, at first, he liked David well enough, he got increasingly to resent his presence in our lives and household. What made me feel free to introduce David into our daily routine—the fact that we were not sleeping together—made it from my husband's point of view so much the worse. It was only too clear that I preferred David's company to his, even without sex.

David, too, had needs and desires I found not entirely convenient. He seemed to want to make people think we were actually having an affair when we weren't. He came to my office too often, too ostentatiously. He touched me in public, although he never did in private.

Things became uncomfortable. When he treated me seductively in public, I was seduced. I thought he had changed his mind and meant to make love to me. I became obsessed with making love with him as I had not been before. I thought if only the circumstances were right, if it was easy enough, relaxed enough, we would fall in bed together and I would save him for women. That nothing about our situation was easy or relaxed did not occur to me. In my rescue fantasy, only ideal circumstances prevailed.

I thought obsessively about homosexuality. Before I'd met David, I believed homosexuality was a choice you made, like the choice of whether or not to take up golf. Now I could see it was not so simple. He liked to think he was free to choose, but I wasn't sure. Often he seemed to want to make love to me but was more afraid of failing at it than he was interested in trying. He told me that his relationship with me had made him see how delicious it would be to live with a woman and raise a family. He said he intended to do just that, when he was forty, after the pleasures of sex had waned. He said this as a politican might talk about the joys of raising begonias in the country—after he was no longer electable.

At about this time, Carolyn Heilbrun published a book about something she called "the ideal of androgyny." Lytton Strachey, the flamboyantly homosexual author of *Eminent Victorians*, who had asked Virginia Woolf to marry him one day and taken it back the next, was an example of the androgynous ideal. I was in the middle of writing a book about Virginia Woolf and had my own thoughts about Lytton Strachey. When my colleagues in the English Department and I discussed Heilbrun's book, I pooh-poohed the idea of Lytton Strachey as androgynous. "He was a queer," I said with some feeling, at a time when the word was not politically correct, "maintaining a fiction of heterosexuality. Carrington was in love with him, he was in love with Carrington's husband, Carrington's husband was in love with Carrington. No one was satisfied. Androgynous ideal, my foot!"

And yet, it sometimes seemed to me that David represented something new—not just in my life, but within the range of possibilities for masculine life in America. It seemed to me that he was an antidote, not just to my husband, but to an ideal of masculinity in America that had become unsatisfying, both to the men who lived it out and to the women who lived with them. In those heady years of hippie culture, communes, sexual experiment, new forms of marriage, and breakthroughs for women, it seemed possible that a new kind of man could come into being, one less focused on the classic success track, more open to emotional experience and to expressing emotion, clinging less to the traditional division between work (male) and family (female), defining himself less by aggressiveness and domination than the classic patriarchal male and willing to cede some of what had been male turf to women. A blending of masculine and feminine, a new man for the new woman, the woman who worked and who had no intention of playing a merely supportive role to her husband.

It was hard for me in those years—and I suspect for others—to separate what was happening to me from what was happening to my generation, what was personal experience and what was historical. We were so aware of living at a time of change. My marriage was a mess. But it also seemed Marriage as an institution was in crisis. There was a new man in my life, very different from my husband. Was there a New Man evolving, different from the traditional patriarchal male? It seemed possible.

The New Man, of course, could be exasperating. Sometimes his theatricality seemed no more than narcissism. One day we had a date to play tennis. It turned out that he didn't play tennis, but he'd always wanted to arrive at the tennis court in a sports car and emerge in whites twirling his racket. So we played that scene. But it bothered me. In retrospect I'd say it bothered me more to play at playing tennis than it did to play at having an affair. Maybe because I knew I knew what tennis was, but I wasn't so sure about love.

Afterward, back at his house, when he changed from his tennis clothes into regular clothes, he came from his bedroom into the living room to display himself at every stage, first with blue jeans and no shirt, then jeans and unbuttoned shirt, then with his shirt neatly tucked in, all ready to go. He wanted, I felt, to make me desire him. He also wanted me to make no move, to accept his unavailability. I complied. I admired.

I had assured him that sex didn't matter. At first, it didn't. When sex came to matter, the first and passionate stage of our relationship had to end. I had to sort out in my own mind whether David had alienated me from my husband, or whether my alienation from my husband had made me receptive to him. When I decided that the latter was true, it was only a matter of time and gathering courage before the marriage ended.

Some friendships are the beautiful fossilized remains of love affairs that did not evolve in the usual ways, into marriage, memory, or nothing. David and I, friends for twenty years now, are fossilized in more ways than one. We have taken and ignored each other's advice, we have solved and complicated each other's problems, we have done each other favors, given each other gifts, and provided each other with new friends. We have traveled together, entertained together, subscribed to the opera together, had Thanksgiving dinner together, jointly found baby-sitters for Teddy, who calls him "Uncle," exchanged clothes, and fantasized about sharing our declining years. If I valued David when we first met for his sense of play, I value him equally now for his managerial skills. He talks to me about health insurance, taxes, mutual funds, wills, art deals, parking spaces, storage, ticket booking, real estate, and university politics. He can and will take charge when we travel, tell me when my hair needs professional help and when a dress is unflattering, design an invitation to a party and get it printed, or decide what restaurant we'll have dinner at with no hesitation, apologies, or after-you-Alphonsing. He lets me experience passivity, a feminine pleasure I rarely allow myself.

Women and gay men are sometimes imagined as chatting "like girls" about men, but I find David too romantic to talk with about romance. Besides, he's unreliable, sometimes taking the man's side, as a woman friend would never do. His stories of his own amours are tedious. He's as obsessive about glances, smiles, and pregnant remarks as a teenaged girl and turns every attraction and crush into what my mother would call a major production. He's most interesting when he gets to the nitty-gritty of sex, the actual physical details of what he did and what was done to him, but although I'm fascinated by this, I'm simultaneously appalled. Once he was telling me about the mechanics of anal penetration, how if you push gently at the anal sphincter, knock at the door as it were, it will relax so you can enter. A strange look must have passed over my face, because David said, "Do you mind my being so graphic?" and I said, "No. I don't mind at all disgusting these things."

A few years ago, when my mother could still leave her apartment, she wanted to go to a reception at the Metropolitan Museum of Art. For various reasons, none of her three children could go with her. Since she could not manage it alone and very much wanted to go, I asked David if he would take her and he kindly agreed. Their date was a success. Mother, taking David's arm, had no trouble negotiating steps, turns, and obstacles that would have impeded or intimidated her alone. She said she felt like she had wings. To people she knew, she introduced David ceremonially, "This is my friend," and she gave his name. "He is a professor of art." Even secondhand, I could feel the wonder in Mother's acquaintances and sense how suddenly more glamorous she must have seemed to them. What was she doing with this younger man who looked like a Gypsy and was certainly not her son? Could it be that Minnie, though hampered by a heart condition, winded, half-blind, shrunken with age, and bent from osteoperosis, could Minnie nonetheless have been visited by Venus? That old gay magic had cast its spell again, spreading the glitter of uncertainty or what might be called in the pages of the *PMLA* "epistemological doubt."

•   •   •

L. and I started living together eleven years after my first marriage ended. From the start he had to assert his rights in the face of so long-standing a friendship as mine with David and establish that our house was *our* house, that David couldn't come into it any time he wanted. He had to establish that we are a pair, not two parts of a triangle.

I say that L. has had to assert his rights in the face of so long-standing a friendship, but he has not felt the need to make a similar assertion to my female friends, no matter how long-standing our friendships. If I spend an hour on the phone with Wendy, for example, he thinks that's entirely my business. If I spend that much time on the phone with David, he resents it. David is a man, after all. Old patterns of jealousy and suspicion die hard. Perhaps, too, David presumes on a privileged position, managing at times to give the impression—as unwelcome to me as to L.—that the real and enduring tie is between me and him, with my husband an episode, a temporary interlude.

A gay man was also attached to L.'s household during his first marriage. He was a famous novelist, a brilliant talker, and a world-class charmer. Easy to see why anyone would want him around. L., who's always suffered from a sense of inadequacy as a conversationalist, was happy to have such backup. If Proust had been alive in our time, if his sensibility had embodied itself in a contemporary writer, he might well, if he had not crossmated with Elizabeth Bishop and become James Merrill, have crossmated with Vladimir Nabokov and become Edmund White. Edmund has the nuanced and cleansed objectivity of Proust the writer, as well as the surpassing sweetness and kindness of Marcel the character. Everyone who knows him is fond of Edmund in the same way that everyone in *Lost Time* is fond of Marcel, and probably for the same reason, a total absence of self-importance and resentment. Marcel says of himself, "I was in my heart of hearts entirely on the side of the weaker party, and of anyone who was in trouble," and the same, I believe, is true of Edmund.

He had already moved to Paris when I appeared there in 1985 to do six months' research for the biography of Josephine Baker. He was already best friends with L.'s first wife, who I suspect is a model for Hélène in the title story of *Skinned Alive*, the book of Edmund's stories that appeared this year. Deep-voiced Hélène, so sophisticated, so Parisian, who wears Japanese clothes and blue-tinted glasses, who is bilingual in English and French, who reads the livelong day and affects a total immersion in her imagined life, saying "I am in China," or "Today it's the Palais-Royal," depending on what she's reading, who sees a hunky young man at a reading, nudges the narrator, and says, "There's one for you."

We were a foursome for a while, L., his wife, Edmund, and I. I loved all three of them. We would go out to dinner together or sometimes have a "family dinner" at home; that meant the four of us and someone else "amusing." So sophisticated was "Hélène" that I thought she was even more sophisticated than she was, and when, before a long weekend in May, she called and asked me to go out with her husband while she went to the country, I thought, "I am in over my head." I imagined that she was a manipulator on the order of Madame de Merteuil in *Les Liaisons Dangereuses* or Madame de Mauve in *The Portrait of a Lady*, and I was the innocent who risked being chewed up and spewed out by Parisian sophistication. I easily developed toward her the anger you need to have toward someone you are hurting badly. Even after L. decided to leave her and come to the States to live with me and everyone but my friends saw me as a scarlet woman and a home-wrecker, I could not see myself as anything but—save for good fortune and the purity of L.'s love—the designated victim, the injured party.

It took L. four years to get a divorce, and as soon as he did, we were married.

I married into an extraordinary family. L.'s father was Jean de Brunhoff, the author and illustrator of the *Babar* books I had loved so much as a child. L. and his brother, Mathieu, barely a year younger than himself, now a beloved pediatrician in Paris, were the little boys for whom the story of Babar was originally invented, by their mother, Cécile. The boys told their mother's wonderful story to their father, a painter, and asked him to illustrate it, which he did, writing a text and slightly modifying the story his wife had told, adding, for example The Old Lady. That is uncanny, because Madame de Brunhoff, my mother-in-law, although she was young at the time and looked nothing like The Old Lady, has come more and more to resemble the woman her husband drew in 1931, as though he could imagine her changing in time, like those computer projections of lost children. Jean de Brunhoff died of tuberculosis when he was thirty-seven, leaving his widow with three small boys. L. was twelve, Mathieu eleven, and Thierry just three. Alone, never remarrying, Madame de Brunhoff got them through the war and brought them up. She was a pianist and taught at the École Normale de Musique.

L. inherited his father's talent and became a painter, living the classic artist's life in a studio in Montparnasse, until, at the age of twenty-one, he resurrected Babar and began himself to write and illustrate books about the lovable elephant, at least in part, he says, as a way of resurrecting his father and continuing imaginatively the family life of his childhood. Many readers were not aware of any change in the authorship of the Babar books, partly because the war had intervened to explain any gap, and partly because L. had trained himself so well to draw elephants in the style of his father.

Thierry inherited his mother's musical talent and became, initially trained by her, a concert pianist, well known in France in the 1960s. By the time I met L., Thierry was legendary in Paris for his talent, looks, and charm and the glamorous life he had led before abruptly retiring from the world and becoming a monk at the age of forty. Within his own family he was both deeply loved and respected. So it was painful to me, and of course to L., that he refused to see me before L. and I were married. But after our marriage, he agreed to let us visit him.

This was the summer of 1990, and at the time, Thierry had left his monastery outside Bordeaux for a hermitage in the Pyrenees. It was remote, but not as remote as I imagined it, my idea of hermits dating to the time of St. Jerome. In my mind's eye I saw them living on columns in the desert or hauling supplies in baskets up by ropes to their handhewn caves. Whereas Thierry lived on the grounds of a convent in a special bungalow enclave built for hermits, and he could have visitors.

L. and I, who were having a late honeymoon in Provence, drove down to see him in an air-conditioned BMW which L. had somehow imagined from the figures Avis gave him was no more expensive to rent than a Ford Escort. From Avignon, it was about two hours on the highway that runs by Nimes, Montpellier, and Perpignan, along the route that the Romans pioneered and that countless tourists now follow on their way to Spain. We traveled at 90 mph the whole way, not feeling the speed, with *Cosi Fan Tutte* on the stereo. Everyone except Mercedes, other BMWs, and very aggressive little R5s and Peugeot 205s moved out of our way. At the last exit in France, we left the autoroute and headed toward the high peaks of the Pyrenees. Soon, following Thierry's directions to the mountain hamlet near which he lived, we were in desolate country, covered with scrub and stunted oaks. The whole mountainside had burned a few years before, but the dense scrub underbrush was already back.

Thierry said he would wait for us on the road, and as we came up over a rise at the appointed hour, we saw him walking toward us. He was dressed not in the brown burlap hermit garb I was stupidly expecting but in ordinary corduroy pants and a green cotton shirt, and, like us, wore sandals. A figure recognizably of L.'s family, handsome, elegant, Parisian, he looked out of place in that wilderness. I had to swallow tears. Loving him from my first glimpse of him through the windshield, I felt an immediate and wrenching sense of loss, something like the grief of mourning, and found it hard to bear that he had chosen to sequester himself this way. I could only imagine this grief more strongly felt by those who knew him better.

We took him to our hotel for lunch and talked all through lunch and for hours after, waiting for the heat of the day to abate before going back to his hermitage. Then we talked more. In all, we spent seven hours talking that day, beginning with reassuringly worldly matters like appreciation of our car. Gradually Thierry began to talk about himself. Although his life was lived almost entirely in silence and secrecy, he wanted to explain how he had come to where he was in life, understanding there would not be many chances for us to meet and know each other.

His had been a lonely childhood. He was three when his father died, so he did not even have memories of him. Madame de Brunhoff rarely talked about him. While Thierry was growing up, she was distant, absorbed in her music and in her continuing grief. His brothers and cousins, almost a decade older, seemed to belong to a different generation.

As a gifted musician, he moved into a world of performers and connoisseurs. At the precocious age of fifteen, he was already leading a sophisticated, worldly life, and by the time he was eighteen, he had had enough of it and wanted solitude. He went to live alone in the country, where he stayed for four years before resuming his highly social existence. For the next ten years, Thierry became more and more known as a pianist, giving concerts, making recordings. Like his mother, he taught at the École Normale de Musique.

Then a distressing event interrupted the momentum of his life. A house he had lived in and used for storage burned. The fire destroyed all the family souvenirs that meant so much to him, including many of his father's paintings, his grandfather's memoirs, and all his music. It shook him very much. It was, he said, his first shedding, his first deprivation, using the word *dépouillement*, which means the skinning of an animal.

He was analyzed, but analysis didn't help much with his inner turmoil, and he had no religion to turn to. His father had been Protestant and his mother, though technically Catholic, really believed only in music. Still, an object that meant a great deal to him was his father's Bible. He took it with him everywhere and looked through it frequently. Jean had underlined it heavily in places. One day, looking through the New Testament, Thierry found a passage that had been underlined so often that the paper was nearly falling apart. It struck him in that moment that his father had really believed, that these words in the Gospel had been important to him.

Around that time, a woman he knew died suddenly at the age of forty. Her husband was a very religious man, and Thierry was struck by the funeral he arranged. There was grief, of course, but there was also a beautiful faith, serenity, and acceptance. As time went by and his thoughts turned more to religion, he had no one to talk to. He got in touch with the husband of the woman who died, and the man recommended Thierry speak to the priest who had conducted the funeral service. They met a couple of times, at which point the priest announced he was leaving for vacation in Brittany. Easter was coming. Thierry didn't want to go through the holiday without having taken Communion, so the priest suggested that he come to Brittany and take First Communion there. He knew a Trappist monastery at which he could stay.

Thierry liked that monastery in Brittany so much that he almost became a Trappist monk, which would have meant never seeing his family or talking to anyone outside the monastery again. Eventually he decided against it, in part because Trappist life is too communal for someone who loves privacy as much as he does, and in part because the total, brutal break with the world that Trappists are required to make would have caused too much pain to his family and friends.

A few people he knew told him about Roissac, which is a Benedictine monastery. He went to look at it and liked it. He made a second, longer stay at Roissac, but remained tempted by the Trappists. The Abbot of Roissac told him not to worry about it, but to go home and wind up his affairs and when the answer was in place, he would know it. So he returned to Paris for a year or two, taking no more students, but bringing all the ones he had through to the end of their studies. In time he decided to enter the Benedictine monastery. He didn't tell many people what he was planning to do, so when he did announce it, it seemed to many abrupt. But in truth it wasn't. Before he left Paris, he gave away all his possessions and stopped accepting bookings. He performed his last concert a few days before he joined the Benedictines at Roissac. Madame de Brunhoff took his decision hard. Music had been the bond between them and the most important thing in the world to her. His renouncing his musical career seemed to her like choosing death.

At Roissac, Thierry was immediately happy and knew it was where he belonged. He stopped playing the piano. He felt that his religious life demanded complete commitment and so did his music. He had to choose between them. Many of the monks were men of accomplishment—one designed tapestries, another worked in stained glass, another was a ceramicist, another was a composer—and continued to practice their art in the monastery. So Thierry's renunciation was something he imposed on himself.

He became a hermit gradually. The abbot had arranged for a few of the monks to take part in some discussions of spiritual matters at a place outside the monastery where they would be free to concentrate—a kind of retreat—and the place they chose, at the random suggestion of someone who had never been there, was St. Paul. Thierry loved the quiet of the spot. Later, when he went through a period of fatigue so great that the abbot noticed and suggested he take some time off, he chose to return there. He began going there regularly for two weeks a year. Eight years went by. Since he discussed everything with his abbot, the abbot knew that he wanted to leave Roissac and move permanently to St. Paul. They decided he would go back for a month, as a test, choosing January, the hardest month. It was cold, damp, and miserable, but Thierry felt spiritually comfortable there, and eventually the abbot decided to let him move.

Thierry related his tale to us with the intensity he brought to playing Chopin and with an inclusiveness I know from my mother's accounts of her illnesses. As she describes with a reverence that is hard to enter into her dealings with the doctors, the nurses, the orderlies in the hospital, he described meetings with his abbot and consultations with his fellow monks. What came through most clearly to me, in addition to the purity of his commitment to the life he had chosen, was a recurrent need to withdraw from other people, which seemed a response to and perhaps also a source of his intense desirability.

We spent an enormous time at lunch, then sat in the leather chairs of the lounge and talked more. When the sun was lower, we headed back to his hermitage. Past the spot where we'd first met him, the road dipped down and ran alongside the nuns' compound. We drove past that, over a small bridge, around another few bends to a gate where we left the car. Then we walked past a wooden outhouse, a shower shed, a chapel, and up a path, with little houses visible through clearings in the scrub.

The enclave had room for ten hermits, who came for stays of a week to a month, but Thierry was the only one who remained on a permanent basis. The tile-roofed, yellow stucco house in which he had been living for three years when we saw him was about ten-by-ten feet, the size of a large toolshed. Its one room contained a mattress on raised boards, covered with an army blanket, a desk and chair under a wall of windows, which were covered in burlap to keep out the sun, an armoire, also covered in burlap, on top of which was a suitcase and some folders. There was a cross made from two branches roughly nailed together on the wall by the bed. The floor was covered in linoleum-patterned Contac paper. There was an electric lightbulb with a simple metal shade. The roof tiles showed above the supporting beams, and the effect was pleasantly rustic. On the desk was a Bible, prayer books, postcards of religious art, a box containing family photographs. In a bookcase next to the desk, he kept his correspondence, a ceramic disc heater, and an electric pesticide diffuser, as well as books.

Nature is violent in this region. When it rains, torrents come down the mountainside. Sometimes the hermitage was cut off from the sisters by a flash flood that covered the bridge over what was at the time of our visit a totally dry, rock-strewn streambed. The hillside was gashed where water had cut through the land. During the first winter, Thierry had watched the water rise outside the house. When it was a foot deep, he began packing his suitcase. Before he could leave, the door burst open under the force of the flood, and the house was instantly filled with water brown from mud and cow shit. This, he said, was his lowest point.

The cold was intense, but a large old-fashioned heater made it bearable. He hoped the new disc heater would help, too, but wanted to know if it consumed much electricity, because he didn't want to burden the sisters. In the in-between season, everything got wet and stayed that way. Mildew covered the walls, and moisture soaked through from the outside. Three lumberjacks who lived nearby built him a little lean–to or porch at the front of the house, so that rain did not beat directly against his door and window. When we were there, too much heat was the problem. With no foundation and no insulation in the roof, the temperature in the bungalow often reached ninety-five degrees.

"It's a dangerous thing, to be a hermit, because if you're not serious, it quickly becomes ridiculous," he said. He had begun to teach himself Hebrew, to read the Old Testament. But he found that he was spending more and more time at it. Whenever he had a spare moment, he would turn to the Hebrew book. It began to fill his head. So finally he had to stop. Because after all, he wasn't there to learn languages. He had constantly to remember what the purpose of all of it was and stick to it. You can easily become a nature-loving bum, he said, or someone who sleeps a lot.

In fact, he was busy; his time was full. He received letters, many of them enormously long from friends, family, and former students. Answering them was a drain on his energy, and as they were serious letters they had to be answered seriously. People brought him their problems. A friend who twice had tried to commit suicide had just written saying that he urgently wanted to come see him. How could he say no? He had prayers to say several times a day and he went to Mass with the sisters every morning. Since they fed him, preparing a bucket of food which he picked up every morning, he felt he had to pay them back somehow and did it by cutting the brush. He had a large-wheeled brushcutter which he operated in the afternoon—the only free time he had—in the heat of the day, brutal work.

He showed us his view. To the side and in front of the house, across a deep cleft, the land rose sharply to a majestic, rocky ridge. It was like a wave about to crash down, frozen in stone. He had asked the Mother Superior for permission to cut an oak in order to get this view, and L. twitted him. Didn't this smack of aestheticism? It depended on the purpose, Thierry replied. If it's an end in itself, yes. If it aided him in communicating with God, no. He chose renunciation not for renunciation's sake, but in the service of something else, his relationship with God. If things got in the way of that, as music did, then he had to give them up. He couldn't split himself. "But I'm not a Cartusian, bound in by walls so I can look up only to the sky. Whatever helps me is okay. This helps."

One of the things he liked most about his hermitage, he said, was the silence: "Silence is my music now." He could pick up the small sounds of the wind in the leaves, the sounds of insects and animals. Sometimes when the wind was strong, it blew the sound of the traffic on the autoroute to him. He liked it. He liked to think of all the people going on with their lives and to think of himself as in a sense staying where he was for their sakes. "Like a lighthouse keeper."

He said he had done a little writing, but he was wary of it. It becomes "*gargarisme*," throat-gargling. You begin to think you're important. You write things up, inflate them. You moussify inside, that is, I guess, foam up like egg whites. (At this point, I was feeling very shabby, a *gargariste* and moussifier. Moreover, I had every intention of going back to the hotel and writing down what Thierry had said.) Whereas the point of passing time in solitude is to strip yourself bare, to discover what is essential and true. When you're stripped down to this point, you see how little you amount to. But that little is all that God is interested in. He doesn't give a damn about the rest.

The dazzling title story in Edmund White's collection, *Skinned Alive*, is about art and masochism. The narrator, Hélène's friend, an American writer living in Paris, is having an affair with a spoiled French boy, Jean-Loup. Things are not going well. To solace himself, he picks up the hunky guy Hélène has pointed out to him at a reading, who turns out to be an American, a bouncer at a disco, remarkably intelligent and literate despite his brutal looks. Sexually, the two do not match, however, since they both like pain. There is an embedded story which Paul, the bouncer, has written, based on the myth of Marsyas and Apollo. Marsyas, a brilliant musician who can imitate anyone, imitates Apollo, the god of music. The muses have a hard time deciding who is better, but decide finally in favor of Apollo. His reward is to get to flay Marsyas alive. Marsyas, who always knew Apollo was the better musician, seems curiously unconcerned by his own flaying. He sees he has the god's full attention by becoming his victim.

Proust says the great moments—like when he ate the madeleine dipped in tea—are those when we escape time. We do what we do in the present but we experience the same action in the past. Thus we are nowhere, neither in past nor present, "the miracle of an analogy" has freed us from the lockstep of time. He does not explain why this freedom should be so desirable, but presumably it is because time moves only in one direction, toward weakness and death. We embrace those things that allow us to transcend death, artists art, monks God, some people sex, some people television.

By the end of the story, Jean-Loup has left the narrator for Régis, one of the richest men in France, and the narrator focuses his attention on Jean-Loup's ass, recreating it for us and ending the story with a bravura description, done on a dare. It is presented in a witty, faux-objective manner, homage to the prose poems of Francis Ponge in which objects as various as oranges, cigarettes, oysters, and doors are detached from context and held up as interesting in their own right, their physical and moral properties exhaustively catalogued. Ponge on the cigarette: "Let's describe first the desiccated, foggy air and general dishevelment the cigarette creates and, in its tipsy way, dominates. Next its person: a miniature torch bringing less light than smell." On doors: "These high obstacles to entering a room, these rapidly moving objects, thanks to which, in one moment of suspended tread, the body gets a chance to adapt to new quarters." Edmund on Jean-Loup's ass: that "perfunctory transition between spine and legs, a simple cushion for a small body, . . . a neutral support . . . for his big, grown-up penis, always so ready to poke up through his flies and take center stage," with "an anus that makes one think of a Leica lens, shut now but with many possible f-stops. An expensive aperture."

Edmund's fiction up to this has been more discreet, sometimes to the point of concealment. Why, now, the Mapplethorpian display? My guess is AIDS, turning life into a series of strippings and forced renunciations—of one person after another, one friendship after another, one pleasure after another—until those who are left are brought to the essential, whatever the essential is for them.

Call me secular, call me Freudian, but I suspect that Thierry became a hermit in part because he recovered his father in solitude as L. did in drawing elephants. Fortunately or not, it takes less extreme measures for me to experience my father. I feel him powerfully whenever I take the Hutchinson or the Merritt Parkway, roads he taught me to use and appreciate, and sometimes, but less powerfully, on the Massachusetts Turnpike and the FDR Drive.

For many years my father commuted by train, but when I was in high school he bought the red Plymouth convertible which he took every day into Manhattan and back, announcing it at the dinner table whenever he discovered a new shortcut through Queens. He would have thought it as shameful to follow Queens Boulevard straight into the city as my mother thought it was to pay retail for dresses.

My father enjoyed driving and had a fine sense of the road. He taught me that the drive from New York to Boston was easier, more natural, than the drive from Boston to New York, because, starting from New York, the fast part came at the end, when you were warmed up and ready for it, whereas, leaving Boston, you immediately had to accelerate to high speed on the Massachusetts Turnpike, and you weren't psychologically prepared. He also taught me to stay in the middle lane of the FDR Drive at all times, except when exiting. You maintained your flexibility that way, he said, and for some reason, in the long run, the center lane of the FDR Drive moved fastest. Such was the wisdom my father passed on to me, as fresh and true now as it was thirty years ago.

Not long ago, driving into New York from Connecticut, I missed the turnoff for the Hutchinson. Actually, I didn't miss it. I was blocked from taking it by an incompetent driver who, at the last minute, cut in front of me from the right. (My father would have said, in a spirit of both insult and curse, "New Jersey driver!") I certainly didn't want to take the Cross County Parkway and end up on the West Side Highway, and that seemed to be where the road I had been forced onto was taking me, but, like a jazz musician launching into a solo, I trusted I would think of something and I did. I saw signs for the Major Deegan heading south and took that. To my delight, I came into the Triboro Bridge approach just before the turnoff for Manhattan, thereby avoiding the whole of Bruckner Boulevard. I thought of how interested my father would have been in this new shortcut, how proud of me for finding it. But in fact, it's just as likely he would have said, "What? You didn't know you could do that? You usually take the Bruckner? I wouldn't be caught dead taking the Bruckner into the city. You young people, nobody knows how to get around this city anymore." For in his later years, he developed a need to assert not just that he knew best, but that the rest of us knew very little.

He had little sympathy for me when Mark and I got divorced. "Don't you young people know how to live anymore? Your mother and I had fights, but we made them up. Who do you think you are? How much happiness do you think you have a right to?" (Versus my mother's, "Don't worry, dear. There are other fish in the sea. You're entitled to some happiness.") He had no sympathy when I despaired of graduate work and then despaired of teaching and thought about going into business. "Well, every corporation has a token woman, I suppose." (Versus my mother's, "Bless you, darling, I never thought I'd live to see the day when women could do the same work as men.") He lived to say, "If you decide to do something creative, honey, Mom and I will back you to the hilt," but also lived long enough for me to see this was mostly rhetoric. He would have hated the messy start to my life with L., but he would have loved L. and the French connection. His favorite client, the one who brought the most glamour to his labors, was the impresario of the Châtelet Theater in Paris, who hired him during the war to prove that his American wife was not Jewish so the Nazis could not confiscate their property, and whose daughters and grandsons were kind to me when I was in Paris, unhappily in love.

At about the time I realized that my father was not just the cuddly, lovable, upstanding man I had adored as a child, but was simultaneously self-satisfied and self-righteous and had a deeply patriarchal need to be central, he died, and for a year I could not keep my mind on anything else or get through a day without crying.

If you had told me when I was fifteen, twenty-five, even thirty-five, that my parents would crisscross in my estimation, and I would increasingly value my mother and, while never ceasing to love him, see more and more that was not so admirable in my father, as though the very nature of my vision had changed, as though I'd been given a different prescription lens or developed colorblindness, I would not have believed it possible. I guess if life goes on long enough, we complicate our opinions of everybody. Most of us father-worshippers are in for a disillusionment. In this sense, Geoffrey Wolff's *The Duke of Deception*, about discovering that his father was a con man, is the story of us all, only for most of us the deception isn't the fathers' fault but ours, love-struck dupes who can rarely hold onto our innocence.

I cannot forget the events of over a decade ago, the worst time of my life, when I was in Paris and in love with L. Often it happened that we would see each other alone at my apartment in the afternoon and then have dinner with "Hélène" at night. The dinners were so uncomfortable for me, such performances, that I actually felt stage fright before walking through their door, that high obstacle to my torment. Did she know about us or not? If not, I felt like a cheat and a liar. But if she knew, if she tacitly gave her permission, I felt used and humiliated. The natural person to tell me was Edmund. Repeatedly I asked him to my place for private chats, prepared to confess everything in return for certainty about what Hélène knew. But at the point of confession I could never forget he was her friend more than mine and stayed silent, continuing to suffer equally from guilt and from the conviction that I would be the one to pay in the end.

I ate too much and got fat. I could read nothing but Roland

Barthes's *A Lover's Discourse*. I felt this was my heart's last outward movement, the elastic was gone, I could never love again, and it was going to end badly. Alone, I would return to Middletown, and although I'd been happy there before, how could I be happy there now? After I'd seen Paree? The worst part was, I had no one to confide in. My best friends were across the Atlantic. I decided finally to make do with what confidence was available locally. I couldn't keep it inside myself anymore.

At a feminist gathering, I had met an Iranian woman who lived in Paris and spoke perfect English, a lawyer, very tough, very ideological, whom I liked and saw occasionally for dinner. She had read my book about marriage and admired it. One night, after dinner, as we walked along the river, I blurted out that I was having an affair with a married man.

"How old is he?" was her first, surprising question.

"Older than me. Seventeen years."

She blew up at me. "I can't believe you! How can you do this? You betray another woman for this old man who is just exploiting your youth? I hate these old men who rejuvenate themselves at the expense of younger women! It's the oldest story in the world. And you talk in your book about how we need new plots, new scenarios! Then you go and re-enact the oldest scenario in the world! How can you do it?"

I tried somebody else, a man.

"What do you want him for?" he asked. "I don't think the family has much money."

Finally I found someone whose words seemed appropriate to my deep state of being in love. She had spent her youth as a dedicated party girl. She had married three times. She knew whereof she spoke. "Real love is a miracle," she said. "You wait and wait for it to happen but it almost never does. If it happens, it's a gift from God. No rules apply. You don't owe anybody anything."

I told L. that I was going back to the States at the end of the summer, and if he didn't come with me, he would never see me again. He was clear about the impossibility of doing that, and yet he said he loved me.

I thought I knew him. If he said he loved me, he loved me, and if he loved me, he would come to live with me. It was just that simple.

One day he said, "If I were to leave Paris, there would be an earthquake." Then I knew it was only a matter of time. I felt bold enough to call my mother and tell her what was going on. Naturally, she was dismayed.

"If you think he's going to leave his wife for you, darling, you're living in a fool's paradise."

She continued to distrust L. and to view my involvement with him as a disaster, even after he announced he would join me in the States, even after he arrived in New York, until the very moment that she first laid eyes on him as she stood on a corner on lower Fifth Avenue waiting to meet us for Sunday brunch. With that first sighting, her heart became his. She never worried about me again, and now, whenever I say as I sometimes do that I wish I hadn't written my book about Josephine Baker, she gets indignant, as though I were being ungrateful to a benefactor. "Don't you dare say that. If it hadn't been for that book, you would never have met L."

Dream: L. and I are in a car. He's driving. He keeps going the wrong way, and I reach over to grab the steering wheel. We swerve all around. In a crowded piazza, we hit several pedestrians. It's hard to bring the car to a halt. We go quite a ways beyond the piazza, park the car on a side street, walk back. The police are already there. Also medical personnel to care for the injured. The police say, "It's a good thing you came back. You already have one citation for leaving the scene of an accident." Dr. S. thought this dream referred to my divorce from Mark, all the years I spent not thinking about it, leaving the scene of the accident. Finally, in therapy, I was returning to confront what happened. Well, that may have been my first citation. But the scene of my most recent accident was Paris.

After our all-day talk with Thierry, we had another session the following morning about L.'s and my tainted romance. We told our story. In passing, I referred to that time in Paris as the worst in my life. Thierry looked pleased. "You see? Already that changes things for me. I didn't know you suffered. I have to confess that I blamed you very much. But now I forgive you. I accept you as my sister." I burst into tears, on the one hand relieved to be forgiven, on the other sickened to find myself in a situation where forgiveness was mine to seek and others to bestow.

7

The Who-Needs-Mother Cookbook

"Let a certain period of time elapse, and you will see (just as, in politics, former ministries reappear, or, in the theatre, forgotten plays are revived) friendships renewed between the same persons as before, after long years of interruption, and renewed with pleasure. After ten years, the reasons which made one party love too passionately, the other unable to endure a too exacting despotism, no longer exist. The affinity alone survives, and everything that Gilberte would have refused me in the past, that had seemed to her intolerable, impossible, she granted me quite readily—doubtless because I no longer desired it." *The Fugitive*

PERHAPS I SHOULD APPLY TO myself Proust's insight about aging artists starting to value themselves on their secondary talents. Perhaps I make too much of my cooking. I know I'm not an inventive cook. Eggs Beatrice is the only dish I ever wholly made up, pouring Hollandaise sauce over shirred eggs and throwing on top some caviar L. got from flying Air France.

What can be said is that L. and I make a good team in the kitchen. I am the executive, he is the sous-chef. I conceptualize the dishes and do the actual cooking. He prepares the ingredients, peeling, coring, slicing, chopping. He likes the focus and discipline of his work. I like the quick changes and three-ring-circus quality of mine. Without him, I would not cook. I do not have the patience to peel potatoes, wash and chop parsley, clean and slice mushrooms. Without him, I would have nothing but hamburgers or steak for dinner, with Lindt chocolate bars for dessert.

I work from cookbooks, simplifying recipes as I go along, cutting out steps and ingredients. Because L. is allergic to garlic, I always cut out the garlic, often substituting shallots. In the course of time, the recipe becomes personalized. I have to remind myself that my picadillo came originally from Linda Gassenheimer's *Keys Cuisine*. I have made it so many times now that it feels as much mine as my toothbrush, which I only realize is an Oral B when I go to buy a new one. Then, too, raisins, which Linda Gassenheimer says are optional, are essential to me. These are the small touches that define personal style.

At first, I carefully attribute my recipes to their sources, like a responsible scholar. After a while, the sources drop away unless the recipe is a friend's. Then I try to retain her name in the name of the dish, as in Annie's Thai Fish or her Java Beef, Salmon Linda Holtzschue, and Anne Bernays's Lamb and Rice Casserole. In this way, scrolling through The Who-Needs-Mother Cookbook is as full of pleasant memories as flipping through my address book. Annie gave me the name for one of my signature dishes, combining her affectionate name for me, Mouse, with my own name, to produce Fettucini Phyllmouse. This is made with peas, mushrooms, and little chunks of ham.

I started compiling The Who-Needs-Mother Cookbook when I stopped writing, in about 1990. The computer made it possible. I began storing recipes electronically and printing out whichever one I wanted to cook from. This meant I could give guests a copy of the recipe I cooked for them; I could easily revise and change; I could splatter all over it and make a fresh copy as needed. Using the index function of WordPerfect, I made a more or less accurate index for the whole thing and printed it out in 1992, as a Christmas present for Teddy. He was then a junior at Harvard and starting to cook, already trying out dishes like steamed fiddlehead ferns, a year younger than I had been when I discovered grilled lamb chops.

In addition to recipes, The Who-Needs-Mother Cookbook contains advice on food preparation, for example: resist the temptation to buy the best cut of meat for hamburger. It has the least fat, but fat is what makes hamburgers taste good. Also, add a little olive oil to the water in which you cook pasta. It keeps the pasta from sticking together. On the other hand, it keeps whatever sauce you prepare from adhering well. (The lesson cooking teaches over and over is, no matter how thin you make a pancake, there are always two sides.)

Teddy appreciated the advice. "How did you know, Mom, that I'd be tempted to buy the most expensive chopped meat?" His willingness to attribute to me clairvoyance is one of his many adorable traits. But what he liked best of all was the hardcore information, what temperature to roast a chicken at, what temperature for roast beef and pot roast, how long for grilling fish, and a question I had not addressed in The Who-Needs-Mother Cookbook, how long do you cook a lobster? This should be an easy question for a parent to handle, far from the toddler's *Why?*, the adolescent's *Why me?*, the young adult's *What next?* Yet it produces some anxiety in me, because I've never been sure how long you cook a lobster. I always get it mixed up with corn.

Teddy will be a good cook. At any rate, he will cook. He will be able to take care of himself. I have done my job as a mother, for my time and my place. Like the tribal people I studied in Anthropology 1B, who taught their children how to find witchety grubs or how to cook a kangaroo using its own skin as a stew pot, I have taught Teddy how to cook a hamburger and pasta. I have passed on the knowledge that mushrooms absorb fat and then give it up. The Who-Needs-Mother Cookbook was, in that sense, a graduation present to myself, something I did to signal that my job as a parent was just about over. I had brought my little portion of the next generation to the point of self-sufficiency.

Teddy recently made a pesto (basil, olive oil, parmesan cheese, garlic) to which he added mushrooms. The mushrooms couldn't be tasted. He often uses too many ingredients, to my way of thinking. If pears and blue cheese are good, wouldn't they be even better with tomatoes? It isn't just Teddy. From what I've seen of student cooking, his whole generation seems to believe that the more ingredients you put in a dish the better it will taste. Is this urge to multiplicity a sign of the age they are living in or the age they're at? Is Teddy's generation taking the lesson of multiculturalism into a realm where it doesn't belong, trying to turn the melting pot into kitchen equipment? Or do these young people, at a time when they want more experience, more variety, more friends, more places, more sensations, also naturally want more ingredients in every dish? Perhaps they haven't yet learned the elegance of definition, limitation, and clarity of taste. For that, I offer the example of the lemon pasta of my friend Daniele Scalise, whose sauce consists simply of butter, cream, parmesan cheese, a touch of nutmeg, salt, and pepper, and, off the heat, at the very last minute, the juice of a lemon. Of course, Daniele is a Roman, comfortable with exactly who he is.

It's only a matter of time before people start reading recipes as texts. Barthes on Japanese bento boxes, Lévi-Stauss on the raw and the cooked—these are steps on the way to close readings of recipes themselves. The food of the recent past I most admire is Ben and Jerry's Chocolate Chip Cookie Dough ice cream, with its brilliant allusion to childhood days when our mothers allowed us to clean the cookie dough bowl with our fingers, a treat which in my household was called "licking the bowl." How many of us did not prefer the uncooked dough to the finished cookie? But who, besides Ben and Jerry, would have had the inspiration and the daring to present the raw ingredients as the principal dish? I aspire to write a book like Chocolate Chip Cookie Dough ice cream, counter-conventional, paradoxical, and true to the lived experience of our times. But such a book might have to be completely non-narrative, a collection of recipes, phone numbers, e-mail, answering machine messages, jottings on notepads, *TV Guide* listings, tax returns, newspaper clippings, and reading lists.

This came by fax, from L.'s lawyer. She got it by fax from someone else. Lawyers, stockbrokers, and other people who are on the phone a lot have a responsibility, which they seem to respect, to keep the rest of us up to speed on humor. These purport to be signs, in English, discovered around the world.

In a Leipzig elevator: Do not enter the lift backwards and only when lit up.

In a Bucharest hotel lobby: The lift is being fixed for the next day. During that time we regret that you will be unbearable.

On the menu of a Polish hotel: Salad of a firm's own make; limpid red beet soup with cheesy dumplings in the form of a finger; roasted duck let loose; beef rashers beaten up in the country people's fashion.

In Germany's Black Forest: It is strictly forbidden on our black forest camping site that people of different sex, for instance, men and women, live together in one tent unless they are married with each other for that purpose.

In a Rome laundry: Ladies, leave your clothes here and spend the afternoon having a good time.

In a Bangkok temple: It is forbidden to enter a woman even a foreigner if dressed as a man.

This document arrived in Key West at a good time. I needed a laugh.

Bob Stone was acting mysteriously. He had asked me to give a dinner party for his friend Sonny Mehta, the head of Knopf, and his wife Gita, who were coming to Key West with some friends. I agreed without hesitation. I would do just about anything for Bob. It didn't seem strange that he wanted me to give a dinner for his friends the Mehtas, even though I'd never met them, because our house is big and on the water and I like to cook. But I told him that our table could seat no more than eight, and that seemed to bother him. Couldn't we fit in six or eight more? Not without renting tables and hiring a caterer, I said, like we do for our annual brunches. The evening was going to be "memorable," he kept saying, a special evening for literature. He mumbled about the importance of doing this right. He didn't make any sense.

This went on for a few days. I thought he was drinking in the morning. I thought he was having a mental collapse. Why make such a big deal over a dinner party? Why get in such a tizzy? He was deep into writing a novel. Maybe the intensity of his fiction was spilling over into his daily life. If it wasn't that, then the nervous breakdown or alcoholism theory was the only one. He couldn't even give me any information about the friends the Mehtas were bringing, first two people, then only one.

"Who are they?" I asked when they were still two.

"Couldn't say."

" 'Couldn't say?' You mean you don't know or you can't say?"

He thought. "I don't know."

When we were down to one guest, I asked the sex. Bob was evasive. Then he committed to male.

"Sonny's lover?" I asked.

Bob erupted. "Good God. The man is traveling with his wife. Would he bring a lover along? Anyway, what makes you think he's gay?"

"I don't think he's gay. I'm just throwing out ideas. I don't know anything about him. I haven't a clue whether or not he would travel with his lover and his wife. I don't know these people at all. They're said to be very sophisticated."

I made my plans for the evening with a sinking heart. It lacked the clarity I need to function well. I was told that Sonny was a Sikh and Gita Hindu, but I was ignorant of the food restrictions for each, and Bob couldn't tell me anything about what the guest ate or didn't eat. I hoped my shrimp with rum and mint would do, but I wasn't sure at all. Lots of people are allergic to shellfish, and orthodox Jews don't eat it. Do Sikhs? Do Hindus?

I invited Alison, and Bill Wright, who can talk to anyone and gives me comfort, but it didn't seem that Bob was happy with the guest list and Janice kept saying she would stay home so I could invite someone else. The week before the party, I wasn't sleeping well, a rarity for me. I woke up not even in the middle of the night, but at the start, at one o'clock and two. Something was going on I couldn't understand.

I discussed my uneasiness with Alison.

"I worry about Bob," I said. "I think he's having a nervous breakdown. He keeps saying this dinner for Sonny Mehta is going to be an important evening for literature. Two weeks ago at Bill Wright's house, he lay down on the sofa during dinner and fell asleep."

"Yes, that's worrisome," said Alison.

"Maybe he'll get better when he finishes his book."

"That's very likely," she said comfortingly.

That day, as I was bicycling back from the gym, I saw Irving Weinman coming in the other direction, looking like the actor Alan Rickman who played Colonel Brandon in *Sense and Sensibility*, tall, dark, a hairsbreadth off conventionally handsome and all the more attractive for it. I waved. He waved. We passed each other. He stopped and called back, "You know, everyone thinks your mystery guest is Salman Rushdie."

Suddenly, as when the precipitate was added to the chemical solution in high school science and the beakerful of murky blue liquid turned clear and transparent, I experienced a tremendous sense of relief. Things were falling into place. The chord was resolved. The mysteries disappeared. Everything made sense. Bob Stone wasn't going crazy. Salman Rushdie was coming for dinner. He was still in hiding, living under a death threat. Security was an issue. Stone didn't tell me because he wasn't allowed to tell me. Moreover, the secrecy and danger would appeal to his imagination. He might even exaggerate them. That it would be a memorable evening for literature was true. It would be memorable for the Key West writers to meet Rushdie. And the meeting ought to be special. A great writer, a martyr to art, was owed a special evening.

Now I understood Stone's discontent with my modest dinner for eight. If only I had paid attention to what he had not said, rather than what he'd said, the pause I'd heard before he answered my question, "Can't say who it is or don't know?" with "Don't know." The pause was the answer. In the windstorm of flying perceptions and insights, half grasped, half ignored, here one moment and blown across the Gulf of Mexico the next that is the life of the mind, I had known for a split second that Stone was lying, but I was too lazy to hang on to this fragment of awareness as it hurtled across my mental field, too lazy to wrestle it to the ground, work out what it meant, and act on it. I had flunked the test of Proust. I had flubbed the hard, minute work of perception. I let the insight go out of my mind so entirely that I hadn't even realized there was a "mystery guest." Of course, if there was a mystery guest his identity, given that Rushdie was in South Florida on a book tour for *The Moor's Last Sigh*, was obvious. But I had never said to myself, "We have a mystery guest." I had said, "We have a publisher coming for dinner," and, "We have a friend going crazy." Lighthearted now, I peddled home quickly to call a caterer and invite more people. My way was clear.

This was Thursday. The dinner was Saturday. But it was not hard to arrange. Fortunately, Doug at Louie's Island Pantry wasn't busy that night. Dinner would be buffet. There would be two men to prepare the food, serve drinks, and clear. Doug promised to try to hire Dan, who had served at our brunches the preceding two years. I ordered snapper baked in banana leaves, which seemed appropriately tropical, and jerk chicken for the people who didn't like fish, with black bean salad and key lime cheesecake for dessert. We would set up two tables of ten on the porch facing the ocean. We would put spotlights on the coconut palms, running extension cords to the house. I would buy Kmart orchids for the tables and to hang from the eaves. Almost everyone I called and invited was free. It would cost what we usually spent on brunch for many fewer people. But there was no question it had to be done. We owed it to literature and to freedom of expression.

When everything was set and I was relaxing by playing minesweeper on the computer, Annie called from Connecticut.

"Bad news," she said. "They've found spots on my lungs. Do you know the name of a thoracic surgeon in New Haven?"

For the basic emotional states—notably grief and depression—it's hard to come up with new metaphors. My stomach sank. I felt turned to lead, such was my sudden weight of grief, my anticipatory sense of loss. Annie smoked. She smoked a lot. Why had I not always seen that she would die young? Now it was only too clear that she was one of those special personalities, super-compacted, incandescent, which made a huge impression in a short time and then were gone. Foreseeing the loss of her, I appreciated her in a way I had not since I first met her and first felt the impact of her mind and personality, before habit dulled my appreciation and the opposition at the vital center of our friendship had made me wary.

She was in her thirties when we met but she had already won a Pulitzer Prize for *Pilgrim at Tinker Creek*. I was in charge of hiring for the Wesleyan English Department, and I recruited her to teach writing at Wesleyan. But to say I recruited her is to give a misleading sense of Annie's style. She is not a person to be recruited, to accept a job, or even a phone call—even a compliment—except at her own good time. What actually happened was that I wrote her asking if she would be interested in our position and she wrote back that she was not. "A writer should be rooted," she wrote, did I not agree? And she was rooted in Western Washington. Some time later she called to say she had changed her mind, wanted to move East, and wondered if the position was still available. It was not. Who had been appointed? The poet, Mark Strand. Would it be all right with us if she could convince him to split the appointment with her? Once conceived, the thing was done: she does not take no for an answer. That was how we came to meet, and to become neighbors and friends.

At first we couldn't get enough of each other's company. We had the feeling lovers sometimes do of being two versions of the same person. We both knew the lyrics to Gilbert and Sullivan, fifties rock 'n' roll, and folk songs. We both revered jokes, hated sloppy writing, had been married and divorced, were personally ambitious, one of three children in a middle-class family, highly energetic, competent, sociable, and blonde. We were Protestant and Jewish editions of the same woman. We divided the world between us. She knew the names of trees; I knew the names of flowers and shrubs. She was at home in the wilderness; I was at home in the city. I was fundamentally secular; she was profoundly religious. I could advise on clothes; she could advise on medications. My cooking tended to the French and Italian, hers to the Thai and the Mexican.

We don't look much alike, but people started confusing us. We were, after all, two women, two writers, two blondes, working in the same department, living on the same street. When we both started going to Key West, the same thing happened there. We both came from Connecticut and were about the same age. A friend on the board of the Monroe County Public Library last winter called to say he'd arranged for me to use the Florida Reference Room. I didn't hesitate. "It must be Annie Dillard who wants to use the Florida Reference Room. I don't know a thing about it."

I think it was my idea to go to Key West, but she probably thinks it was hers. This is an example, typical in its insignificance, of the kind of competitiveness that exists between us. Who found Key West? Who is more at home there? Who is more friendly with X or Z? Nothing is beyond the range of competition. Whose posture is worse? (This has positive value, as indicating greater commitment to writing.) And (reverse value) which of us is responsible for this competitiveness?

She is, I say. She is so competitive, she is even competitive about virtue, trying so hard to be a good person and make other people believe in their own goodness that she ends by claiming goodness as her shop. In praising me, Annie, as I feel it, claims my action and makes it over in her own image. "Oh, how good of you to call your mother." And I inevitably accept the praise, even as I feel that it betrays the character of my act, which was produced by a mishmash of motives, including habit, guilt, generosity, cowardice, superstition, love, and no small measure of pleasure-seeking. If I said this to her, she would very likely agree, for she wouldn't want me to have had an idea she hadn't already thought of, but she would take it further, perhaps like this: "I shouldn't ever open my mouth. Whatever comes out is disastrous. Someone ought to tape my mouth up." For exaggeration is another of her modes of possessing, and she loves to apologize.

There's another side to the pancake.

When I introduced her to my friend and Key West gym teacher, Bill Y., she stuck her hand out to shake his. "Pleased to meet you," she said. "Thank you for being so kind to Greg and Angel."

Greg, a hairy, hunky, sweet-natured young man, who had worked on the tourist catamaran and was now assisting Bill at the gym, had recently married Angel, diminutive and angelic as her name and seven months pregnant. Two lovable waifs who occasionally baby-sat for Annie's daughter, they had no place to live, and Bill had been letting them stay with him in his tiny cottage.

"They've found their own place now," Bill said.

"Yes, I heard. Just in time," said Annie. "Joseph and Mary. They found a manger."

Now when Annie said, "Thank you for being so kind to Greg and Angel," I thought, "There she goes again, as though all the world's kindness were in her jurisdiction. Can't anyone do something decent without Annie thanking them?" But when she compared Greg and Angel to Joseph and Mary, I drew in my breath, acknowledging inspiration. This, too, was just like her, and you didn't get one without the other. Every hour with Annie is likely to contain such a one-two punch. Watch out! Moral posturing coming in at ten o'clock. But hold on: wit and brilliance are right behind.

Annie converted to Catholicism some years ago, a move which seemed to me perfectly normal and even predictable given her constant battle to tame her unruly self. The entire weight of Saint Peter's Basilica is hardly enough to keep down a personality and a personal assertiveness that have the resilience of a banana plant, on top of which you could park a van and have it pop up again, the load removed. From my point of view, which is that of Cardinal Newman, the Church of Rome is the natural endpoint of all Christian religions which aim at the subjection of self to a higher authority, just as Quakerism is the natural endpoint of all those others that seek the higher authority in the self. If Annie took religion seriously, and she did, she would naturally, given her temperament, become a Catholic sooner or later. You can't say it took *me* by surprise.

Our friendship, over time, had become complicated. Each thought of the other as a difficult person, someone to be treated gingerly. Annie used to say we managed to stay friends so long because we did not talk about the hurts we inflicted on each other. This pronouncement had the force of a prohibition: I was not to mention it if she did something that bothered me. It worked, in a way, but slowed down the molecules of the friendship, giving it prolonged life but a certain immobility, like frozen apple sauce. Years could go by in which I brooded over a slight, in which we would not be so close. At times I forgot why we weren't so close anymore, forgot the slight, was left only with the feeling of estrangement. Periodically I rediscovered the fun it is to be with her. Warmth between us revived. I can only assume that she was going through the same cycle, although, since we never talked about it, I do not know. Our friendship developed an overall fuzziness, the result of countless individual acts of willed ignorance, silence, blurring, and erasure. I counted on it for the long term, but at any given moment it could be on or off, the temperature up or down.

Proust says that people in time forget the specific causes of their resentments and so confront other people as though in a dream, where one may feel insulted but not be sure by whom. You'd need to consult a register, he says, to remember your feelings about each person you know, your past interactions. As at a big party, you approach people you haven't seen in a long time with benevolence and perhaps a little too much joy, fearing that you've forgotten how close you were, in a long friendship, you might approach your friend with a tentativeness and uncertainty unwarranted by the degree of affection you feel for her, but understandable in the light of human forgetfulness and the complexity of your particular exchanges. And so, with time, the ebullience and joy of your early encounters is gone, replaced by delicacy and courtesy.

Annie had charged me to tell people about the spots on her lungs. Over the next couple of days, I did. They reacted variously, one with strength, one with lugubrious mien and excessive emotion, one with a firm sense of other priorities: "Oh, that's terrible. Can you come to dinner on the sixth?"

Annie's pain, and my pain about Annie, wound its way through the next week like the bougainvillea boughs—a whole Birnam Wood of bougainvillea harvested in rubber gloves and carried over to our house in her car by the intrepid Rollie M.—which we twined through the porch railings for the big dinner.

Bob, who is a good friend of Annie's, hardly seemed to hear what I was saying when I told him about her problem, so focused was he on the Rushdie visit. So it annoyed me when, in the middle of this supposed-to-be-memorable dinner, instead of making the brilliant conversation I thought was his duty and my due, he brought up the spots on Annie's lungs. What could the great writer and martyr for art do on being informed that a woman he did not know very likely had lung cancer except to offer, as he did, conventional words of sorrow?

For me the whole dinner was like that. It kept getting away from me. It wasn't what I'd hoped. I had planned for the guests to change places at dessert, so more people would have a chance to talk with the visitors, but Sonny Mehta, who wasn't feeling well, didn't show up, throwing off my seating plan and making the whole exercise irrelevant.

Of all the forms of creativity, hostessing is one of the most treacherous. Your materials are people, who don't always behave as you need them to. Sometimes acting like dairy products that spoil quickly unless refrigerated, people can go off in the course of the evening. Someone who can be counted on to be charming at the start of dinner may be drunk, sloppy, confused, and potentially obnoxious by dessert. Another, whom you expect to be incisive and dazzling in conversation, may lapse into a fit of sentimentality or, even worse, develop an absorbing and inappropriate interest in his food. A woman who has put a lot of energy into drawing out the man sitting next to her may suddenly get fed up and say no more. On the other hand, someone on whom you were not especially relying will amuse the whole table with stories, stories you laugh at all the harder because you are so grateful to have the air-

space above the table filled with happy laughter and the simu-
lacrum of dazzling conversation.

At the table on the other side of the porch, the conversation
got on to elephants and never got off, everyone adding another bit
of fact or fancy about elephants to the communal store. When
everything that could possibly be said about elephants had been
said, someone discovered in some dim recess of his mind even
more. They clung to elephants as people do who fear that if they
let this subject go, no other subject will emerge to take its place
and they will sit in mortifying silence.

It was true that all of Key West talked about the party afterward, but the subject of general discussion was who had paid for
it. Most people knew for a fact or had it on excellent authority
that Sonny Mehta had paid. A few partisans, my closest friends,
insisted that I had paid, but they were taken to be not disinterested in the matter. Even people who had asked me this indiscreet
question directly and whom I had frankly told that L. and I were
footing the bill still preferred to believe that Sonny Mehta had
done so, I suppose because Sonny, a remote figure, was easy to
imagine as a host. Moreover, if the party was "business," no special gratitude was in order on the part of the guests, and it's a rule
in Proust that people will perform any psychic action rather than
feel gratitude. I think that for a long time Bob himself believed
that Sonny paid for the dinner (or would eventually pay for it)
because he so much hoped that this was the case.

Annie was operated on soon after, and they found no cancer.
Nor did she have TB. There seemed to be nothing wrong with
her at all. But they had spread her ribs to operate on her lungs,
and the pain was awful. When I reached her by phone, in the hospital, she sounded as though she was being drawn and quartered.
There was a limit to the amount of painkiller she could be given;
at a certain point it would inhibit breathing.

"She's lucky!" people said.

I had rarely been as grumpy in my life. In Bob's eyes I could
see the absence of response which indicates that a friendship has
become problematic. He didn't understand why I wasn't grateful
for the historic role he had handed me. I didn't understand why he

wasn't grateful for the party I had given on his behalf. Another friend was being tortured for no reason and people called her lucky. As a hostess, I was dissatisfied. The dinner party hadn't come up to my own expectations. I wished I had it to do over again so I could do it better. I kept thinking of things I should have done differently. I should have ordered more jerk chicken, less fish. I should have made people change places even though Sonny wasn't there. What with grinding over one thing and another, I was still waking up on the hour all night long.

It was at this point that the fax came from L.'s lawyer. I read parts of it to Annie over the phone and she gave the dry sound of air being sucked through clenched teeth, a sound like sawing through stringy wood, which was what she could manage of laughter without hurting her ribs. "I've always loved that one about the Black Forest," she said, to indicate that I wasn't telling her anything she didn't already know. " 'Different sexes, for instance, men and women.' Very funny!"

At Bill Wright's lunch the following weekend, I was in a foul mood. I didn't feel sociable. I didn't want to be out at lunchtime. I was down on writers. I joined a small group only to find that the subject under discussion was whether writers made good company. Edmund White was citing Proust on the matter. Proust, of all people! When Proust belonged to me! When the whole subject was mine, one I'd earned by not sleeping for ten nights. At first I felt too much to speak. When I spoke, the words that came from my mouth—"Sometimes they are good company and sometimes they're not"—did not reflect the depth of my thoughts on the subject, although I felt them to be profound.

Let's get down to cases, I was thinking. Here's Bob Stone, whose genius has this paranoid sense of danger at the heart of it. Most of the time he's a great friend and great company, and the contrast between the taut and scary world he inhabits imaginatively and the world he lives in, where he drops his poker hand and the scariest thing you can do with him is to let him drive you to the beach, is amusing and touching. But every now and then, his imagination, which ought to stay in his work, applies itself to his daily life, and then he's disturbing company and a troublesome

friend. He really should have told me Salman Rushdie was coming for dinner.

And as for you, Edmund, you're sweet as pie, and everybody
loves you. You're everybody's teddy bear. But it's tiresome and
painful that you refuse to come to our house out of loyalty to
"Hélène." I'm through trying to prove that I'm not hurt by your
behavior, which is in fact hurtful.

I got my revenge. I managed to derail the nice conversation
Edmund, Bill S., and Ann B. had been having about whether writers make good friends into the much shallower waters of whether
writers are good-looking, which quickly led to Tom McGuane, a
very good-looking writer who had recently been in Key West for
the annual literary seminar. Edmund revealed that he and
McGuane had gone to school together. Edmund had written
about McGuane, and McGuane told him he'd gotten it wrong.
He wasn't self-confident, as Edmund depicted him. He was shy.
But then, we all said, the shallow stream becoming now a familiar
drip from the faucet, who isn't shy? Does it mean anything to say
you're shy? Don't we all just compensate for our shyness in different ways? Having ruined this conversation, I drifted to another
group, where the talk was about *Primary Colors*, which none of us
had read.

Mother thought I was entertaining too much. Every evening
when she asked by phone what I'd be doing later, if I said I was
giving a dinner party, she would say, in an unmistakable tone of
reproach, "Again?" In this, she was on Proust's wavelength. Like
an old-fashioned soccer coach who tells his athletes to abstain
from sex in order to keep their energy up, Mother—like Proust—
seems to think that energy devoted to social activity takes away
from the energies available for art.

"People who have the capacity to do so . . . also have the duty
to live for themselves. And friendship is a dispensation from this
duty, an abdication of self. Even conversation, which is friendship's mode of expression, is a superficial digression which gives us
nothing worth acquiring." (Vol. 2, p. 664)

According to Proust, the creative life is solitary and hard. Any right-thinking person will avoid it if possible. He will convince himself that whatever he is doing (for example, watching the O. J. Simpson trial on TV) is more important than his art, or will eventually contribute to it. But the only thing really necessary is sitting down and pulling out of the inner darkness the exact words in the exact order needed to body forth truth. In the section on Marcel's friendship with Saint-Loup, where Proust goes most deeply into the seductions of friendship, he makes clear how little respect he has for it. He also has no sympathy for the common wisdom which expects artists to profit most from other artists as friends and to seek most energetically the company of the greatest artists. While the Duchess of Guermantes was shocked that Marcel would rather spend time with a shallow girl like Albertine than a great artist like Elstir, Marcel himself saw there was no contest. Elstir could not make him feel the things that would stimulate him to create and Albertine could.

Nevertheless, Proust spent a lot of time on his own friendships and considered artists the best friends to have. For a nobleman or society person, he wrote, will seek always to charm his friends, whereas an artist will seek to give them something.

The party for Salman Rushdie got better the farther it was in the past, for Bob Stone had been right: there was a historic role to be savored. All my friends and business associates up north wanted to hear about it. What was Rushdie like? Splendid. Courteous. Pleased to be complimented on *Midnight's Children*. A writer. (I use writer as a term of approbation, the way my mother uses mensch.) Were there bodyguards? Yes. Two former navy Seals blocking the driveway. (Not, as Stone had allowed me to believe, three or four active Seals in scuba gear somewhere in the ocean in front of the house.) Was he going to have to live this way forever? I certainly hoped not. I wanted to see more of him in Key West. Within the week *The New Yorker* ran a cartoon by Roz Chast: What to do if Salman Rushdie drops by your place. Her advice was get out the frozen lasagna and settle down with him for some good TV ("Mr.

Rushdie loves daytime soaps"). Honor M., who had heard my tale, faxed me some additions: have Rollie cut some bougainvillea to twine through the porch railings ("Mr. Rushdie loves bougainvillea"); don't imagine that he's someone's secret lover, just because no one will tell you who he is.

I was on the phone with Indira K. in Connecticut, telling her about the evening. She especially wanted to hear about Gita Mehta, whose novel, *The River Sutra*, she had liked, and I was enthusiastically describing Gita's beauty and elegance when the BellSouth operator interrupted to say that my brother was trying to reach me and wondered if the phone was out of order because I'd been talking so long. My stomach sank. That meant serious trouble with Mother.

"Come immediately," Richard said. "But she won't be alive when you get here. They say there's no way she can last more than another hour or two."

He called at four thirty. I left on a seven o'clock flight out of Key West. She was still alive when I left the house. At Miami, where I had to change planes, I called again. She was still alive. We took off, not for La Guardia, which was fogged in, but for Newark. On route, I used an airplane phone to call again. She was still alive. Moreover, she seemed to have turned a corner. She would probably pull through.

We landed at Newark after midnight. I had been at the back of the plane, having booked late, and by the time I joined the line of people waiting for taxis, it was already long. There was fog. I figured it would be half an hour before I got a cab, but one stopped just after pulling out, and the driver shouted, "One more for Manhattan?" Everyone else was in pairs. I grabbed it. There were three passengers already, a young couple and a man up front. I took my place with the couple in back.

The young man said to the driver, "Another one? Does this mean we split the fare four ways? What is the fare? Thirty-two? With all these other people in the cab? This is my cab. You have an obligation to consult me if you take more people and you didn't. I'm giving you twenty and not a cent more." He was young and afraid of being cheated.

The driver reacted strongly. "You got some big mouth. With a big mouth like that you're gonna find your throat cut some day. Who the hell do you think you are? I'm doing you a favor. It's a foggy night. There's a long line. Where do you think you are, New York? This is not a New York cab. Do you see New York plates on this cab? This is a Jersey cab. What? Big shot. You're only gonna give me twenty? You're making all this fuss for a lousy ten dollars? Big shot. You're lucky I know how to drive in this fog."

In his anger, he careened from one side of the empty highway to the other.

"If it makes you feel any better," I said to the young man, "my mother's in the hospital and I'm trying to get there as fast as possible. I really appreciate the ride."

"I, too, appreciate the ride," said the man in front, who was English. "I could have been waiting there another half an hour."

"I don't mind at all having you here. It's the principle," the young man said. He was rigid with righteous indignation. He took out a piece of paper and a pen and wrote down the cabbie's license number, while the driver continued his angry monologue.

When I got home, the last to be dropped off, afraid to drive across the park with the crazy cabbie, but seeing no other taxis on the streets, I called the cardiac intensive care station and was told Mother was resting comfortably. I could see her during regular visiting hours next day. I went to sleep, more wrought up about the ride from the airport than I was about Mother, as though I had flown up all the way from Florida to witness this drama in a taxi cab rather than to see her, so hard is it to keep from being distracted by the sideshows of life.

Or was it a sideshow? The next morning, too, beautiful and springlike, I took my time about getting to the hospital and went for a walk in Central Park, thinking about the set-to between the young man and the cabbie. What was so fascinating about this midnight ride? Why did it make me feel bereft? I decided to treat it as a dream.

I am on an unfamiliar road, coming from an unfamiliar airport, on an emergency mission. I am in the hands of a madman.

Will I get where I'm going? Can I do what I'm supposed to? The young man, who doesn't know how to deal with the situation, who only makes it worse by his legalistic, prissy response is clearly me. Cars, roads. Who was at the wheel? Suddenly I saw. The imagery was my father's, like his leitmotif in an opera. But where was Daddy? I was on roads he hadn't taught me to travel. The cabbie was The New Jersey Driver he'd always warned me about. The young man was my own incapacity for dealing with things, the cab ride itself or my mother's dying. "Don't you young people know how to *schmeikhl* anymore?" (*Schmeikling* is the art of catching flies with honey.) "Am I the last man in New York who can talk to people?" So where was he when I needed him?

Before heading to the hospital, I bought a babka at William Greenberg and a *New York Times* from the Indian newsseller on Lexington and went home for a pleasant breakfast. Always, the first part of the *Times* I read after the front page is the obituaries. I need to know who is alive and who isn't. I consider this fundamental information without which I cannot orient myself, and in Key West I had worked out a way of getting to the *Times* through America Online just so I could read the obituaries. The rest of the news would reach me somehow.

That morning I read in the obituaries that Jill R. had died, at the age of fifty-two, of cancer. She was one of Kathy's closest friends. The irony of my mother outfoxing death yet again while a woman my own age died hardly needed going into. It was as though every time Mother had an attack, somewhere else in my world Death grabbed someone younger, like a corrupt recruiting officer who would accept any replacement for the soldier drafted, whether they were fit for service or not. I called Kathy to offer my condolences, but she was with Jill's family, her housekeeper said.

As for Mother, I had seen her in worse shape. However, the longer she stayed in the cardiac intensive care unit, the worse she seemed to get. Her roommate was a Mrs. Bennett, the most literate lady I've ever run into in a medical emergency situation. If we'd met under other circumstances, I felt I would have liked her a lot. She had many visitors, most of them young and bright, whom she questioned about their reading. What had they read of

Jane Austen? Had they read any Salman Rushdie? She herself was reading *The Moor's Last Sigh*.

Salman Rushdie. Salman Rushdie. The name recurred all afternoon long, at first amusing (if only she knew that I, the obscure person sitting at the foot of the bed of the patient next to her, had just two weeks before entertained this very Salman Rushdie in my own home!) and then excruciating in its repetition, each "Salman Rushdie" detonating in my brain like a drop of water in the Chinese torture, which begins by being cooling and pleasant before it becomes a misery. Would she never shut up? Would she never be querulous and kvetchy? Her sanity and good nature were driving me nuts. What was a person who talked so thoughtfully doing in intensive care? Mother never got a minute's rest. Moreover, Mrs. Bennett was so charming that the nurses flocked to her, with hardly a glance at Mother.

Mother's lunch sat untouched at the foot of her bed. She didn't know it was there. She couldn't see it. She could not have reached it anyway. When I tried to feed her, she spat it out. It was inedible.

In the late afternoon, I went out for a walk. When I came back to her room at six, nothing had changed except that Mother was even more tired. Her dinner was at the foot of her bed. It turned out to be the untouched lunch, never removed. Visiting hours were almost over, but before my eyes, Mother had some kind of attack. Her lungs seemed to be filling up again. She couldn't breathe. The nurses—can I be remembering this right?—were sitting in a group just outside her door, ignoring the monitors, chatting and eating from a box of chocolates. I had to shout to get their attention. "There's something wrong with my mother! Please get a doctor! She can't breathe." Eventually they got her an oxygen mask. A resident came and gave her a shot of Lasix. She was still gasping, long whooping intakes of air, behind the oxygen mask, when an intern came and earnestly questioned her. "What is the nature of your discomfort?" Gasp, gasp, mumble, gasp. "Please describe for me the nature of your discomfort."

By the end of the day, I was exhausted. This was a full-time job, and not one for which I was temperamentally qualified. Nor could I get a private-duty nurse to take my place. You are not allowed to have a private nurse in the cardiac intensive care unit, where, theoretically, the nursing is so high-powered that another nurse would only get in the way.

When I called the nursing station to check on Mother's condition next morning, they said she was fine, only unfortunately during the night her hearing aids had been thrown away.

"I want her out of there!" I said to Dr. Franklin, when, after a three-hour wait for his callback I finally reached him by telling his secretary it was an emergency. "I want her home or at the very least on a floor where she can have her own nurse. They're ignoring her in intensive care."

"They're geared for emergencies," said Dr. F.

"Yes, but the emergency is over. She needs to sleep. By the way, thank you for saving her life again."

"My pleasure."

In the hospital that afternoon, the Salman Rushdie torture continued, as a mighty stream of enthusiastic young people in publishing, theater, and finance came to visit Mrs. Bennett. In between visitors, she spoke on the phone. "I hate to impose on you, but would you bring me that hairbrush I keep in the bathroom drawer, darling? Well, that would be too kind of you, really." Damn the woman's courtesy! Mother, in contrast, had greeted me by saying, "You and Susan treat your dogs better than you treat me."

I had brought her whitefish salad, herring, and mushroom and barley salad, hoping these old-fashioned foods would comfort her, but she hardly had the strength to eat and found what she ate too salty. She had gotten no sleep. They woke her up to take her temperature, then to reinsert an IV which had fallen out, and then there was the business of the hearing aids. "I will say this for them. They ripped the place apart looking for them."

A good intern came in. You could tell at a glance how capable he was. He listened to Mother's chest. I made my pitch for moving her to another floor. Capable Dr. W. went away, came back, and said, "There's good news and there's good news." She would be moved to the regular cardiac floor and into a private room.

The room was sunny and quiet. There was a list of incapacities over her bed, each engraved on a different color-coded plastic plaque—Visually Impaired, Hearing Impaired, Allergies, Requires Feeding Assistance, Falls Prevention—reminding me of the placards listing specialties you see outside restaurants in Paris: Croque Monsieur, Omelette aux Fines Herbes, Steak Frites, Tartines Beurrées. This boded well. I got her set up with a private nurse from four to midnight and another from midnight to eight in the morning. When the nurse came on, I left. But as soon as I got home, the phone rang. Mother was asking me to come back.

She'd convinced herself that when the nurses changed shifts at midnight, they would wake her up. By this time she was like a cranky baby in a crying jag, too tired to sleep, too hungry to eat, so sleep-deprived and starved that she was barely rational and carried on about the change of nurses as though they proposed to amputate a leg without anesthesia. By the time I got back to the hospital, the private-duty nurse had agreed to stay on through the night, to placate her. "She was hyperventilating," said the nurse. "I didn't want her to have another heart attack."

She was a wonderful nurse. She sent away Mother's awful dinner and ordered her a better one, which she fed her thoughtfully, sensitively, with infinite patience. Mother ate the soup with animal hunger, her lips pushed forward to the rim of the bowl, totally focused on the next mouthful. Then she ate the rice, merely greedily, a few spoonfuls, then wanted to stop. The nurse kept coaxing her to eat just one more spoonful, as Mother herself had coaxed me through a bowl of oatmeal when I was a child, cutting highways through it, inviting me to eat one neighborhood at a time. I could see her calm down before my eyes with every bit of food the nurse managed to get into her. After that she insisted on Mother's taking a few steps around the room so she would be tired enough to sleep. When I left, the lights were out and the nurse was posted in a chair at the door to keep anyone from waking Mother up.

She got a good night's sleep and was feeling much better the next morning when Susan came to visit. Susan didn't know what all the fuss had been about.

•　　•　　•

The night I got back to Key West, Rollie came over to celebrate. We drank my signature rum punch, one-third orange juice, one-third pineapple juice, one-third cranberry juice, with rum to taste. I boiled up two pounds of Key West pinks with crab boil spices and served them with mustard sauce. We went through the whole two pounds except for three pieces which L. gave to Rollie to give to Foufou, her cat, who had developed a taste for shrimp. Afterward, we went to see *Broken Arrow* with John Travolta and Christian Slater as fighter pilots, fighting over thermonuclear warheads in the Utah desert. I loved it. In the movies now, people jump from planes and land on moving trains with no difficulty.

In New York, I had stopped at the bead store next to Mortimer's on the way back from the hospital and bought myself some beads to string. Now, in Key West, I sat on the porch stringing beads. That was all I wanted to do. I could sense I was letting L. down. He wanted me to be happier to be home, fuller of the energy of reunion, than I was. I wanted only silence and order. I wanted to sink to the bottom of my own mind, into clear waters, leaving behind on the surface the scummy business of old age and death.

But phone calls kept coming in from my closest friends.

Annie's father, who had been dying of lymphoma for two or three years, had died. Still in pain from her own operation, she had gone to Pittsburgh the weekend before, thinking he was about to die, but he had lived. Three days after she got home, he died, and she went back again for the memorial service.

Wendy's father, ninety-one years old and living in Madrid, was not doing well, couldn't walk, was in constant pain and making life difficult for everyone around him, but it was his wife, Wendy's stepmother, some fifteen years younger, who suddenly had a stroke and died. Who would take care of her father now? He begged Wendy to come to Madrid.

"They will live forever," Wendy and I agreed. "We will carry them on our backs into the next century."

On my second day home, L. and I were sitting on the porch while I made calls on the cordless phone.

Mother was back from the hospital, doing fine. She had Claire's cousin Olive staying with her. Disconcertingly, she remembered quite well saying what I had chalked up to medication and sleep deprivation. "You remember how I said I was being treated worse than your dogs? Well, now I'm being treated like the queen of England."

Annie was back from the memorial service in Pittsburgh. I reached her in Connecticut. Over the phone, her anguish was intense, so intense and unexpected that I got up from where I was sitting with L. and moved to the other side of the porch, the way you move when you stub your toe, uselessly but instinctively, to counteract the pain. She said that everyone was so concerned about her lung cancer scare, so upset by her operation, so glad she was okay, that no one seemed to notice that her father had died, and she was overwhelmed by grief, even though she'd known it was coming, even though he'd been suffering so much that you could only wish for his death. The mail was filled with letters wishing her a speedy recovery or rejoicing to hear she was fine, while she was grief-stricken.

"There is no preparation for this. I just keep breaking down, thinking about my adorable father. Girls and their fathers. I remember how you suffered when your father died. I don't think I was sympathetic enough. Now I understand. The pain is unbelievable. I don't know how I'd get through it without my religion. Is there any up side?"

"No. The only thing is that now and then they come back in your dreams. You get to spend more time with them."

I put on Callas to make dinner by and broiled the yellowtail with flour and butter. I didn't deglaze it with wine, the way some people, especially the French, prefer it. I myself like it dry. I also made a salad, arugula, tangerine, fennel in a balsamic vinaigrette sauce, based on one I had had in New York with Wendy a few days before.

"It should have a few shrimp, though," I said to L. "The ones you gave to Foufou."

And so it came out, how angry he was at me, how angry I was at him. He was angry because I had stood up and moved to the other side of the porch when I was talking to Annie, as though I didn't want him to hear what I was saying. He was also hurt by my lack of interest in his work. He had done a painting he especially liked while I was gone, and I hadn't even noticed it.

I replied, "All I've wanted to do is string beads. I don't think you've made much effort to understand how I feel or to help me. The hot water heater was broken when I left and it's still broken."

"Yes. I could see that was important to you. I don't know why."

"And you didn't change the message on the answering machine when I got back. You expect me to come home and over-whelm you with attention, when I'm tired out and would like some attention myself."

"Yes, perhaps I'm selfish and self-centered."

This, for L., was a prolonged and cleansing bout of anger.

Finally I succeeded in reaching Kathy. She was, as I knew she would be, devastated by her friend's death. She told me about Jill's final weeks of life. "She retained her quality of life up until the end. She wasn't in terrible pain. She just had no energy. At the very end, she hardly had the strength to talk, so she asked me to do all the talking. She asked me to tell her everything that was happening in the world. She never tuned out of life. She was interested in everything. I told her all the dumb little details of my day, every stupid thing I did. I even told her about your dinner for Salman Rushdie."

I read Hemingway's letters to see what Key West was like for him. The ocean was full of fish. Hemingway went out every afternoon and caught them: tarpon, amberjack, marlin, snapper. He was writing *A Farewell to Arms*, then *To Have and Have Not*. He was writing another book, too, set in Chicago, based on a medieval ballad, which he thought was great while he was writing it and sounds awful and which has never been published. Writing to Maxwell Perkins, his editor at Scribner's, he said F. Scott Fitzgerald was taking too long on the follow-up book to *Great Gatsby*. He should write more, more quickly, not brood. Some of the books would be good and some would be bad and it wouldn't matter in the end, the bad would drop away and only the good would be left.

One night at a dinner party, Irving and Bob discussed whether or not it was true that Hemingway punched Wallace Stevens. Bob said it was true, according to Kenneth Lynn's biography of Hemingway. Irving said no. The real story was, there was an academic in town who said that Wallace Stevens was the best writer in Key West and Hemingway punched *him*. Bob agreed that this story had the ring of truth.

It was more than sixty years ago that Hemingway for some eight years spent his winters in Key West, and the town still lives partly on his fumes. Almost every tourist in Key West visits the Hemingway house on Whitehead Street. It is an unusually large two-story house with wrap-around verandas on both floors, a formidable fortress in the battle against heat. I have never been inside. I do not think of the house as Hemingway's but as his wife's. Pauline's family money bought it, and she had the enormous swimming pool built, which Hemingway found an embarrassment.

I do not enjoy seeing writers' houses unless the writers are in residence. I see no point in walking through the rooms Hemingway lived in when the whole atmosphere in which he lived has changed. Wallace Stevens would no longer perch at the Casa Marina. It is filled with conventions and sales conferences. The raffish town is a thing of the past. Gone are the sailors who attracted Tennessee Williams, closed the cigar factories which intrigued Hemingway. The ocean is fished out, the reefs are dying, and the waters of Florida Bay are changed irreparably by the chemical runoff from the sugar plantations and the urban sprawl at the edge of the Everglades. And no writer, in any case, can now afford the luxury of taking a boat out every afternoon. I feel more in Hemingway's presence when I sit in my own kitchen eating Product 19 and drinking my coffee, reading his letters at breakfast, than I would walking with a tour group through the house on Whitehead Street.

In fact, it was Hemingway's house that drove Hemingway

from Key West. Pauline wanted people around. Naturally they made noise. The swimming pool acted like a sounding board. The road brought in "every son of a bitch I ever knew or who ever read a line I wrote." He was writing *For Whom the Bell Tolls*. He had to go to Cuba for some peace and quiet. He checked into a hotel to work. That was his advice: live in a hotel. Tell everyone you're living in one hotel, then go and live in another. When they find you, move to the country. When they find you in the country, move again.

In the spring we can no longer occupy our house on the Wesleyan campus until the students are gone. It is too noisy to think in the daytime, often too noisy to sleep at night. They have moved the steel band classes (!) into the old building across the street that used to house the gym. The building is not soundproofed, and the whole thing resonates, sending tidal waves of sound crashing against my house. The steel drums themselves make too thin and high-pitched a sound to bother me, but the band has an accompanist on a snare drum set. He stays after class sometimes and bangs away to release frustration. This one student on his one set of drums comes across the street like an Albert Hall full of drummers.

Then, too, drummers practice on the field in front of our house. The wind blows their banging into my ears, inside my brain. I can think of nothing but my own irritation. Several times a day, when I am in residence, I go outside and ask the drummers to cease and desist. I try to be polite. My opposition has become, like so much else, more tentative with time. I used to be uncompromising about student noise. Now I find myself less sure of my moral ground and also more afraid of wounding young egos. I always start by telling the drummers that I'm sure I'd like their music under other circumstances. Still, my sense of beleaguerment comes through. I identify with Betsy Trotwood, David Copperfield's aunt, chasing the donkeys away from her door.

At night, there are parties. Many students consider it a kindness to make their music public. All assume that the sounds of happiness are happy sounds to all. The drums, or, what is just as bad, the thumping bass of the amplified music, can go on until two. One party whose noise we could hear even over the television at midnight was a fashion show and rap music party for minority pre-freshmen. Welcome to Wesleyan, where we wear hip-hop clothes and party!

What is happening to the university? Why has it gotten so noisy? Why has partying become central to the educational enterprise? Teddy says the culprit is late-stage capitalism. The university cannot market the life of the mind. It has to market fun and parties.

It's true that we tend to substitute easy transactions for hard ones. Sometimes we buy a book so we don't have to read it. We buy Calphalon pots, Cajun spices, a breadmaker, a pasta machine, we sign up for a cooking school in Tuscany, so we don't have to cook. That philistine bully, Late-Stage Capitalism, must encourage all this substitution as he certainly profits from it. Perhaps it's also his doing that people revere Hemingway for his fishing, his shooting, his drinking, his houses—everything we have learned to call life-style and to consume—rather than for his sentences.

8

Florida Landscape Plants

"We lack the sense of our own visibility as we lack that of distances, imagining as quite close to us the interested attention of people who on the contrary never give us a thought, and not suspecting that we are at the same moment the sole preoccupation of others. Thus M. de Charlus lived in a fool's paradise like the fish that thinks that the water in which it is swimming extends beyond the glass wall of its aquarium."

Sodom and Gomorrah

As soon as we pulled in the driveway, I sensed that everything was different. It took me a minute or so to know why. The drive from Orlando had taken eight hours. We were tired. It was dusk. Then I saw. The trees were gone.

Between the house and the street there had been a wild area, about fifteen hundred square feet, large for Key West, with a giant tamarind tree at the center whose roots spread all over the yard, making parking difficult and getting out of the car and walking to the house a climbing-Everest-like ordeal to my mother on her one visit. A hawk and mourning doves roosted in the upper branches and regularly befouled our car below. An unused wooden boat rotted in one corner of the yard, serving as a hiding place for the *Miami Herald*s that were thrown over the wall in the morning. It was a rich little ecosystem.

When we first discovered this house, I didn't immediately

appreciate its distinction. The high branches, the hanging vines, the undergrowth all kept the sun off the yard. Leaves fell on a daily basis. On the other side of the house, facing the ocean, a derelict car blocked the view. The house itself was little more than a shack on a large scale. It had started out as a carriage house at the turn of the century and gradually been made into living quarters, but I don't think anyone planned for people to spend the winter inside. You could see the ocean in the gaps between the boards. The walls were unfinished wood. The effect was dark. Outside, on the porch, boards were missing from the floor, the paint was always peeling, the railings, which one might have expected to run horizontally, took sudden unpredictable dips.

Without ever adopting the local spirit which had created the way this place looked, a spirit completely opposed to my way of worrying about everything in advance and upsetting myself before bad things happened to make sure they never did, I nevertheless came, in my own way, quickly to see a use for it. Who would want to rob a house that looked like ours did? I felt safe behind the peeling paint, the rotting porch, the derelict yard.

In a matter of a few months precisely the qualities I'd made excuses for came to seem most beautiful to me. Our place, I told visitors, was a piece of Old Florida. It was the Florida of Marjorie Stoneman Douglas and Marjorie Kinnan Rawlings, the true Florida of bungalows with porches open to the breeze, not the spurious one of golf courses and air-conditioned condos. By then, late-stage capitalism's aesthetic advance men were nipping at my heels. A museum show in Miami touted "cracker vernacular" as one of five native Florida styles. Cutting-edge designers purveyed "shabby chic." I had stumbled on a look ("Southern derelict"?) as viable as, and more politically correct than, Plantation or British Colonial, the 1990s successors to the Early American or French Provincial of my mother's generation as the middle-class decor of choice. Such was the politico-aesthetic transformation which had taken place in me to enable me to stand at the kitchen sink and look out into our dank and messy yard with satisfaction, veiled by vines and undergrowth and carelessly parked cars from the tourists who walked by on their way to the Southernmost Point and those who rode on the Conch Train.

But now the undergrowth was gone. The roots were gone. The tree was gone. The house was exposed to the traffic on the street. A load of bark mulch had been brought in and spread as a substitute for gravel. It was onto its unappealing, rough surface that I stepped from Greta Garbo to go talk to our landlady, who stood waiting to greet us.

She is dainty, pale, dark-haired, beautiful, an exotic flower from Central America. Our landlord, Mr. Quinn, a native Key Wester, met her on a business trip and managed to transplant her to Florida. Now they have three beautiful children. Our house shares the oceanfront, the dock, the yards, and the driveway with theirs, a two-story stucco which may lack the rustic charm I find in ours but is certainly more comfortable to live in. From our porch we can see through their window the screens of the kids' computers and the large television set in their living room.

"What happened?" I said to Mrs. Quinn, after a perfunctory hug and greeting. "What happened to the trees?"

"We cut them down," she said smiling. "We are going to plant fruit trees."

"Isn't it illegal?" In Key West you cannot cut so much as an avocado tree without the approval of the Tree Commission.

"We got all the permits," Mrs. Quinn said. "It was hard, but we said we would put in rare local trees."

"How can you replace that tamarind? It was so old."

"We will have very nice trees," she said. Her smile was wearing thin. "It will be very beautiful."

"It looks awful."

"It will be beautiful," she said firmly, and walked into her house.

I was aware even as I said to Mrs. Quinn "It looks awful" that I was setting in motion something whose consequences I could not see but which would be many and serious. As soon as the remark was out of my mouth, I regretted it. I knew I would pay for it. But I could not call it back, and no apology or retraction I offered would be able to erase the remark or wholly counteract its effect. What happened instead is what happens when you leave a message you regret on an answering machine. You erase what you can erase. Since you can't erase the message, your mind erases the memory of it or its effect. Either it didn't happen, or if it did happen, it gave no offense. In situations like this, I attribute superhuman powers of understanding to my victims: Mrs. Quinn would understand I was tired after my long drive. She would know I meant no offense. She was too generous a person to take offense when none was meant. There must be mad messianic murderers who imagine that the people they kill see the larger picture and feel honored to fall beneath their blows, just as I had been capable of imagining that a friend whose wife had died would realize he had all my sympathy without my writing a condolence note or that the editor for whom I'd agreed to write a piece I no longer wanted to write was too smart to think it was a good idea and didn't really want it after all. So I convinced myself that, thanks to Mrs. Quinn's magnanimity and my own insignificance in the greater scheme of things, the effects of my hasty and rude remark, which I knew would be catastrophic, would be negligible.

For my insult that was no insult I apologized with a gift that was no gift. I bought three areca palms, excellent for screening, a pretty round pygmy date palm, a broad-leaved Chinese fan palm, two large birds of paradise, several heliconia, and many anthurium, shoved them, still in their containers, into the small space between the kitchen window and the mulch-covered parking lot to screen us from the street. With an especially big smile on my face, as though giddy with my own Dickensian generosity, I told Mrs. Quinn that this landscaping was a Christmas present to her.

"Oh no, Phyllis, you mustn't do that," she said in genuine horror which I responded to as polite demurral.

"But I want to. Please. You've done so much for us over the years. The refrigerator. The dishwashing machine. The washer and dryer. The king-size bed."

"It is too expensive."

"I want you to have them."

"We want to plant fruit trees there."

"I'll leave them in their containers. You can move them anywhere you want to after we go home."

"Well, if you promise not to put them in the ground."

Even as I smiled and pretended to be generous, I felt uncomfortable. A new falsity had entered our heretofore cordial relations with the Quinns. But over the next few weeks I didn't admit it to myself. An unattributed, free-floating sense of guilt stayed with me all day every day, as a blemish in my consciousness. There was something I had missed, something to go back to and explore, a pebble in the stream of time, something interrupting the smooth flow of existence. Likeable people, the people whose company we enjoy, register these disruptive moments and speak about them immediately, as a joke if possible, putting them in the front of the mind where they can be cleansed by the flow of events rather than at the back, where they get caught like grit in gears or dirt in the gas line, bringing the whole automobile to a stop.

The Key West Literary Seminar this year was on the subject of "American Writers and the Natural World." Annie gave the keynote address, even though she goes up and down on being thought of as a nature writer. Part of her thinks that what she does, even when writing about frogs, weasels, eclipses, and trees, is theology. Part of her worries, as every writer does, about being ghettoized, finding one audience at the expense of all others. (I would be happy to be thought of as a nature writer like Proust, but that's another matter.)

For three days, distinguished writers held forth about the environment to a wrapt audience of hundreds. Since everyone present—talkers and listeners—was in favor of the environment, you might have thought there would be no controversy. But there's no greater potential for dispute than within groups of people who fundamentally agree.

Terry Tempest Williams, a naturalist from Utah, was the

moderator of the panel on writers and advocacy. Williams wrote a wonderful book called *Refuge*, about a year in which the Great Salt Lake flooded, inundating a bird sanctuary she especially loved. No one was to blame for the disaster. Periodically the Great Salt Lake just rises. This natural catastrophe is paired in *Refuge* with another, Williams's mother's death from cancer. It's a powerful book, and I read it to the end, even though I'm no longer keen to read about the slow deaths of other people's parents.

Williams is also an advocate for environmental causes, which isn't easy in Utah. Pipelines are the Tempest family business, and one of their biggest projects was held up because it threatened the existence of a certain desert-dwelling turtle. To stand up for the turtle in a construction family must have taken as much courage as fighting for the Union in a family of rebels. On another occasion, she testified in Congress. A congressman from her state pointedly ignored her during her testimony and when she called him on it said by way of explanation, "For some reason, Mrs. Williams, I cannot hear your voice."

Of the others on the panel—John Nichols, Doug Peacock, Rick Bass, Joy Williams, and Tom McGuane—the most uncompromising was John Nichols, author of *The Sterile Cuckoo* and *The Milagro Beanfield War*. Smiling an eerie, uncheerful, revolutionary's smile, speaking thinly so you had to focus all your attention on him to hear, he said that every one of us was responsible for destroying the environment by using the products of capitalism. We should, like him, ride bikes, instead of driving cars. Travel was wasteful. We should stay in one place. We should not try to make money. He looked patrician, puritan in every sense, as though he came of people who owned thousands of acres of virgin forest that is now prime metropolitan real estate. Easy for him to say give up capitalism, give up wealth.

Tom McGuane, who lives in Montana, in addition to writing novels runs a cattle ranch. He belongs to the Stockmen's Association. In that group, he counts as a radical. In this group, he's provocatively sympathetic to the ranchers. Understanding both those who want to make a buck and can't eat scenery and those who think the land is a sacred trust, he went right to the class issue which underlies these discussions of environment as the San Andreas Fault underlies Northern California. It's hard, he said, for people who never leave the land to be told by rich people from the East who come to vacation on it for three months a year what they should or should not do with it. Locals find elitist many of the city people's pleasures. Hiking seems elitist. Right-thinking itself can seem elitist. He turned the self-righteous, anticapitalist prescriptions of John Nichols on their head without being so inelegant as to mention them. He recalled to us a moment when, with his son, looking out over the Montana landscape, he bemoaned the disfiguring presence of double-wide trailers. How ugly. What eyesores. "Dad," said his son. "Quit it. Those are my friends' homes."

McGuane opined that literature should mind its own business, whatever that happens to be, and not try to tell other people what to do. His was a unique position at the Key West Literary Seminar. My friend and fellow Key Wester, Joy Williams, who is a passionate advocate for the environment as well as a masterful writer of fiction, spoke next, about the reception given by the NRA and others to a piece she had published about hunting. She hates hunters. She is so gentle and kind-hearted that the idea of doing violence to any animal really pains her. To her, hunting is so much macho nonsense and she doesn't think that animals should die to feed male egos.

"That's just what I mean," McGuane interrupted her to say. "Joy Williams is a great writer. Joy Williams is one of the finest short story writers in America. And she never wrote worse than in that piece about hunting. What condescension! What bunkum! Does she really believe that men pick up a gun to make themselves feel more masculine? She is better than that! That's what happens to good writers when they indulge in advocacy."

At his words, many of us in the audience entered the frozen zone of panic. These sessions are usually as full of mutual compliment and back-patting as a Kiwanis dinner. No speaker attacks another speaker. Those present are always exempt from an otherwise near universal scorn and disapproval. To suggest that anyone present could write badly in any circumstance was unprecedented.

The shock silenced the audience, suspending even program rattling. But Joy herself was unruffled. She continued to smile and began to speak again. She didn't turn her remarks against McGuane personally, as she easily might have done, but went back to her critique of hunting. Hardly were two sentences out of her mouth, however, before McGuane interrupted her again.

"My point—" he began to say.

Terry Tempest Williams cut him off. "You're interrupting Joy Williams. Let her finish."

Joy started speaking again. McGuane again interrupted. "If I may just make a point."

"No," said Terry Tempest Williams, with great force and emphasis. "You may not." And with that, as though overwhelmed by the effort of calming the mighty forces of battle, she started to cry.

"Now I've made our gentle moderator cry and I've offended my distinguished fellow panelist. It's an odd position to find myself in. I seem to be the panel bully, defending art for art's sake. I'm the dandy with a shotgun."

I liked McGuane. I was happy to have him puncture the seminar air balloon, wafting into the stratosphere on the updrafts of preaching to the converted. But why hadn't he interrupted John Nichols? Why choose Joy to pick on? It was as clear as the rifle on your gunrack to all the women I discussed it with later: this was a man-woman thing. Men listen to other men and not to women. Men they reply to. Women they interrupt. Women's voices, as the congressman said to Terry Tempest Williams, can't be heard. Our little do-good microcosm was repeating the story we'd all heard of how, within the 1960s civil rights movement, women were second-class citizens. Men might be capitalists or socialists, real estate developers or Earth Firsters, they might want to save turtles or poison possums. The one thing they could all agree on was that their opinions were serious and women's were not.

A group of writers participating in the seminar gathered spontaneously at Annie's for brunch, and she kindly called to ask me to join them. Jim and Lois Welch were there. Jim is a novelist from Montana, a Blackfeet Indian, and Lois teaches French literature at the university. Gretel Ehrlich, the writer laureate of Wyoming, who wrote *The Solace of Open Spaces*, was there, too. We were discussing the virtues of Polartec. Each of us has a piece or two, but Gretel has a wardrobe, because she is on the board of directors of the Polartec corporation. Every time the board meets, she gets another piece. She even has a Polartec blanket.

This winter the Massachusetts factory that manufactures Polartec burned down. In the ordinary course of events, hundreds of workers would have been out of jobs. But the factory owner, in a benevolent act which attracted a great deal of attention from the media, as being so opposed to the prevailing spirit in capitalism, vowed to keep meeting his payroll until the factory was reopened and the jobs restored. When pressed to explain the philosophical sources of his charity, the man cited his religion, Judaism.

Annie said that her stepdaughter Carin had been reading about this act of Good Samaritanism in the newspaper. It said that the factory owner, "an observant Jew," had learned from his father about the responsibilities a person had to his neighbors. Carin didn't understand the term "observant Jew," the equivalent of "practicing Catholic."

"Does it mean that he observed his neighbors closely?"

Later David adopted this as a code joke. If I asked him how he knew something, he would hoot at the chance to reply, "I know that because I am an observant Jew." According to him, Proust was the most observant Jew there's ever been.

If, on the one side of us, we have old Key West, a real Conch gentleman, a Spanish-speaking lawyer and magistrate, with ties to Cuba and Latin America, rooted in local life and local politics, training his sons to play in the Little League and on the high school football team, on the other side we have wealthy people from the North who own homes in several other places and spend no more than three months a year in Florida.

Some days after my "gift" of the palm trees, I was at my desk when a man knocked on the door and introduced himself as Christopher, the Garretts' property manager. He had a pager clipped to his belt and a cellular phone in his pocket. His introductory chitchat consisted of letting me know what a job it was getting so many properties in such farflung parts of America up and running, and he seemed to assume that those of us who had nothing better to do than to live in only one house or two needed to do our bit to help with the great work. Specifically, what he wanted was water for the Garretts' pool. They were arriving in two days. The pool had been emptied for resurfacing, and now it wasn't filling up quickly enough from their hoses. Could he add ours?

"You'd have to speak to our landlord. Water costs a lot down here."

"No problem with him, if it's okay with you. You won't have any water pressure all day, is all."

"Well, I was going to do the laundry, but I guess I won't."

I wanted to suggest that I was making a sacrifice in order to help him. I was trying to provoke an "I'd really appreciate it," or "That would be kind of you," but all I got was, "Yeah, right!" Presumably he was unable to imagine me doing my own laundry.

I went outside with him to connect the hoses and loop them over the coral fence between us and the Garretts. I would kill him with kindness. But he never did say thank you. Instead he told me, in his valley girl phrasings and tone, how horrified he and the Garretts' gardener had been by the cutting down of the trees, which left a bit of the Garretts' house, too, visible at an angle from the street.

"Like, 'hello'! If you cut down the trees, you're gonna see the houses."

"I don't think they care about that. They want to put in fruit trees."

"So, come on. Where are all these fruit trees? The meter's ticking!"

The Garretts' yard, the space between their house and the street, is thickly planted. Palms are crowded on palms. Even the undergrowth is planted. It's a little bit of jungle, and it used to hide the house from the street completely. But when the Quinns cleared their yard, Christopher told me, the Garretts' gardener had to bring in a load of very large palms to make up for the lost protection.

The root balls were so big they couldn't get them through the gate from the street, so he'd gotten Mr. Quinn's permission to carry them through his yard and hoist them over the fence to the Garretts'. He had left the trees on the Quinns' side overnight before he could haul them over, and Mrs. Quinn got furious about it, for no reason he could understand. "She went, like, berserk. I gather she's crazy."

"She isn't crazy!"

"But, 'hello'! Did I miss something? Her husband said we could leave them there. What's her problem? Okay?"

Once you got used to his assumption of privilege, his ruling passion (service to the Garretts), and his grating urban style, he really wasn't so bad. When I showed him how much of the Garretts' house was visible from our front yard, he offered to buy some more palm trees and have the Garretts' landscape man plant them for us on our side.

"You let me know what you want. They'll be in by next week."

"I have to check with my landlady first."

As I knew but didn't know that I had wounded her and then added insult to injury by making her a gift of palms, I knew but did not know that the offer of landscaping from the Garretts was bound to cause trouble. Tact and wisdom would have rejected Christopher's offer on the spot. But thrift and willful innocence impelled me to try to accept it.

When I reached her the next day, my landlady was not happy about the Garretts' offer.

"Why don't they put them in on their own side?" she asked.

"They will," I said. "But the more the better. We'd be happy for the privacy. They'd be doing it as a gift."

The word exasperated her. "I cannot accept these gifts. It is one thing from you, Phyllis," she said, making a courteous exception, "but quite another thing from people I do not know."

It wasn't going to work. When Christopher got back in touch

with me about the plantings, I'd have to decline. But he never did get back in touch. Nor did he ever retract and restore to us the hoses. The demands of home maintenance, of keeping three residences up and running, had swept him away and left us behind.

Anxious dreams substituted one neighbor for the other. L. and I had to tour all the Garretts' houses, not just the one in Key West but houses I dreamed they maintained in Jamaica, Cuernavaca, Puerto Rico, and Barbados. We paraded through room after room in house after house, admiring and praising as we went, the effort considerable. In one room Mr. G. played the drums for me. The drums made no sound. L. came to get me. We both wanted to go home. L. said that first we had to say good-bye to the Garretts "to make our peace." "Make our peace for what?" I said. "What have we done wrong?"

Just as an incision heals and makes a hard discolored lump on the skin, a psychic tear makes its presence felt as a lump in the texture of a relationship. I could no longer repress the knowledge that something was wrong between us and the Quinns. I talked about it to all our friends, putting ourselves in the right. "They cut down the trees. I couldn't conceal my feelings. I think I offended them. It was an old tamarind. A hawk lived in it." I played shamelessly to their environmental protectionist beliefs, and Joy, especially, was sympathetic. "What kind of people cut down a tree that a hawk lives in?" I accepted the partisan response. One of the nicest things friends can offer friends is the refusal to look at both sides. I didn't think it was my place to tell Joy about the mess the hawk used to make on our car or reveal that I was therefore of two minds about its disappearance, however I felt about the trees.

The jungle look is in in Florida landscaping. Cosmopolitan people favor it, as much as, in the eighteenth century, English people of sophisticated tastes preferred the asymmetrical, pseudonatural designs of Humphrey Repton to the fusty old symmetries and formality of French landscape design. My northern neighbors and their expensive gardener were up to the moment in their landscape design. My other neighbors, with their cravings for open spaces and alleys of fruit trees, were something else. That was how I saw it: all about looks. I had clearly heard and even said that the Quinns wanted to plant fruit trees, but I did not understand that they wanted fruit trees not because they liked the look of fruit trees, as would be the case with me, but because they wanted fruit.

One day (the very day that Teddy had to leave abruptly because of his grandfather's death) my landlady reached me by phone and started bawling me out.

"What have you done now? You promised me you would not plant things. Is my English not good enough? Did I not make myself clear? I told you not to plant them. Why have you planted them?"

I didn't know what she meant. I hadn't planted the palm trees. I had only planted the ground covers, the anthurium, and the heliconia. They were so insignificant they did not count in my mind as plantings.

Even when I realized what she was talking about, I could not take the problem seriously. Her fury made no sense to me.

"They're only anthurium."

"You don't know how things grow here. The people across the street had to take out things they put in because they grew so big."

"These won't hurt anything. But if worse comes to worse, take them out."

"How can I do that? You gave them to me," she wailed. "As a present."

The way that Tom Cruise in *A Few Good Men*, playing the prosecutor, so outrages Jack Nicholson, the defendant, that he trumpets an admission of his guilt, revealing in a moment the secret he has stolidly and cagily been protecting for months, my landlady now, pushed beyond politeness and restraint by my stupidity, revealed the true story of her rage.

Mr. Quinn, she explained, wanted to raise banana trees. They had been given a couple of shoots of a very unusual banana. One he had planted near the wall adjacent to the Garretts' property, the other was in front of our house. When the Garretts' gardener unloaded the new palm trees on the Quinn side of the wall, he left them right on top of one of the banana shoots, so small it went unnoticed. Mrs. Quinn had gotten very angry. (Read: "She went, like, berserk.") Then we had come and put our own load of palms on top of the other banana plant.

"Oh God. I'm so sorry. I didn't know it was there. How can I ever apologize?"

I had to stifle my urge to offer to buy new banana plants, big banana plants, to replace the ones Mr. Quinn had put in. Even I could see that money was part of the problem here, money, arrogance, and a way of growing things that started in the middle, as unnatural from one point of view as adopting a child when it had already won the Nobel Prize.

Just at that moment, Mr. Quinn himself drove up in his truck. I ran out to talk to him, glad to see him, eager to apologize. I really felt terrible.

"I just heard about your banana plants. Please forgive me. I had no idea. I wouldn't have hurt them for the world."

Mr. Quinn had been a football star in college. Dark-haired, blue-eyed, movie-star handsome, as a young man he had a small role in a film which was shot in Key West. He might have had a movie career, but he thought it would be more interesting to be a lawyer. He speaks in a voice that to me is irresistibly southern and caressing, and he has the southern gentleman's delicious habit of calling every woman he talks to "darlin'." But in the colloquy that followed, he didn't call me darlin' once, which I took as a measure of his disaffection.

"He made fun of my banana plants," said Mr. Quinn. "When I complained about his putting their root balls on top of my banana, he didn't apologize at all. He mocked me."

"You mean Christopher, their manager?" The failure to apologize seemed perfectly consistent with his failure to thank.

"No, he's not so bad. The other one. The gardener. He was dismissive to me, and he made fun of my banana plant. The next morning I found the other shoot had been cut, sliced right off."

"No! How awful! Are you sure it didn't just break off? Could I have done it when I was moving the plants around?"

"You weren't even here yet, and there's no way a banana plant can break. They're tough. You can bend them any which way. There is nothing you can do to break it. Believe me, this was cut, sliced right off, done intentionally, vandalized. Let me show you."

He knelt down by the patch of earth underneath our kitchen window, picked up a piece of coral, and scratched the ground with it. After a while, he found what he was looking for, a pale-colored shoot swelling at the middle and tapering at the top, rather like an endive, hardly visible until he dug down and disrobed it of dirt to show it to me. Adjusting my gaze to the size, I could see that the shoot had been lovingly planted, with some kind of protection encircling it.

"We plant them in sponges, to keep in the water. See how tough it is?"

He grabbed the little shoot and bent it back on itself in every direction. He was right. No way this was going to break.

"See there? That's where he sliced it. But there's nothing you can do to a banana plant that'll keep it down. It's coming back."

Spunky little native banana plant resisting foreign aggression! Me, allied with the barbarian invaders, crude, materialist, throwing their money around, demanding instant gratification. What could I do but beg forgiveness?

"I know you wouldn't have done that," said Mr. Quinn graciously and then gave me his philosophy of landscaping.

"We want to put three banana trees here, and another couple by the wall. We want to put a soursop, a mango, an orange, a guava. My uncle gave me these banana shoots. They're a very special kind, and he's going to get us some more. We'll put in a row of bougainvillea along the street wall. The tourists like that. But the rest of the yard will be fruit trees. I don't see the point," he said pointedly, looking me in the eye, "of any tree that doesn't bear fruit."

When I had taken that in, he said he'd like to show me his garden. Was I interested? You bet! We had rented next door for five years, and I'd never noticed their garden.

I was expecting a bed of heliconia, colorful ginger plants, anthurium, perhaps lantana. What he showed me, leading me to the side of their house, was a piece of earth inside a low stucco containing wall with chicken-wire siding, filled with tomatoes, peppers, and herbs. As a visual statement, it wasn't much.

"You put the tomatoes in October, they can go to March. Then the white fly gets them. You can't grow tomatoes in this climate past March. But in March, they are sweet! You throw them in a pot with the peppers, the basil, you have a great spaghetti sauce. You put in some conch, you can make a conch stew. My conch stew is delicious."

"I'm sure it is. I'd love to taste it. Could you give me the recipe?" But then I couldn't resist an attempt to reassert my dignity. "The basil tastes better if you don't let it flower. Just keep snipping the top off. It isn't so bitter."

"I throw it in, flowers and all. It tastes just fine," he said.

Two little tomato plants sat unplanted in four-inch plastic pots at the edge of the garden. He picked them up and held them out to me. "You take these. When do you leave? The first week in April? They should give you tomatoes by then. This one's a Beefsteak. This one's a Big Boy. Just put them in the sun and give them lots of water. Take them. As a present."

What is natural? In *Winter's Tale*, the young hero berates the heroine for putting on makeup. She defends herself. It's human nature to want to improve things. Hybrid flowers improve on the species they were bred from, but they are still flowers. Human nature is nature, too, and art is part of human nature.

In Middletown, L. and I have a little garden. It consists of an L-shaped bed, about twenty feet long, with the bottom of the L about four feet. It wasn't always this big. We started by digging just a small trench, parallel to the street. Every year I'd encourage L. to dig me another few feet. (As with our collaboration in the kitchen, I draw up the plans, and he puts in the work.) We started with peonies, daylilies, columbine, flax, poppies, and every year added more plants as they caught our eye at the garden center or in the catalogues. I ordered tulip bulbs and planted them in the fall, Apricot Beauty, Angelique, which is multifloral, and Queen of the Night, which is almost black. We put in rose bushes, the hybrid tea rose, Peace, for L., and less elegant but more abundant everblooming roses for me. After a couple of years, I started ordering dahlias, which bloom spectacularly in the fall, but have to be dug up and packed away for the winter. For me they only last one season. I've never succeeded in bringing them through the winter and getting them to bloom again. We put in Siberian iris which did so well they threatened to take over the garden. We divided them, with great effort, using a machete and even a saw to cut the roots apart. We've also divided rudbeckia and coreopsis, so a band of yellow continues throughout much of the garden in the summer.

Everything does well because the garden faces full south. It gets so warm that we have pansies and sometimes even roses blooming all the way to Christmas, and the pansies sometimes start to flower again as early as April. We often leave for Florida with flowers blooming and find them blooming again when we come back.

The worst time of the year for our garden is July, when the Japanese beetles take over. We have tried everything to keep them under control. We bought Japanese beetle traps, which are loaded with a scent that Japanese beetles are supposed to find irresistible. Theoretically, you put these upwind from your garden and the beetles will go to the traps and not to your roses. But we found that the traps attracted more beetles than we had had before, and although some went to the odor source, most stayed chewing away on our roses.

The only thing that really works with Japanese beetles is to pick them off one by one and drop them into a solution of dish-washing detergent and water. But this is a labor of despair. You can pick the leaves clean of beetles one minute, baring all the tattered lacework they have chewed, only to have your plants shimmering with beetles half an hour later. For several summers, I would knock off work every hour or so to go outside and drown Japanese beetles, but now I just turn the garden over to them in midsummer and look forward to fall, when they die off naturally with the colder air.

Our garden is highly visible. We overlook Wesleyan's central open space, Andrus Field, where graduation ceremonies take place, football games are played, reunion classes gather, and undergraduates cavort and sunbathe. We are directly across the field from the library, from whose windows our white clapboard house is a landmark. The street we live on is a one-way street which goes past the major entrance to the administration buildings and the arts center before it gets to our house and on out again to the outside world. All administrators who drive to work have to pass our house once a day, and much of the student body walks by, either on the way to the dorms or to the dining hall. All visitors who take a campus tour or schedule an interview at the Admissions Office pass our house. Most people get pleasure from our garden. Some take the trouble to compliment us or to ask the name of a flower. We enjoy the attention the garden gets. I make sure to have it looking especially good for graduation and reunion weekends. I hope that the spectacular poppy, in Wesleyan's colors of cardinal red and black, blooms, as it often does, just in time for the spring festivities.

A few years ago, as I was standing in the kitchen looking out the window toward the garden, I saw an undergraduate step up to the flower bed and stare at it. The Apricot Beauty tulips were blooming, as well as some Greenlands, which are greenish white with green stripes. I thought he was lost in admiration. Then he bent over and starting picking himself a bouquet. By the time I made it outside, he had helped himself to half a dozen tulips and was walking toward the Foss Hill dorms. I saw him enter the door as I made it to the sidewalk, shouting, "Stop, stop! Come back here!"

By the time I tracked down the flower thief, he was in his room, with the door closed, and the tulips were already in a vase on one of his stereo speakers. He turned out to be so stoned that I could get no satisfaction from rebuking him. But in my search through the dorm ("Have you seen a guy with a bunch of tulips?") I had attracted quite a crowd of students, by no means all of whom were sympathetic to my position.

"Who does she think she is? Does she think she owns the flowers?" one student said to another.

It was on this one I turned.

"You bet I think I own them."

"You don't own them," the kid said.

"Oh yeah? Who owns them?"

"We all own them," he said. "They're nature. God made them."

Every one of his sentences outraged me. It was a wonder I could talk.

"God made them? You think God made them? Did God call White Flower Farm and order the bulbs? Did God put it on his credit card? Did God dig holes for the bulbs in the fall and mix bonemeal in the dirt to feed them and cover them with mulch in the winter? If you think God did that, you're an idiot!"

"What's your problem, lady? Chill!"

"What's my problem? Kids who think the world belongs to them. Stupidity. That's my problem. Even if I believed that God made my garden and even if I conceded that that meant we should all share it, aren't we sharing it by looking at it? Enjoying it? And isn't your friend preventing us from doing that by taking the flowers for himself and putting them in a vase in his own room? Why is private property okay for him but not for me? What would you do if I told you that God made your stereo system and therefore I have a right to it?"

"A stereo system's not a garden."

"But it's a product of human ingenuity, and human ingenuity is, if you believe in God, God's creation. People make gardens. People make stereos. What's the difference?"

And so we continued for several vivacious minutes, engaging in what the Wesleyan Bulletin calls education outside the classroom.

Mr. Quinn's gift of tomatoes gave me nothing but grief, a fair exchange for the present I'd given his wife. In fact, I came to think that the seemingly offhand gift had been a finely calculated object lesson, brilliantly conceived to teach me the arrogance of gifts of living things. I called myself a gardener? Because I went out and bought fully grown arecas and Chinese fan palms and watered them whenever it occurred to me? Let me try to get two tomato plants through a couple of months in the tropics, and, if I wanted to aim a little higher, let me get them to produce tomatoes.

First I had to transplant them. They couldn't stay in their little containers. They needed more room. I went to the garden center and bought big clay pots for them, as well as potting soil to grow them in. They said I would need to get wire cages for the vines to twine on, and I had seen that Mr. Quinn had such contraptions, but I had already spent, to buy the pots and the soil, about fifteen dollars for tomato plants that had probably cost no more than two dollars apiece. I could not bring myself to pay another eight or ten for wire cages. Fortunately, a few days later I found some beat-up ones on sale at KMart for a dollar apiece and grabbed them.

By that time I knew I had a problem about where to put the plants. We had started out putting them in the full sun of the yard, in the angle made by the street wall and the Garretts' wall. But a rabbit who had taken up residence beneath Greta Garbo dined on the leaves, seeming to prefer them to his previous diet of anthurium. The Quinn tomatoes were protected on the outside by a tall picket fence and more immediately by chicken wire. If we wanted to leave our plants in the yard, we would have to surround them with chicken wire, which, in addition to the cost, would be unsightly.

Ordinarily, I would have cut my losses at this point and thrown the tomato plants out. I did not feel I could do that, however, because they had been a present. That was when I realized the devilish cleverness, the O. Henry-like ingenuity of Mr. Quinn's "gift." I could not, as one does with most unwelcome gifts, leave it in its wrapping and keep it in the basement, the attic, a capacious closet. I had to keep the damned thing alive. I had to give it time and attention, as Mrs. Quinn had had to do for the palms I had given her that she did not want.

The tomato plants had to be moved to the porch, not the accessible downstairs porch, where we spent a lot of time, which was covered and therefore too dark, but the upstairs porch, off our bedroom, which was open to the sun. On this porch there was no hose hookup, no water source. Like Jean de Florette carrying water bucket by bucket up the dry, hot Provençal hill from a distant stream to his vegetable patch, I had to carry water container by container from our bathroom, across the bedroom, out the door, to the sundeck. The bathroom sink was not deep. The largest container we could fill there held perhaps a pint. It took four trips between the bathroom and the porch to water the tomato plants, and, Bill Y., our tomato consultant, assured us we had to do that two or even three times a day.

Despite our labors the tomato plants—a few pathetic leaves on a lengthening vine—yellowed and declined. Were they getting too much water or too little? Did they need fertilizer? Had they become infested? Bill Y. insisted we bring samples to the gym for analysis. He looked closely at the leaves we brought, leaves we could ill afford to remove from the plant, but could find no bugs or blight. He couldn't tell us what was wrong. Ever more hopelessly, we continued to water the plants. Every time I sunbathed on the upper porch, I was depressed by those wretched plants, which resisted all my efforts to please them, yet whenever I felt tempted to discard them, they said, "Not so fast, sister! *We* are a gift."

One evening, toward the end of our stay in Key West, we were sitting by the seawall watching the sunset and having a drink with another couple, visitors from New York. Our attention was focused on the water, on the clouds, the sun, and pelicans diving for fish, gulping deeply when they'd caught one, returning to the derelict pier stumps to sit and think about their next sortie. So we did not notice a child heading across the yard toward us until he was halfway upon us. It was the Quinns' youngest child, a beautiful dark-haired boy on the verge of adolescence, and he was carrying something before him in the palms of his hands, like the page in the tarot deck or a Venetian painting. What he bore before him was a huge, red, smooth-skinned perfect tomato.

"My father said this is for you."

When he returned to the house, our friend Paul said, "What was that about?"

"It's a long story."

"I thought you weren't getting along with your landlord. Something about trees?"

"This is part of it."

"I thought it had the look of a peace offering," said Paul.

"Possibly," I said. "Possibly a taunt."

Ever since I started coming to Florida, I've been reading Marjorie Kinnan Rawlings, first *Cross Creek*, then *The Yearling*, then *South Moon Under* and "Jacob's Ladder," reversing the order in which they were written as one does on discovering a writer through her best-known books and working backward. Rawlings was a newspaperwoman from the North who moved to Florida in 1928 to escape city life, to try to make a living by running an orange grove, and to concentrate on her writing, which until then had been unimpressive.

She moved to a remote place called Cross Creek, near Gainesville and Ocala, where the small chunks of arable land were surrounded by thousands of acres of swampy wilderness or the dry, low brush which she called in her fiction The Big Scrub. She had an old wooden farmhouse with big porches, onto which she would bring her typewriter to work.

At first Rawlings lived there with her husband, but the marriage was unhappy. He was a difficult man with a mediocre talent (he, too, wanted to write), and he blamed her for his failure. Feeling inferior to her, he criticized every thing she did all day long. He called attention to her every fault. He bullied, berated, and mocked her. When he finally left her, unable to stand the isolation and backwardness of their new home, she found it a pleasure to wake up in the morning and think, "Nobody's going to give me Hell today!"

Her neighbors, black and white, because of their isolation and poverty, inhabited a world the rest of America had left behind. It took her awhile to see them as subjects for literature. When she first wrote about her cracker neighbors, her attitude was unsympathetic and stereotyped. They were shiftless, half-drunk, prone to violence. But the more she learned about them, the more she came to respect them. Especially the people of the scrub.

She came to see them as living with beautiful simplicity, attuned to the harsh world around them without adopting the harshness. She admired their wit and energy. She understood their dignity and appreciated their resourcefulness. Scrub-dwellers made a meager living from whatever they did, trapping, fishing, or moonshining. They were not lawless people, but none of the ways in which they could make a living was legal. Based on her expeditions to the scrub and her observation of its people, she wrote "Jacob's Ladder" and *South Moon Under,* both little master-pieces. She had found her subject, the spiritual beauty of lives, however hard, lived in harmony with nature.

In 1930, she started working with Maxwell Perkins, the legendary editor who also worked with Hemingway, Fitzgerald, and Thomas Wolfe. Starved for literary companionship, she spent long hours talking to him through the mail, discussing her own work and the work of contemporaries. She was competing with Hemingway and Fitzgerald for Perkins's attention and respect, jealous that Perkins went to Key West to visit Hemingway but did not come to Cross Creek to visit her.

It was Perkins who suggested she write something of the same sort as *South Moon Under,* about the people of the scrub, but with a young boy as the central character. He imagined something for a juvenile audience that adults could also read with pleasure, something like *Treasure Island* or *Huckleberry Finn.* At first she was offended by the suggestion that she write a "juvenile." But gradu-ally she got to like the idea. "Do you realize," she wrote Perkins, "how calmly you sat up there in your office and announced that you were expecting a boy's *classic* of me?" And she did write a clas-sic. *The Yearling* was a best-seller and won the Pulitzer Prize, mak-ing Rawlings one of the most successful, beloved writers in America.

Rawlings's life at Cross Creek in many ways was idyllic. By our standards, she was well taken care of by servants, although the more you read about women writers' lives before World War II the more you realize that managing the servants was as much work as running the laundry through the washing machine, doing the dishes, and going over the house with a vacuum yourself could ever be. Rawlings liked to cook and energetically entertained friends from St. Augustine, one of whom, a hotel manager, Norton Baskin, she would later marry.

Besides her research trips in the scrub, she went on excursions with wealthy friends. Yachting in the Bahamas, she finally met Hemingway and described him in a long letter to Perkins as someone who seemed needlessly defensive for such a great writer. She speculated that his sporting friends did not understand his artistic and literary side and that that was the root of his problem (?!). On another expedition with a woman friend she boated the entire length of the St. John River, northern Florida's Amazon.

Until her books started selling she didn't have much money. She depended on the orange crop, and it was a precarious support. She was about as far north as you can be and still try to raise oranges. Periodically the groves froze. When her books started selling, she had other problems, not the least of which was answering her mail. The sheer volume was daunting. And she couldn't get the tone right, cordial but distant. Either she was too cool and heard later she was considered "high-hat," or she was too warm, and couldn't get the correspondents to stop pestering her.

In the same way that Annie sometimes worries about being known only as a nature writer, Rawlings worried about being known only as a regionalist. Even in her most productive years, she was torn between her love of the Florida material and her fear of being seen as just a local writer. Many of the noblest works of literature are regionalist, she said in a lecture on the subject, in the sense that in them an artist used for his own purposes a background he knew well and deeply loved. But it would belittle these writers to consider them regionalist. Hardy was her example. The problem of regionalism bothered her so much that every now and then she would write a book about English aristocrats or a historical novel about Northerners, as though to prove she wasn't limited to writing about Florida crackers. These books were harder to write and never as good as the others.

The good ones, like *The Yearling*, came easily. She went off to the mountains of North Carolina to get started on it, taking along her pointer and her Proust. Her admiration of Proust only seems incongruous if you think of her as a woman with a raccoon on her shoulder feeding a deer. She was a sophisticated literary creature, whose stories appeared in *The New Yorker* and *Scribner's Magazine*. In North Carolina, escaping the summer heat of Florida and working on *The Yearling*, she took time off, at Perkins's request, to pay a call on F. Scott Fitzgerald, who was at a hospital near Ashville recovering from the effects of alcoholism. Though alcohol was strictly forbidden, they drank sherry and talked all afternoon and evening.

Cross Creek, her book about her life on the orange grove, opens with the observation that it is possible to rise to the universal through a close consideration of the particular, but that you never get to the particular by considering the general. She wanted the book to have a "Proustian deepness and intimacy." Whether or not it achieves that, it is, as a memoir, wholly original, a collection of sketches and stories connected by the locale and by Rawlings's personality.

My favorite chapter is "A Pig is Paid For." A neighbor's pig has been getting onto Rawlings's property and eating her fluffy-ruffle petunias. After many warnings, she picks up her rifle and shoots it. Then she invites her friends from St. Augustine to join her in a festive barbecue. Eventually, word reaches her that Mr. Martin, the neighbor who owned the pig, is hopping mad. She visits him and offers to pay for the pig. The visit mollifies him somewhat. It was the callousness of her eating the pig at a drunken party with her friends that upset him most. But she won't repent, and he won't take money for his beloved pig, so the matter is left hanging.

Meanwhile, various neighbors indulge in various acts of the bartering that constitutes the local economy. They "borrow" gas from Rawlings's truck; in return they leave offerings of game birds they've shot. One Mr. Higgenbotham, a frog and snake hunter, needs a new license for his truck but doesn't have the six dollars he needs to pay for it. Rawlings gives him the money in exchange for work on her groves. He never does the work, however, and when she reproaches him, he turns up with a sow in his truck.

"Can't think of nobody now you owe a pig to?"

Mr. Higgenbotham is taking the sow to someone who owns a boar. He has a dollar in his pocket for the stud fee. Sows are unpredictable, but if she accepts the boar and if she gets pregnant, Mr. Martin will take her in exchange for the pig that was shot.

Rawlings never hears any more about the matter until she runs into Mr. Martin at the general store and he invites her to go duck hunting with him.

"Did she take? Are we all square, you and Mr. Higgenbotham and I?"

"Mis' Rawlings," he said, "the pig is paid for."

Most people I question about Marjorie Kinnan Rawlings have only read *The Yearling* and that only as youngsters in school. Maxwell Perkins's great idea has proved her undoing. She is ghettoized after all, as a children's book writer. Ironically, if anything has saved her, it's regionalism. In Florida, Marjorie Kinnan Rawlings's works are available in every bookstore. Everything she wrote, including her letters and all her stories, is in print. The University of Florida has published even a memoir by her maid, Idella Parker. Were she alive, Rawlings would be in despair. The only worse thing that could have happened to this proud and self-consciously literary writer would have been to be rescued by feminism. So let me preemptively argue that regionalism has worked on behalf of women writers, saving them in quiet coves of literary reputation until the slow-moving wheels of purely aesthetic appreciation (or a new set of political concerns) can make their way to them. Willa Cather, writer laureate of New Mexico, is another case in point.

Rawlings's later career is sad to contemplate. After *Cross Creek*, published in 1942 (the year of my birth, the year that other three-named lady published *Our Hearts Were Young and Gay*), there was no first-rate work, except her calorie-laden, delicious cookbook, *Cross Creek Cookery*. She married Norton Baskin and moved with him into an apartment at the top of his hotel in St. Augustine. She was happy with him but missed her life at Cross Creek. She spent much time in sociability, entertaining Baskin's friends and business associates. She drank too much. Idella Parker describes picking her up off the floor more than once. Her health was poor. The war came. Baskin served for a year and a half, and Rawlings worried about him. He came home seriously ill, and she nursed him. She spent too much time writing letters to servicemen who wrote to her about *The Yearling* and *Cross Creek*. Everything seemed to turn against her as a writer: her happy marriage, which distracted her; her own literary ambitions, which led her up false paths; her very success, which increased the demands the public made on her; her decency and sense of responsibility, which made her susceptible to the demands. To say nothing of her alcoholism and her generally poor health. But the most damaging thing of all was a lawsuit, inspired by the publication of *Cross Creek*.

Zelma Cason, one of her neighbors, the local postmistress and a friend, was not happy with the way she had been portrayed in Rawlings's memoir:

> Zelma is an ageless spinster resembling an angry and efficient canary. She manages her orange grove and as much of the village and county as needs management or will submit to it. I cannot decide whether she should have been a man or a mother. She combines the more violent characteristics of both and those who ask for or accept her manifold ministrations think nothing of being cursed loudly at the very instant of being tenderly fed, clothed, nursed or guided through their troubles.

Miss Cason sued for libel, retaining a brilliant young lawyer from Palatka, Kate Walton, to represent her. It took eighteen months to determine if there were grounds for trial, with the court deciding that there were if the charge was changed from libel to "invasion of privacy," a principle which had only recently been announced by Justice Brandeis.

Even before she wrote *Cross Creek*, Rawlings had been unusually concerned about how her writing would affect her neighbors. The Lant family in *South Moon Under* was based on the family of Leonard Fiddia, moonshiners and poachers, who had been her hosts in the scrub. Her concern was specific. If she identified these people too closely, they could have gotten in trouble with the law, and Fiddia, for one, was grateful for her discretion.

For the rest, she had seen both sides of people's response to being written about. The children of Barney Dillard, another old hunter whose stories she mined for her fiction, resented her, feeling that she was stealing his life's story, which they believed had some tangible value, like cash. On the other hand, when she offered to split the proceeds from her story, "Alligators," with Fred Tompkins, who had given her much of the material on which the story was based, his wife refused to accept it. The story could not have been written without Fred's anecdotes, Rawlings reminded Mrs. Tompkins, who replied, "I know, honey, but tellin' is one thing and composin' is another."

With *Cross Creek*, Rawlings was concerned about libel. (Invasion of privacy was so new a concept it didn't occur to her as a problem.) She raised the matter in a letter to Perkins, and when he replied that she must be the judge of her neighbors' reactions, she went back through the manuscript to pick out people who might be offended. She figured Mr. Martin, the pig owner, was the most likely to be upset by his portrayal, so she took her manuscript in hand and actually read "A Pig is Paid For" to him and his wife in their home. When Rawlings was finished, Mr. Martin chuckled and said, "That's okay." Rawlings consulted in one way or another with many of her neighbors, but not Zelma Cason. In individual lives as in human history, it is always the things we don't know are important that overwhelm and undermine us and change everything for us, and it never occurred to Rawlings that Zelma Cason, one of her closer friends in Cross Creek and one of the town's more sophisticated residents, would be upset.

The case went to trial in 1946 and was a major event in northern Florida. Much of Cross Creek testified. Marjorie Kinnan Rawlings was on the stand for two days. She gave a complete accounting of her life and work. "I was in great despair about my writings. I had been trying to do so-called 'popular' writings . . . and they were just not any good; and when I came to Florida and was so enchanted with the country and the people, I put all thought of writing from a popular angle for a woman's magazine and that kind of thing behind me, and I decided to get at this new material in an entirely different way."

She was forced to account for line after line of her own writing, under the most literalist attack. Every word she had written could be used against her, a Dantesque punishment. She had to explain that although she had enjoyed killing her neighbor's pig, she did not enjoy flouting the law. She had to justify every metaphor in the description of Zelma. What did she mean, an angry canary? In what way did Miss Cason look like a canary?

Finally, after half an hour of deliberation, the jury found the defendant not liable. "We just didn't believe this had gone beyond free speech and had invaded private rights," one juryman said, and Rawlings said, "I'm glad that a jury has upheld a principle of factual writing."

Could you write about your own life or couldn't you? This was the principle Rawlings felt was at stake. Repeatedly Cason's lawyers's questions implied that the only material belonging in an autobiography or memoir was personal. What business, they asked, did this anecdote or that story have in an autobiography? Was it "about" Rawlings? The question Rawlings wanted to pose was, How can you write about your own life without writing about the human environment in which your life unfolds?

Kate Walton filed an appeal. The case continued all told for five and half years, destroying Rawlings's concentration and peace of mind. It was finally settled when the Florida Supreme Court overturned the decision of the lower court, saying that too much attention had been paid in the first trial to Rawlings's prominence. Her stature as a writer did not make the invasion of privacy any less real or more justified. However, they also found that Cason had not been materially damaged, and they awarded her only token damages of a dollar.

When she lost the suit, Rawlings believed that a serious blow had been struck against literature: memoirs would cease to be written. But for whatever reason the Cross Creek trial did not have the impact Rawlings feared, except on her own life and her own writing. After it, she stayed far away from the material of daily life. Her last novel, *The Sojourner*, published in 1953, was set in Michigan after the Civil War.

If we knew the major changes in our life were major changes which would forever destroy a kind of peace and contentment that had allowed us to flourish, naturally we wouldn't make them. If we saw, "This is the line not to cross," we might not cross it (although we might). But when things are going well, we are lured into thinking they might go even better. Willa Cather had a little apartment in Greenwich Village which she shared with her friend Miss Lewis. There she produced her best work. When she found other, better quarters, she was never as happy or productive again. For Marjorie Kinnan Rawlings, Cross Creek was a little paradise, her Walden Pond, the small patch of earth she could work to produce big art, the beloved particular through which she could rise to the glorious general. It was Eden, and no one threw her out of it. She herself chose to leave, for domestic happiness, for a hotel in St. Augustine.

A month before our scheduled departure from Key West, Mrs. Quinn stopped me as I was getting out of Greta Garbo with bags of groceries and started to chat, about the cold winter we had had, about work they were having done on the roof and the porches, about nothing at all out of the ordinary, except that she seemed to have said that they didn't want to rent the house to us next year.

"Wait a minute! Did you say you won't rent us the house again?"

"Not long-term. Only for two weeks. It is so much trouble. We really don't make enough money to make it worthwhile."

As my mind worked to take this in, I said things, I don't remember what, and Mrs. Quinn replied to what I said. "You suffer so much from the cold. More than I do." "Your kitchen now is better than ours." The gist was, we would be better off in a more comfortable house. ("But we like this house!") Later, as I tried to make sense of our expulsion, the sentences came back to me. Had we used too much electricity in a futile attempt to keep warm? Should I not have asked to have the water heater fixed?

In my mind's eye, the scene changes. Instead of Mrs. Quinn and I standing in the driveway, me with my arms full of grocery bags, she in her denim skirt and white rayon blouse with shoulder pads, standing demurely with her hands clasped behind her, I see a version of Masaccio's Adam and Eve expelled from Eden. Mrs. Quinn's long black hair falls by her face and her arm is outstretched, her finger pointed, like the angry deity. "Go!" she is saying. L. and I are seen from the side, heads bowed in shame, in T-shirts, shorts, and Birkenstocks, to be sure, but in Renaissance fresco colors, slinking away. What have we done? Was it the water, the electricity, their need for more space, our superior kitchen, my complaints, my rudeness, or the thing I'd always known or feared it would be, the thing that probably made God so mad when Adam and Eve ate the fruit from his tree—an outraged sense of proprietorship. As He may have felt about His uppity tenants, as the postmistress of Cross Creek felt on finding herself caricatured in the Northerner's memoir, as I felt when the stoned student picked my tulips, as all gardeners must feel in the face of selfish trespassers and all year-rounders in the face of seasonal residents: "Whose place is this anyway?"

The worst had happened. We had lost our house. After the blow, what L. and I felt was relief. The world lay all before us where to choose our place of rest. We could travel. We could spend the next winter somewhere else. We thought about seeing Indochina, California, Mexico, Saba. Even staying in Middletown sounded good. We didn't have to come back to Key West. We were giddy with freedom. Now that our house was down, we could see the moon.

I started to give away or place on extended loan all the possessions we'd accumulated in the five winters we'd stayed in the house. To Bill W. went our driftwood lamp, our patio umbrella and water-weighted umbrella base, the king-sized sheets and electric blanket, the bread box, the parrot painting, the reproduction of Botticelli's *Spring*, and much, much else. Janice helped me clear

9

An Unwritten Novel

"He would have scorned to invent what he reports as so acute or so colourful when said by Mme. Cornuel or Louis XIV. . . . In the state of mind in which we 'observe' we are a long way below the level to which we rise when we create."

Within a Budding Grove

"Memory has no power of invention. . . . It is powerless to desire anything else, let alone anything better, than what we have already possessed."

The Fugitive

As a college professor, as a literary critic, I should have been more ashamed than I was not to have read Proust. While I taught my students that a literary work is an experience in time and that novels are the richest, most detailed and uncondensable of literary experiences, while I told them that there is no shortcut for the slow movement of the reading mind from word to word and sentence to sentence, I fell victim to an error I was trying to eradicate—that a novelist's work is a point on a finite line inscribed by the history of the novel. Probably this came from studying Erich Auerbach at too impressionable an age and accepting as truth his description of the novel's changing objects of representation. From reading just the first fifty pages of *Swann's Way*, I thought I knew what Proust was "about," where he stood, what he stood for. He was in the camp of the free associaters, the stream-of-consciousness people, interested in how one thing leads to another in the mind and how that, rather than anything external, is reality. Throw in a Parisian setting, some observations about society people in whom I had very little interest, that famous structured world which we are told over and over was brought to an end by the first World War, an obsession with mother, the past, time, and memory, and there you had Proust.

Just as when you have a sensitive tooth, you learn to move your food to the other side of your mouth, or when you are suffering from pain in the lower back, you almost unthinkingly shift your weight onto other parts of your body and other muscles, so I had adjusted to my literary weakness. I never pretended I had read Proust. When people began talking about him—which they rarely did—I was silent, and the conversation soon went away. In my experience, most of the people who talked about Proust were gay men, and their love of Proust was so intimate and treasured a part of their sexual identity that they did not seem to mind when a straight person did not share it, any more than I would mind if a WASP or Latino didn't know what mensch meant or mispronounced kvetch.

David was an exception. He pestered me to read Proust. He referred constantly, exasperatingly, to Odette and Charlus and Swann, as though they were old friends of his from Brown or Yale Art School whom I didn't know but about whom I inexplicably wanted to be kept informed. He pestered me to read Proust the way Teddy, with quicker success, had pestered me to give up smoking. Finally he pressed the right button. "How can you write a historical novel about the 1890s in Paris without having read Proust?" he asked, referring to a novel I had in mind about a Belle Époque courtesan. The button David pushed was not shame, that ineffectual feeling which ought to have gotten me to read Proust before I pontificated about *To the Lighthouse* and *Ulysses*, but procrastination. If I had to read all of Proust before I wrote the novel, I could put off for at least several months that unnerving and potentially demanding business. The novel was figured out. All I had to do was sit down and write it. Surely it couldn't hurt to postpone for some months the mechanical inscription of something whose existence in my mind was so vivid and complete.

This book had come to me in a dream: I was married to Mark, but it was late in life. Teddy was grown. I had a new baby, a daughter named Thea. Mark's mother was taking care of her so I could work, but I felt bereft. In the dream, I had an epiphany: "I can take care of the baby myself." Suddenly, I felt wonderful. I could take care of the baby myself! There was no other job I had to do.

Now I see it as a menopause dream like a couple of others I had at about that time in which I had a second baby, different from Teddy. Teddy always appeared as complete and satisfactory, while the second one was problematic. One dream baby was ugly and deformed, suffering from a motor disease that made it twitch. I loved it anyway and said to myself, "Teddy was beautiful. I can live with an ugly one. The tics aren't all that bad." One phase of my life was over, but progeny of another sort lay ahead, with an appeal of their own to me, however ugly in the eyes of the world.

Immediately upon waking, I took the dream as a message from my subconscious to my conscious self. "I could take care of the baby myself" meant I could and should write another book. It had been a while since the last one, but whatever "job" I had been doing while I wasn't writing was now over.

Literally following the lead of my dream, I gave the name Thea to my heroine. She would be, like the Byzantine empress Theodora, a courtesan who becomes a head of state. She would live in late nineteenth-century Paris and would partake of the character of the Belle Époque courtesans, Liane de Pougy, Emilienne d'Alençon, Cléo de Mérode, La Belle Otéro, self-employed, entrepreneurial celebrities trading in beauty and glamour, their clothing, jewelry, and love affairs all covered in the press—precursors of movie stars. In one episode, a theater owner, knowing that the queen of Sweden was attending a performance at his theater, would hire Thea to appear, ermine-draped, jewels ablaze, to stand up in her box and receive the applause of the audience. He knew Thea would look more like a queen than the real queen, a mousy, modestly dressed lady sitting unnoticed in an opposite box. This episode I had taken wholesale from Liane de Pougy's enchanting account of her own life, *My Blue Notebooks*. In another scene I intended to crib from the same source, Liane, in her ongoing competition with other courtesans, appeared at a party with no jewels at all. Her maid walked behind her, carrying on a pillow a diamond necklace and earrings.

At thirty-six, Liane de Pougy (the name was manufactured) had succeeded in getting the weak and good-for-nothing but genuinely blueblooded Prince Georges Ghurka of Romania to marry her, making her a princess. My Thea would do better. Instead of marrying a pathetic alcoholic who happened to be of noble blood, she would marry someone who really had a country to run, as Theodora helped Justinian to rule the Byzantine Empire.

Theodora, whose face and figure are immortalized in the mosaics at Ravenna, first grabbed the public's attention (according to Procopius) by appearing naked in a lewd *tableau vivant* of Leda and the Swan, having trained a bird to perform what appeared to be oral sex. In turn-of-the-century Paris, the empress was again in fashion. Sardou wrote a play about her. Sarah Bernhardt played her. Mucha did a poster. The Empress Theodora was the patron saint of all those upwardly mobile women, like Liane de Pougy, who rose so surely to the top that a later generation, seeing their splendor, seeing their centrality to Parisian society, would never guess where they began, any more than someone new to New York could imagine that the fabulously wealthy old ladies who endow so generously the museums and libraries and lend their august names to the benefit committees of worthwhile charities were ever ravishing, adorable nobodies from nowhere—secretaries, models, schoolteachers, au pair girls, wives of other men—who caught the eye and heart of some man in possession of a fortune who felt himself so much in want of a wife of exactly her sort that he would give anything he had to secure her. So money changes hands, from men to women, from age to youth, propelled by the vagaries of love as often as by drearily predictable inheritance. So men, unimaginative, derivative creatures, renew themselves by tapping into the social energy of women.

Over and over in Belle Époque Paris, you see the same story, with the passing back and forth of titles added to that of money to make the game more complicated, like double Dutch jump rope, in which two ropes are deployed instead of one. The Contesse de

Loynes began as a factory worker, caught the eye of a newspaper mogul, became his mistress. He found her so fascinating that he gave her the money to run a salon and brought his most interesting acquaintances to meet her. In her twenties, she fell in love with a man who had made a fortune in South American mines. When he was killed in the Franco-Prussian War, he left her everything, mine shares, bank shares, and a sugar refinery, which she hired young Conte de Loynes to run. He fell in love with her and married her, and although his horrified family got the marriage annulled, they could not strip her of her title. So the bottlewasher became a countess, using her money, position, and wit to run one of the most dazzling salons in Paris.

In addition to Thea, I had another character in mind, based on a man whose existence I learned about when I searched for "Belle Époque" on the Wesleyan library computer and found *Paul Delesalle: Un Anarchiste de la Belle Époque*. Delesalle, who came from a desperately poor working-class family, at the age of thirteen went into the same foundry his father worked in, undertaking, as was common at the time, a three-year unpaid apprenticeship. His father begrudged him books, education, even religion—any food for the soul. It was Dickens in the blacking factory all over again.

He became a machinist, a meticulous craftsman. However, he hated his work, called his factory "the forced labor camp," and in 1897 quit to devote himself full-time to anarchism. So many anarchist bombs exploded in Paris in the mid-1890s that there seemed to be a terrorist epidemic. Two were placed at restaurants. One, made of nails packed in an iron casserole, was sent to a mining company office but exploded in a police station. One was thrown in the Chamber of Deputies and one in a crowded working-class café. Many people thought Paul Delesalle was responsible for a bomb that was thrown into a restaurant opposite the Luxembourg Gardens in 1894, a bomb which hurt only one person, ironically an anarchist himself.

Delesalle was uncompromising in his politics. He had no interest whatsoever in legal reforms or parliamentary action, only in the complete destruction of the social system. As he got older, however, he turned from political action to collecting political literature, specializing in ephemera—printed material that is quickly destroyed, like pamphlets and posters. He opened a bookstore in the Rue Monsieur le Prince and, after years of running it, retired with his wife to a quiet suburban house where his biographer found him at the age of seventy-five living with a huge library of socialist, communist, and anarchist tracts. My anarchist, too, would have a long and placid life, bomber turned bibliophile. He and my buoyant courtesan would be brother and sister.

Everything was falling into place. The company Delesalle worked for made custom-tooled precision instruments; their greatest honor had been to construct, for the Lumière Brothers, the first motion picture camera. Upon learning this, I grew quivery with excitement. I saw the first lightbulbs going on in Paris in 1889. I saw the Lumières presenting the first moving picture show in 1895. I saw circuses and dance halls, café-concerts and the Folies-Bergère. I saw people playing tennis for the first time and taking their first wobbling rides on bicycles. I saw people working in factories and labor unions born. I saw emigrants from Eastern Europe, Jews who went to France instead of America, and worked their way up.

I began to see a grand historical theme for my novel, the beginnings then of now, in social mobility, in the polarization of work and play, in the deep anarchic resentment of organized society which produced, in this year while I was reading Proust, the brutal bombing at Oklahoma City by government-hating militants and the desperate last bids for attention, the Luddite rantings, of the Unabomber. And if O. J. Simpson's acquittal was hard to swallow, was it more egregious, was the behavior of the defense counsels any more outrageous than in the 1914 trial of Henriette Caillaux for the murder of Gaston Calmette?

Calmette was the editor of Le Figaro, and Madame Caillaux, upset by the newspaper's attacks on her husband, the Minister of Finance, walked into his office, reached into her handbag, pulled out a pistol, and shot him. The defense attorneys made the case that responsibility for Calmette's death lay not with Madame Caillaux, who shot the fatal bullet, but with the victim's physicians, who had decided to postpone surgery until his heartbeat stabilized. They also claimed that Madame Caillaux had not aimed at Monsieur Calmette, but that he had hurled himself in the path of the bullet she had fired at the floor. She was found innocent. Gaston Calmette, whose murder went unpunished, was the person to whom Marcel Proust, the year before, had dedicated the first volume of *A la recherche du temps perdu.*

So many tantalizing connections! Karl Marx's son-in-law preached against work and lived it up on a fortune inherited from Engels. The horrible 1896 fire in the charity bazaar which killed so many women of fashion including the greatest lady of France, the Duchess d'Alençon (the real Madame d'Alençon, not the courtesan who borrowed her name), had been started by a malfunctioning movie projector. An ether lamp exploded and the flimsy building that had been erected for the event went up in flames, men trampling women to get out first. The ironies of history were so astonishing that I almost thought it was a shame to write this as fiction.

I reread Marguerite Yourcenar's *Memoirs of Hadrian* to learn how to write a historical novel with dignity and weight. I did and didn't get what I was looking for. If anything the book was too marmoreal, too dignified for its own good. But it did show a way to avoid the hokiness of many historical novels, which was to deemphasize scene and incident and emphasize consciousness. It's written in the first person from the point of view of a man of enormous power, the Emperor Hadrian, at the moment of death, looking back on his life. Amazingly little happens. There is only that voice, that mind, ruminating on the past, tolerant, worldly, wise:

> Catastrophe and ruin will come; disorder will triumph, but order will too, from time to time. Peace will again establish itself between two periods of war; the words *humanity, liberty,* and *justice* will here and there regain the meaning which we have tried to give them. Not all our books will perish, nor all our statues, if broken, lie unrepaired. (p. 245)

Unless you believed in the narrator's importance, reflective-ness like Hadrian's could seem downright pompous. Could I pull it off in a female character? Wouldn't she sound like a school-marm? Could I make her global role believable? Could I insert into the already crowded map of Europe a fictive country whose fate convincingly mattered?

These, I felt, were literalist problems, unworthy of my great vision of then and now, men and women, work and play, anarchy and regimentation. Somehow, it was Marguerite Yourcenar's fault. I suspected she didn't believe it possible to write a serious book about a woman, and I clung to my courtesan. I decided to read a more up-to-date historical novel, E. L. Doctorow's *Ragtime*, which is set at about the time that interested me, the turn of the century, in New York.

Right away, I felt better. I loved the short sentences, the unabashed generalizations. "Everyone wore white in summer. Tennis racquets were hefty and the racquet faces elliptical. There was a lot of sexual fainting. There were no Negroes." Much of the art was in timing. He didn't linger on anything long. He cut quickly from general to specific—"There were no Negroes. There were no immigrants. On Sunday, after dinner, Father and Mother went upstairs and closed the bedroom door"—and then from specific to general—"Evelyn fainted. Her underclothes were white. Her husband habitually whipped her. She happened once to meet Emma Goldman, the revolutionary. Goldman lashed her with her tongue. Apparently there *were* Negroes. There *were* immigrants."

At the level of plot, the cuts were similarly quick. Evelyn Nes-bit, the real-life showgirl, married a millionaire, Harry K. Thaw, who killed her former lover, the architect and bon vivant Stanford White. She meets the real-life revolutionary Emma Goldman on the Lower East Side, in a presumably fictional encounter. This gives way to Mother finding a black baby on her doorstep in New Rochelle, which gives way to Father at the North Pole with Peary, which gives way to Mother's Younger Brother's love for Evelyn Nesbit and his involvement with militants who threaten to blow up the Morgan Library. Houdini appears, as does a fictional Jewish immigrant who goes from a meager living cutting silhouette portraits to wealth and success in the infant movie business.

It occurred to me that with Evelyn Nesbit, Doctorow did much of what I wanted to do with my courtesan. I rejected the thought. Doctorow's Evelyn, I told myself, exists to be the object of Emma Goldman's intelligence and her analysis of women's place in capitalist society.

It was disturbing that Mother's Younger Brother was an explosives expert, a political extremist, a bomb-throwing militant. Still, he wasn't technically an anarchist.

Who was I kidding? With the revolutionary, the courtesan who marries well, the movie pioneer, I had to admit that my book would be thematically just a rehash of *Ragtime*. Of course, Doctorow's outlook was more political than mine. His novel was more American than mine would be and more epic. My book might be about social mobility, but it wouldn't have Doctorow's brilliant understanding of cultural dynamics, how the early motion picture entrepreneurs, for example, understood that if they could reproduce the effect of Evelyn Nesbit, selling out every newspaper issue her picture appeared in, they could make fortunes. "The value of the duplicable event was everywhere perceived." I couldn't write a sentence like that. So my book wouldn't be anything like Doctorow's. That was a relief.

I should have known I was in trouble when I heard myself describe the novel as a cross between *Memoirs of Hadrian* and *Ragtime*. I had never had anything but scorn for people who described a project as a mixture—it was always a mixture, never a flat-out copy—of one work of art and another, using the success of creations whose fundamental quirkiness and originality I doubted they understood to market literary products. I had sunk to the level of Hollywood pitchsters, magazine editors, grant proposal writers, and others who dealt in illusionist ideas of works of art rather than their painstaking, timeconsuming, word-by-word production. "Real books," says Proust, "are the offspring of darkness and silence, not of daylight and casual talk."

In my heart of hearts, if I had looked there, I would have known that my idea for the Belle Époque novel was too thought out, a dried grain, unlikely to blossom. But I did not want to know, so I did not look. It had been a long time since I had worked on a book, even a long time since I'd wanted to. It felt good, when people asked what I was working on, to reply succinctly "a historical novel, a cross between *Memoirs of Hadrian* and *Ragtime*, about a courtesan who becomes a queen, set in 1890s Paris." However I suspect there is an inverse ratio between how good (clear, presentable) an idea is for a book and the book that emerges, the best books being the product of such a private vision that no one else can imagine what will be there until the author has actually brought it into being, just as L. and I, standing in our yard in Connecticut, looking with pride at a trenchful of dirt, saw the peonies, daylilies, poppies, columbine, tulips, irises, and pansies that we knew we would grow there, but a friend, passing by, stopped to see what was wrong because we looked so peculiar staring at the bare ground.

In a notebook, as I "worked on" *Thea*, that is, wrote the book in my head without putting a word on paper, I kept track of ideas for other writing I might do, a whole conceptual career. I wanted to get to nineteen, because my friend Bob Richardson, when I asked him what he was going to do after finishing his Emerson biography, said, "I have nineteen projects." I wanted to match him. Every time I had an idea, whether for a book demanding years to write or for a six-page essay, I wrote it down and it became one item. "Historical Novel: 1890s (Memoirs of Hadrian + Ragtime)." "Essay, Autobiographical: The Scholar Gypsy." "Essay, Biographical: Marjorie Kinnan Rawlings." "Travel and Disappointment." "The Writing Life: The True Story." "Key West: The Idea of Disorder." "Middletown: A Memoir." "The Reluctant Bigamist." "Reading Proust." "Confessions of a Fag Hag." "Confessions of a Primipara." "Confessions of a Home-wrecker."

My notebook continued to fill also with reading notes on the products of my computer search of "Belle Époque." I was reading Proust in the morning and researching the 1890s in the afternoon. Gradually the research notes trail off. There are fragments, accounts of conversations, dreams—babble. Then only a list of

fish seen on Western Sambo Reef in Key West—angelfish, squir-
relfish, tilefish, porkfish—like the last primitive utterances of the
computer, Hal, in *2001*, as his mind reverts to inactivity. In my
case it was the semisilence and the interrupted breathing that
sounds like a snore which accompanies an intake of breath. The
new breath was Proust. Once I really got caught up in Proust, I
never gave poor Thea and her anarchist brother and her small but
viable European realm another thought. I had become a different
person.

It wasn't that Proust had already written the book I wanted to
write. It never occurred to me to say, "Proust has done what I
wanted to do." He had courtesans and social mobility. He had, in
Odette de Crécy, a character who might have been modeled on
Liane de Pougy, down to her name, so aristocratic as to be tarty.
He had, in the Dreyfus case, the real trial of the century. But none
of this mattered. He made me see the banality of my project. He
showed me, in a way that brought it home more intimately, more
personally than any other writer I had ever read, what literature
should be, what it should do. The important thing was finding a
way to put in words one's vision and sensibility; subject was of no
importance whatever. My best might not equal his, but, at best
and at worst, it would be mine, an embodiment in words,
extracted with difficulty from my inner darkness, of my own sensibility. Nothing else was worth doing. Anything else was copyist's
work, pastiche, more or less skillful, but not original art:

> Style for the writer, no less than colour for the painter, is a
> question not of technique but of vision: it is the revela-
> tion, which by direct and conscious methods would be
> impossible, of the qualitative difference, the uniqueness of
> the fashion in which the world appears to each one of us, a
> difference which, if there were no art, would remain for-
> ever the secret of every individual. Through art alone are
> we able to emerge from ourselves, to know what another
> person sees of a universe which is not the same as our own
> and of which, without art, the landscapes would remain as
> unknown to us as those that may exist on the moon.

Thanks to art, instead of seeing one world only, our own, we see that world multiply itself and we have at our disposal as many worlds as there are original artists, worlds more different one from the other than those which revolve in infinite space, worlds which, centuries after the extinction of the fire from which their light first emanated, whether it is called Rembrandt or Vermeer, send us still each one its special radiance." (Vol. 6, p. 299)

A year after starting Proust, I was at the last volume, *Time Regained*. Marcel returns from his years in a sanatarium to see the people he had known before recognizable but different, seeming to have chosen, out of some perversity of taste, to pretend to be old men and women, wearing masks that were skillfully rendered versions of themselves in some future epoch. Marcel has a vision of Time, its effects on individuals and on society as an organism, that prompts him, after years as a dandy and dilettante, to undertake his great work, causing him to retire from society, immure himself in a cork-lined room, and devote himself to art. It is a symphonic recapitulation of the themes of the whole, and I read it very slowly, savoring every embedded essay on creativity, time, and timelessness.

As I approached the end, David asked if I wasn't sad not to have the whole of *Lost Time* ahead of me. I said no. I would read it again. It wouldn't matter to me whether I was reading it for the first time, the third, or the eighth. I wasn't reading to find out "what happened" to Odette, Gilberte, Marcel, Charlus, and the rest. Revelations about the characters might indeed lose their impact on a second reading, but what I looked forward to most in reading Proust were revelations about myself. The best moments had been those in which I descended most deeply into myself, as though the text were an elevator shooting me down to the lowest levels of a mine, or, to reverse the image, shot me up into the light, so I achieved a sudden clarity of vision. Little in my response depended on surprise, much on the concentration I could muster. If I read with more attentiveness the next time, bringing more of my own experience to bear, Proust would be even better.

Proust understood that every reader, in reading, reads himself. Far from minding this, he saw it as the writer's task to facilitate it. "The writer's work is merely a kind of optical instrument which he offers to the reader to enable him to discern what, without this book, he would perhaps never have perceived in himself. And the recognition by the reader in his own self of what the book says is the proof of its veracity. . . . In order to read with understanding many readers require to read in their own particular fashion, and the author must not be indignant at this; on the contrary he must leave the reader all possible liberty, saying to him: 'Look for yourself, and try whether you see best with this lens or that one or this other.' " (Vol. 6, p. 322)

The more Proust I read, the more of a Victorian scientist he seemed, a truthseeker, Darwinian in outlook and methodology. Marcel's ruminations on social change after his years in the sanatarium are a Parisian *The Origin of Species*. Since society itself evolves very slowly over a very long time and any one person sees only one section, it seems to be immutable, as animal species seemed to be, as the geology of the earth seemed to be, before the long view of the nineteenth-century scientists was directed at them. In Paris, only people with a determinedly long view, like Marcel, see any change at all. Bloch, for example, his hack-intellectual friend, is now at home in drawing rooms where he would not have been received twenty years before. People new to society see as a fixture this man who used to be a pushy upstart.

Individuals disappear; the species survives. The only people to last ultimately are those who bear the permanent, generic name of some great aristocratic family. The Princesse de Guermantes is dead, but the Princesse de Guermantes still rules society, her title now inhabited by the person of she who was once Madame Verdurin. Many of the people Marcel knew and revered, like Swann, were dead and completely forgotten, and Marcel has trouble remembering whether many of the others are ill, retired, dead, or merely absent, they are so fundamentally insignificant. He is, as always, unsentimental to the point of cruelty about the way people take the deaths of their less than dearest friends. No one is upset. On the contrary, there are many reasons to be secretly glad, not the least that you are still alive. "Every death is for others a simplification of life, it spares them the necessity of showing gratitude, the obligation of paying calls."

When I asked myself not what elements of my unwritten novel about 1890s Paris Proust had incorporated but which he had not, I realized that what he left out was chaos. The courtesan-countesses and arrivistes of every stripe in their own way obey social laws, being absorbed and transformed, but Proust has no random bombs, no anarchists. He is interested in the evolution of society, not in aberrations and ineffective protests against it. Even the war, as he brilliantly presents it, obeys rules in its unfolding as in its resolution.

Only the type intrigued him, the general, the recurring, the eternal, whatever transcended Time. As though he could foresee those positivist books which present models, often with photos by Nadar, for each of his characters (Charlus=Robert de Montesquiou, Swann=Charles Haas), suggesting that the historical people were responsible for the brilliance of their fictional incarnations, Proust protests more and more in his last volume that all of his characters and locations are amalgams, all invented, many girls (and indeed one man) combined to make one girl, many churches to make one church, so that he could be said to have made his book "in the same way that Françoise made that *boeuf à la mode* which Monsieur de Norpois had found so delicious, just because she had enriched its jelly with so many carefully chosen pieces of meat." Into each of his characters, many bits of observation of many real people have been combined.

Having nothing but contempt for the specific, Proust sees the diary or journal as a primitive form of literature. The butt of his last volume, the book that he defines his own against, is the journal of the Goncourt Brothers, whose glamorization of their times Proust wickedly parodies in a long, invented passage describing the Verdurin salon in the old days, when Swann was courting Odette. "Prestige of literature!" says Marcel, closing the volume. The Verdurins, the Cottards, the Duc de Guermantes, they had all seemed commonplace people to him. How could Goncourt see so much in them and find their anecdotes so amusing?

> There was in me a personage who knew more or less how to look, but it was an intermittent personage, coming to life only in the presence of some general essence common to a number of things, these essences being its nourishment and joy. Then the personage looked and listened, but at a certain depth only, without my powers of superficial observation being enhanced. Just as a geometer, stripping things of their sensible qualities, sees only the linear substratum beneath them, so the stories people told escaped me, for what interested me was not what they were trying to say but . . . the point that was common to one being and another. As soon as I perceived this my intelligence . . . at once set off joyously in pursuit, but its quarry then, for instance the identity of the Verdurin drawing room in various places and at various times, was situated in the middle distance, behind actual appearances, in a zone that was rather more withdrawn. So the apparent, copiable charm of things and people escape me. . . . If I went to a dinner party, I did not see the guests: when I thought I was looking at them, I was in fact examining them with X-rays. (Vol. 6, p. 40)

This is the big difference between me and Marcel Proust. This is why I was not stupid enough to say, "He has written the book I might have written." The "apparent, copiable charm" of people and things is my province. A diarist by temperament, I must acknowledge descent from the Goncourts. I honor Proust, but I am not of his species. I cannot combine the many into the one. I recall, but I do not invent. I am bound to the concrete. Only in my dreams do I escape and rise to archetype. This is why, like Proust, I value the "nocturnal muse" and its products, dreams, the only literary production in which I escape my thralldom to the particular, my love of the specific, the particular instance, the individual friend.

•   •   •

When Marcel finally gets to Venice, there are no descriptions of architecture in the manner of Ruskin, no history-soaked renderings of present-day charm in the manner of Mary McCarthy or Jan Morris. Proust is the opposite of a travel writer. Where a travel writer will try to locate magic in the alien place, Proust knows that the source of any magic is the traveler's own imagination. If imagined lovers are more gratifying than actual lovers, imagined places are better than places seen, imagined Balbec better than Balbec visited, and longed-for Venice more intriguing even than the city itself. Where travel writing assumes that a place exists apart from the observer in some changeless form which everyone would agree on, Proust assumes there are as many Venices as there are Parisians. Where travel writing is biased toward enthusiasm, Proust understands that enthusiasm is a state travelers may eventually arrive at but only after some time has been spent wrestling with their natural reluctance to embrace a new reality. As a traveler, he's in the tradition of Huysman's Des Esseintes, who gets so excited about his trip to London, imagines so thoroughly the rain, the cold, the imperial gray city, that by the time he gets to the train station, he no longer feels the need to go.

Last year L. and I did a truly decadent thing—decadent not in the Huysmanian sense, but in the old-fashioned, gilding-the-lily sense. From Key West, we went farther south to the Caribbean island of Bonaire, in search of warmer weather and bluer water. Proust says that great art always disappoints at first because we do not have the proper mental tools to savor its originality. We have only the worn-out conventions by which we appreciate an older art, an art which no longer has the capacity to surprise. So, too, a beautiful new place is bound to disappoint. We measure it by the beauty we've seen elsewhere and find it wanting.

On Bonaire, a flat dry island, I looked for St. John's vistas of hilly green islands plunging into the sea, the flowering shrubs of St. Kitts, the cute little yachts in the harbor at Bequia, the turquoise of Bahamian water, the bright coral houses of Bermuda. My mind quickly moved between places it would take months to visit. I remembered one town's main street, the way the sun reflected off the white-washed buildings of another, the fine sand of one place, the offshore rocks of another. From one feature to another my mind raced, creating an oscillating perfection which the stolid present could not match. Every experience of islands I had had in the past went into my disappointment with this one.

When we checked into our hotel room, I saw that it was clean and tasteful in a bland and tasteless way, but I noticed more that the view of the ocean in our supposedly oceanfront room was blocked by Chinese fan palms. I noticed the lack of power in the bathroom sink faucet and the unfinished space beneath the bar. Always my visual tour of the room ended up on the obstructive Chinese fan palms.

Eventually I became attached to them. I got to like the way the fan palms formed a curtain blocking but implying the ocean, as the great velvet curtains of the opera house implied the stage. I enjoyed the way they sounded in the wind, like cardboard blowing against a wall or canvas flapping, as opposed to the clicking of coconut palms. I enjoyed the chirping of the golden warblers as they hopped about the fronds searching for fruit. But it took time for my spirit, which began by registering flaws, to make its way to appreciation.

In the effort to understand a new object, whether a Caribbean island or a pasta stirrer, we compare the object before us with others we have known. Only geniuses, only the most original minds, are capable of direct perception—perception uninfluenced by comparison. And as we compare, we idealize what is not in front of us, whose faults we do not see. The past can be bathed in a radiance the present only has when we're intoxicated, for in the present we are more alive to our own discomfort than we are to our comfort, more attuned to our unhappiness than our happiness. Whereas for the past, the process is reversed, and we have to make an effort to remember the disagreeable feelings we felt. Often we cannot remember them unless we name them, using the name as a hook and rope to drag the feeling up from the waters of unconsciousness.

For example, if I think about St. Lucia, where I went in the early 1980s, I remember a beautiful sandy bay, a charming restaurant right on the water, my own hair in corn rows, the beautiful Pitons, mold in the bathtub (a disagreeable image, but in fact what it says to me was the hotel I stayed at was cheap and the whole vacation a bargain). When I force myself to remember what I felt then, when I force myself to give it a name, I know what I felt was boredom. At the time, I was more bored than I was enthralled by the beauty I now remember so wistfully. I was bored because I wanted the kind of excitement I had been having before I went on vacation—the excitement I precisely wanted a vacation from. My senses, lagging behind my body, were still in New York. I was suffering jet lag of the soul.

Anyone who writes a memoir is a traveler in time. What Lévi-Strauss said about travel is true of memory visits, too: "I have only two possibilities: either I can be like some traveler of olden days, who was faced with a stupendous spectacle, all, or almost all of which eluded him, or worse still, filled him with scorn and disgust; or I can be a modern traveller, chasing after the vestiges of a vanished reality." In relation to the past, I am closer to the benighted traveler of olden days, untouched by the fabulous spectacle he sees, than to the nostalgic searcher. I always regarded my childhood as an imperfect prelude to adult life, a state better left behind, of no interest in itself. I couldn't wait to grow up, and the further I get from my childhood and childhood locales, the happier I have been. So I'm unlikely to get caught up in the search for a vanished reality that powers most reminiscences. I care more about trying to see the present for what it is. But there, too, I run into a problem. Can we see what is right before us, what we're caught up in? Lévi-Strauss has his doubts. He thinks that the most important features of our lives are invisible to us. We're able to see them only in retrospect.

So here's the dilemma: authentic habitation of a place or time involves a kind of blindness, but retrospect tends to set in motion a falsifying nostalgia and an overvaluation of what has disappeared. For Lévi-Strauss, this dilemma was solved by the passage of time. After twenty years, he could look back on his earlier experiences and see the underlying structure. Natural processes (his imagery is geological, of earthquakes, land shifts, and erosion) have reshaped the landscape of his past. Much falls away but the essential remains. So in my literal-minded way I conclude that perhaps there is an ideal time to sit down and try to look back at one's personal past. When, as a college girl, I read in Wordsworth that poetry consisted of emotion recollected in tranquillity, it annoyed me that he didn't say how long exactly you have to wait to be tranquil. How long before clarity sets in? Lévi-Strauss says twenty years.

My sister Susan called me recently, excited. She had been to her high school reunion the night before. She had driven by the house we grew up in. It was for sale. She wanted me to come with her to look at it. I agreed.

Over the next few days I grew nauseous with dread. I did not want to revisit the house I grew up in. I had not been inside— except in my dreams—in thirty-six years. I had not even returned—except in dreams—to the neighborhood. I felt that actually seeing what these places and spaces had become could only ruin the memory I had of them, which had become pleasant with time. If I disliked being a child, why should I now be a nostalgic pilgrim to the childhood shrine? Besides, I didn't want someone else's tiling, lighting fixtures, and wallpaper disfiguring my memory of my mother's decor.

Annie said, "Whatever brings you back to where you began, whatever convinces you that you are one person, makes you stronger and better."

I was flabbergasted. "Whoever told you that? I have to say I don't agree at all."

I couldn't place this idea, which seemed to me nonsense. Was it Freudian? Wordsworthian? The child is the father of the man?

Later, Wendy explained. "It's Christian. 'In our end is our beginning.' Read *The Four Quartets*. That's why Wallace Stevens was such a relief to me. You could invent yourself. You were a fiction. You didn't have to find yourself back where you started, like T. S. Eliot said."

I drove out from the city. Susan came from Rye. As soon as I got south of the airport, I relaxed. There were reeds by the side of the highway, marshes. The air, the land, the space itself felt familiar. I was home, and all it felt was natural.

Inside the house, nothing had changed, except that Mother's wallpaper was gone, painted over, and the stone fireplace was painted white. The linoleum floors my parents had laid down in the 1940s were still there, the ruby red of the breakfast room even deeper and richer in color, the alternating green-and-tan square tiles of the television room still intact. The tole lighting fixtures were still hanging in the dead center of every room. Mother's eight-foot sofa was there, along with the rattan furniture in the sunroom, the clock in the kitchen, the Hotpoint dishwasher, the stove, the Victrola, the Grandma Moses upholstery fabric on the window seat in the living room, books, a glass horse bookend, the chemicals in the darkroom, the GE refrigerator in the basement, the red shag carpet I had chosen for the floor of my bedroom when Richard went to college in 1950 and I moved into his room. Everything was just as we had left it. It was Miss Havisham's house, or Sleeping Beauty's. No one seemed to have lived there for thirty-six years. The mirrored liquor cabinet, into which I would stick my head to see it reflected ten, fifteen times to the left, right, up, and down, and ponder the mysteries of infinite recession, was still available for the same use. No stranger had obliterated my family's traces. By some miracle of nonlife, quite the contrary. The place was like a museum to our family past.

Susan and I gasped in amazement. "The red carpet's still there. Your desk is there. Here is the closet I hid in to listen to 'The Lone Ranger' on your radio. Here is the closet where your crinolines and dressy dresses hung. Here is where I couldn't make it to the toilet and threw up on the floor. Here is the bathroom scale, the very same one!"

It was astonishing, but after the initial shock it seemed strangely superfluous. Of course those things were there. They were all still inside my mind. They didn't seem any more real than my memories. Susan kept asking me how I could walk through so fast. Didn't I want to stop and savor? But I had stopped and savored long before, in reality, in dream, and in recollection. Now I was just checking against my mental inventory, and since it was all exactly as I had it remembered, I could proceed quickly.

Susan was the one suffering from the existential malaise I had expected to feel. This time, the imagination of disaster had worked: by imagining my discomfort in advance, I warded it off.

"It would make a great house for a doctor, or an accountant. You just cut through here, and make a separate entrance here. You join that long room with this room. You block that off. You open this up. You have the fireplace. It could be fabulous," said the kindly real estate agent, who must have suspected she was exercising her arts in vain. We were not interested in the possibilities of the house but in its ghosts.

Afterward, Susan and I drove around the neighborhood together. We knew the roads. We knew each block between our house and elementary school. We had walked those blocks hundreds of time in reality and again in our dreams. Each block had a different aura, some friendly, where the houses of our friends had been, some threatening, some, now all gone, mysterious, where there had been wooded land. In the villages, outside the residential areas, much was changed. Our public elementary school had become a private religious school. The whole town seemed to have been taken over by Orthodox Jews. The blocks seemed small. There were fast food restaurants. Chubby's, the luncheonette, was gone.

"Chubby's isn't there anymore!" Susan was outraged.

"It was forty years ago, Susan. You can't expect Chubby's to be there!"

"But in my mind it's yesterday. In my mind it's just the same."

Meaning, which was reality, her eternal, Platonic memory of Chubby's or its momentary nonexistence? As Proust pointed out, time, which changes the world we knew, does not change the image we have preserved of it.

This is my theory: disgust is caused by a discrepancy between expectation—or memory, which is another form of expectation—and actuality. If things exist in your memory, it is an outrage to the perceptual system, disconcerting and disorienting, not to have them still in existence in the world you see. Our house proved exempt from disgust, because by some bizarre, hilarious fluke it had escaped change. It was a house in a fairy tale, worse for wear, but exactly as we left it, confirming every child's fantasy that the house they lived in would continue the same, unlived in by anyone else. No changes had to be made to my memory map. No architect had messed with the floorplan of my mind. Awake or asleep, I could walk around that house just as I always had. I never had to fear not being able to find my way. I knew where I stood.

Susan said, assessing the visit, "They talk about closure. It's supposed to be good for you. I'm glad we went. I think what I experienced was closure."

I said, "I'm glad we went, too. I don't know about closure."

David was disappointed with my response. He wanted my return to Woodmere to be more "Proustian." He wanted it to have meant more to me that it seemed to, as Susan had wanted me to go more slowly through the house and to find closure, as Annie had wished me to find wholeness in revisiting the past. When I told David that the visit had left me relieved to know I could still find my way around, he said it would be more "poetic" if I said instead that I was reassured to know I could find my way *back*.

On March 19, 1996, I finished reading Proust. I had taken all the winter in Key West to read this final volume, finishing many other books as I read it, putting it down for days and even weeks at a time. Some inner metronome set my pace. I felt anxious to finish at the right time, although I didn't know what the right time was. I remembered my mother's desire to "come out even" when she ate dessert, finding herself with cake left over when she'd finished her coffee, taking more coffee, then finding herself out of cake with coffee to spare.

Having finished, I had to resist the cultural imperative to be especially moved or uplifted by the end. We reserve a special reverence for endings; we expect them to evoke extreme emotions. But the ending of *In Search of Lost Time* evoked in me no more emotion than many other parts along the way, and although I can definitely say that my life was changed by reading Proust, it was changed long before I reached the end. The changes books provoke are gradual and cumulative, so that you are changed by a book—if you are changed at all—as you are reading it and not all at once upon completion, just as you are educated before you graduate from college and not upon being handed the diploma.

Alison had suggested after reading the first chapter of this book that I finish my reading of Proust before writing about him, but I resisted her prudent advice. Even then I knew my life had changed and if I could not convey what I had learned up to that point, I wouldn't be more articulate by knowing more. If I understood Proust, he was concerned with principles, not examples, and by the end of the series of books I would have only more examples of the same principles. More than I feared speaking rashly, I feared reaching a point at which I was so overwhelmed by my respect for Proust and by all the things I wanted to say about him that I wouldn't be able to write at all. A certain ignorance is necessary for creativity, or as Proust said, putting it the other way, erudition is one of the many ways in which we flee from our own lives.

As Proust neared the end of his great work, he was anxious that he might not live long enough to finish it. He felt like a painter walking along a hilltop trying to get a view of the lake below but finding it always blocked by trees. At last he reaches a clearing and sits down to paint, but by then night is falling, the night which no dawn will follow. Proust, carrying his work within him, feared death as he never had before. He was haunted by the image of an unfinished edifice. He reminded himself that some cathedrals were unfinished, then rejected the pompous comparison. His work, he said, was more humble and domestic than a cathedral, more like their family servant's tasks, sewing a dress out of different pieces, patching a window with newspaper, or making a stew.

He passed around some of his sketches and was misunderstood. People praised him for writing under a microscope when he saw himself as having used a telescope. "Those passages in which I was trying to arrive at general laws were described as so much pedantic investigation of detail." But being misunderstood did not bother him as much as not reaching the end of what was within him to say. He knew his audience would catch up with him eventually.

Death dominates the imagery of the last pages. While he is ostensibly describing how he returned to Paris, went to a party, saw the effects of Time on individuals and on society, conceived the idea for his book—that is, how he started his work—his imagery reflects a writer's fears at the end, his fears at the moment of writing, not the moment written about. His feelings for his book are compared to those for her son of a dying mother, who, between bloodlettings and injections, has to make the exhausting effort of looking after him and perhaps still loves him "but it is only in the form of a duty too great for her strength that she is aware of her affection."

The last image is of people living precariously on top of the years they have lived, trying to keep them under control and to incorporate them into the life they are leading, like people trying to walk on stilts. No one takes up much space in the world, but each of us occupies a long length of time.

So we come to the end. I have stretched the year as far as it can go. Works of art are changing as I speak. *Carrie*, which was still a stylish horror film at the start of the year, has turned into a coming-of-age film for women. My narrative has blended two winters into one, and in real life, events are starting to repeat. We have picadillo dinner again, a year later, with Rust, Joy, Bob, and this time, Janice, too. We talk about the work of William Gaddis, Gilbert Sorrentino, Francine Gray.

Rust, who is a gentleman, politely inquires what I'm working on. I take a deep breath and say, "About the experience of reading Proust."

"Ah, does he still apply?" Rust wants to know. "The world he writes about is so different from ours. That society is dead and gone."

"Not at all," I say. "He was a kind of human naturalist. He was interested in laws that govern behavior as much now as then. He would be able to explain exactly how the society of today is the descendant of the one he knew—how it's the same and how it's different. It's amazingly the same. When he describes Balbec, it might as well be Key West."

Rust doesn't see it, even after I try to explain the principle of the marginal being central. It makes him think of friends who moved to Nantucket year round. Now they have time to see the color of water, the quality of light in the rushes at sunset. I think, "That is not what I meant. That is not what I meant at all."

The conversation moves on to Conrad. "What an old bore Marlowe is," says Bob. "He's the English identity Conrad feels he has to establish for himself."

It is an extraordinary evening: writers actually talking about literature, not real estate, not agents, not magazines, not who was invited to Ballast Key or who paid for the dinner for Salman Rushdie.

Now it is Easter again, a gray, rainy day, not a good day for a walk in the park. Besides, L. couldn't make it to Fifth Avenue. He injured his back picking up our junk mail at the Middletown post office when we returned from Key West. He's been in pain for over a week. He's lying in bed, on ibuprophen and Valium. We haven't been out all day. It seems to be getting worse. Two days ago he was still able to walk to the Metropolitan and spend some time at the Treasures of Imperial China show.

I myself especially liked the scroll "Dwelling in the Fu-Ch'un Mountains," one of those twenty-foot-long affairs which are meant to be unrolled a section at a time, from right to left, but which the Met actually had on display at full length. You can't take it in all at once. You have to walk along and look at one section after another, past a forest, past a bridge, into the mountains, past the gathering of scholars, seeing brush strokes become objects then brush strokes again.

The work took many years. The artist described the process in a colophon. In the seventh year of Chih-Cheng (1347), he went to live in the Fu-Ch'un Mountains. One leisurely day he lifted up his brush and sketched out the scroll to the end. He was in a state of extreme exhilaration. He came back to it over and over, filling things in and developing details. Three or four years later it was still not finished. He had left the scroll in the mountains while he went on his travels. "Now I have picked it up again and put it in my traveling bag. Morning and evening, whenever I can catch a free moment, I put my brush to work. Wu-yung is excessively anxious that someone will make off with it. So I hereby inscribe the end of the scroll in advance, to let people know how hard it is to bring to completion."

I talked by phone with my friend Stephen in California. Playing tennis, he rushed the net and tore his Achilles tendon. "A yuppie injury," he calls it, but no joke. These silly injuries have major consequences, big *tsuris* from little acorns. His orthopedist missed the moment when the repair could be simple and had to reconstruct the Achilles tendon using tendon from Steve's big toe. Apparently, we were made to be monkeys, using our feet to cling to branches, and our toes have lots of extra tendon for redistributing. But now his foot has to be in a cast for five months.

I told him about the Chinese Imperial Treasures, and he told me about visiting a museum in China that had one magnificent scroll painting after another. He had copied out the ideograms for the different periods of Chinese art to take with him to the museum, so he could make out from the labels when each work was painted and sometimes the name of the artist as well. He was deeply moved by what he saw. As he left the museum, he ran into a Chinese friend and asked him to translate an ideogram he noticed on all the labels, something like the three connected balls of the pawnbroker, which he hadn't understood. The man told Stephen it meant "reproduction."

Mother must have the last word.

At first she was unenthusiastic about this book. She didn't see the commercial potential of a book with Proust in the title ("Could you at least call it something else?"), and she would really like to see me on the best-seller list before she dies. I explained to her that it took a special gift to write like Danielle Steele and Robert Ludlum. I couldn't do it if I bent my entire mind and talent to it, which, I informed her, I had no desire to do.

"I have to be me, Mother," I said, singing the theme song of our era.

With time, Mother got to like the idea of my writing what she called Proust's memoirs. She saw the book's potential, if not for making money, then for asserting our family's intellectual and educational superiority to certain of her acquaintance, about one of whom she confided, "She's not of our class, dear. She doesn't know Marcel Proust."

"What we have not had to decipher, to elucidate by our own efforts, what was clear before we looked at it, is not ours. From ourselves comes only that which we drag forth from the obscurity which lies within us, that which to others is unknown."

Time Regained

Recommended Reading

Abelove, Henry. *The Evangelist of Desire.*
———, ed. *The Lesbian and Gay Studies Reader.*
Alexander, Shana. *The Pizza Connection.*
Alpers, Svetlana. *The Art of Describing.*
Alpers, Paul. *What Is Pastoral?*
Alter, Robert. *Genesis.*
Alther, Lisa. *Kinflicks.*
Antonaccio, Carla. *An Archaeology of Ancestors.*
Atlas, James. *Delmore Schwartz.*
Bair, Deirdre. *Samuel Beckett.*
Baker, Jean-Claude, and Chris Chase. *Josephine.*
Baker, Nicholson. *U and I.*
Bank, Mirra. *Anonymous Was a Woman.*
Barthes, Roland. *A Lover's Discourse.*
———. *Mythologies.*
Basinger, Jeanine. *The American Cinema.*
Bate, Walter Jackson. *John Keats.*
Battin, Margaret. *Ethics in the Sanctuary.*
Baudelaire, Charles, *Les Fleurs du Mal,* Richard Howard, trans.
Bauer, Douglas. *The Very Air.*
Bausch, Richard. *Rare and Endangered Species.*
Beattie, Ann. *Another You.*
———. *Secrets and Surprises.*
Beatty, Jack. *The Rascal King.*
Bell, Michael Davitt. *The Problem of American Realism.*
Bell, Quentin. *Virginia Woolf.*

Bell, Olivier, ed. *The Diaries of Virginia Woolf.*

Benton, William. *Normal Meanings.*

Berg, Scott. *Maxwell Perkins.*

Bernays, Anne. *Professor Romeo.*

Birkerts, Sven. *The Artificial Wilderness.*

Blais, Marie-Claire. *Deaf to the City.*

Blau, Eve. *Architecture and Its Image.*

Blauner, Peter. *A Slow-Motion Riot.*

Bloch, Don. *Face Value.*

Bloom, Amy. *Come to Me.*

Bloom, Harold. *Shelley's Mythmaking.*

Bloom, Lary. *Notes from the Jewish Infantry.*

Blume, Judy. *Wifey.*

Borges, Jorge Luis. *Labyrinths.*

Bosworth, Patricia. *Diane Arbus.*

Boyd, Blanche. *The Redneck Way of Knowledge.*

Braudy, Leo. *The Frenzy of Renown.*

Braudy, Susan. *Who Killed Sal Mineo?*

Brightman, Carol. *Writing Dangerously.*

Brinnin, John Malcolm. *The Third Rose.*

Brodhead, Richard. *Cultures of Letters.*

Brooks, Peter. *Reading for the Plot.*

Brownmiller, Susan. *Against Our Will.*

Brunhoff, Anne de. *Souls in Stone.*

Brunhoff, Laurent de. *Babar's Little Girl.*

———. *The Rescue of Babar.*

———. *Babar's Visit to Bird Island.*

———. *Babar and the Wully-Wully.*

———. *Babar's Little Library (Air, Earth, Water, Fire,* a boxed set)

———. *Bonhomme.*

Brustein, Robert. *Who Needs Theatre?*

Buckley, Jerome. *The Victorian Temper.*

Burney, Fanny. *Selected Letters and Journals.*

Burt, Robert. *Two Jewish Justices.*

Butler, Jeffrey. *Democratic Liberalism in South Africa.*

Byrd, Max. *Jefferson.*

Cantor, Jay. *The Death of Che Guevara.*

Cantwell, Mary. *American Girl.*

Cather, Willa. *O Pioneers!*

Cavell, Stanley. *Pursuits of Happiness.*

Chaix, Marie. *The Laurels of Lake Constance.*

Cheever, Susan. *Home Before Dark.*

Cholodenko, Marc. *Histoire de Vivant Lanon.*

Ciolkowski, Laura. *Border Crossings.*

Cohen-Solal, Annie. *Sartre.*

Comden, Betty. *Off Stage.*

Conarroe, Joel. *John Berryman.*

Conley, Cort. *Idaho Loners.*

Connor, Tony. *Spirits of the Place.*

Conway, Jill Ker. *The Road from Coorain.*

Cook, Blanche Wiesen. *Eleanor Roosevelt.*

Cooper, George. *Lost Love.*

Craig, Kit. *Gone.*

Crapanzano, Vincent. *Hermes' Dilemma and Hamlet's Desire.*

Crews, Frederick. *The Pooh Perplex.*

Crosby, Christina. *The Ends of History.*

Crowther, Hal. *Unarmed But Dangerous.*

Culler, A. Dwight. *The Victorian Mirror of History.*

Curtiss, Mina. *Other People's Letters.*

D'Oench, Ellen. *Darkness Into Light.*

Davidson, Bruce. *Central Park.*

Denby, David. *Great Books.*

Des Pres, Terrence. *The Survivor.*

Dickason, Christie. *Indochina.*

Dickstein, Morris. *Gates of Eden.*

Dillard, Annie. *An American Childhood.*

———. *The Writing Life.*

———. *Pilgrim at Tinker Creek.*

———. *Encounters with Chinese Writers.*

———. *The Living.*

———. *Teaching a Stone to Talk.*

Dillon, Millicent. *After Egypt.*

Djerassi, Carl. *The Pill, Pygmy Chimps, and Degas' Horse.*

Doctorow, E. L. *Ragtime.*

Doniger, Wendy. *Sexual Masquerades.*

Douglas, Ann. *The Feminization of American Culture.*

Drury, Tom. *The End of Vandalism.*

Duberstein, Larry. *The Marriage Hearse.*

duCille, Anne. *Skin Trade.*

Ehrenreich, Barbara. *The Snarling Citizen.*

Eisler, Benita. *O'Keeffe and Stieglitz.*

Eisler, Colin. *Durer's Animals.*

Eliot, George. *Middlemarch.*

Fabre, Michel. *From Harlem to Paris.*

Faierstein, Linda. *Sexual Violence.*

Famularo, Joe. *Vegetables.*

Farber, Thomas. *Compared to What?*

Feiffer, Jules. *Little Murders.*

Fell, Alison. *The Pillow Boy of the Lady Onogoro.*

Ferrer, Daniel. *Virginia Woolf and the Madness of Language.*

Finkielkraut, Alain. *La Sagesse de l'amour.*

Fitzgerald, Robert, transl. *The Odyssey.*

Fizdale, Robert and Arthur Gold. *Misia.*

Franks, Lucinda. *Wild Apples.*

French, Marilyn. *The Women's Room.*

Frey, Julia. *Toulouse-Lautrec.*

Garber, Marjorie. *Vested Interests.*

Garrett, George. *The Death of the Fox.*

Garrett, Susan. *Taking Care of Our Own.*

Gassenheimer, Linda. *Keys Cuisine.*

Gates, Henry Louis, Jr. *Colored People.*

Gezari, Janet. *Charlotte Bronte and Defensive Conduct.*

Gilot, Francoise. *Matisse and Picasso.*

Gimbel, Wendy. *Havana Dreams.*

Gioia, Dana. *Can Poetry Matter?*

Girodias, Maurice. *J'arrive!*

Glickman, Gary. *Years From Now.*

Goldberg, Vicki. *Margaret Bourke-White.*

Goldfarb, Ronald. *The Writer's Lawyer.*

Goldsmith, Barbara. *Little Gloria . . . Happy At Last.*

Goreau, Angeline. *Reconstructing Aphra.*

Gordon, Mary. *Final Payments.*

Gornick, Vivian. *Fierce Attachments.*

Gould, Lois. *Such Good Friends.*

Gourevitch, Victor, ed. *On Tyranny,* by Leo Strauss.

Graver, Elizabeth. *Have You Seen Me?.*

Gray, Francine. *Lovers and Tyrants.*

Greenblatt, Stephen. *Learning to Curse.*

———. *Marvelous Possessions.*

Greene, Nathanael. *From Versailles to Vichy.*

Grosskurth, Phyllis. *Byron.*

Hallie, Philip. *Lest Innocent Blood Be Shed.*

Hamburger, Philip. *Curious World.*

Harris, Lis. *Holy Days.*

Harrison, Jim. *Legends of the Fall.*

Hartman, Geoffrey. *Criticism in the Wilderness.*

Haskell, Molly. *Holding My Own in No Man's Land.*

Hawes, Elizabeth. *New York, New York.*

Hawkes, Judith. *Julian's House.*

Hedrick, Joan. *Harriet Beecher Stowe.*

Hemingway, Ernest. *A Moveable Feast.*

Herrera, Hayden. *Frida.*

Hills, L. Rust. *How to Do Things Right.*

Hitchcock, Jane. *Trick of the Eye.*

Hoagland, Edward. *The Tugman's Passage.*

Hoffman, Eva. *Lost in Translation.*

Hollander, John. *Rhyme's Reason.*

Holtzschue, Linda. *Understanding Color.*

Horgan, Paul. *Great River.*

Hower, Edward. *Night Train Blues.*

Hughes, Gertrude. *Emerson's Demanding Optimism.*

Huggins, Nathan. *Revelations.*

Hujar, Peter. *Portraits in Life and Death.*

Hunter, Mark. *The Passions of Men.*

Jones, Ann. *Women Who Kill.*

Jong, Erica. *Fear of Flying.*

Joyce, James. *Ulysses.*

Kahn, E. J. *A Year at the The New Yorker.*

Kaplan, Justin. *Mr. Clemens and Mr. Twain.*

Kaplan, Louise. *Female Perversions.*

Kaufelt, David. *The Fat Boy Murders.*

Kaufelt, Lynn. *Key West Writers and Their Houses.*

Kazantzis, Judith. *The Rabbit Magician Plate.*

Kelley, Kitty. *Nancy Reagan.*

Kendall, Elizabeth. *The Runaway Bride.*

Kevorkian, A. J. *The Kevorkian Newsletter.*

Kittredge, William. *Owning It All.*

Koestenbaum, Wayne. *The Queen's Throat.*

Kopit, Arthur. *Oh Dad, Poor Dad, Mama's Hung You in the Closet and I'm Feeling So Sad.*

Kramer, Jane. *Europeans.*

Kundera, Milan. *The Book of Laughter and Forgetting.*

Laidlaw, Brett. *Three Nights in the Heart of the Earth.*

Lambert, Ellen Zetzel. *The Face of Love.*

Laszlo, Pierre. *Organic Spectroscopy.*

Lazan, Marion. *Four Perfect Pebbles.*

Lear, Martha. *Heartsounds.*

Lebergott, Stanley. *Pursuing Happiness.*

Leavitt, David. *Family Dancing.*

Lefort, Colette. *Maigrir à volonté . . . ou sans volonté.*

Leontief, Estelle. *Genia and Wassily.*

Leslie, John. *Havana Hustle.*

Lesser, Wendy. *Pictures at an Execution.*

Levering, Frank and Wanda Urbansky. *Simple Living.*

Lévi-Strauss, Claude. *Tristes Tropiques.*

Levin, Harry. *Playboys and Killjoys.*

Lewis, David Levering. *When Harlem was in Vogue.*

Lewis, R.W.B. *Edith Wharton.*

Liebowitz, Fran. *Metropolitan Life.*

Lifton, Betty Jean. *Journey of the Adopted Self.*

Lifton, Robert. *The Genocidal Mentality.*

Lord, James. *Picasso and Dora.*

Lottman, Herbert. *The Left Bank.*

Love, Susan M., with Karen Lindsey. *Dr. Susan Love's Breast Book.*

Lubow, Arthur. *The Reporter Who Would Be King.*

Lurie, Alison. *Foreign Affairs.*

———. *The War Between the Tates.*

———. *Imaginary Friends.*

———. *Love and Friendship.*

———. *Women and Ghosts.*

Maas, Peter. *The Valachi Papers.*

Malcolm, Janet. *The Silent Woman.*

Mallon, Thomas. *Henry and Clara.*

Manchester, William. *The City of Anger.*

Mandell, Gail Porter. *Life Into Art*

Mason, Felicity (writing as Anne Cumming). *The Love Habit.*

Matheson, Susan. *Ancient Glass in the Collection of the Yale University Art Gallery.*

Mathews, Harry. *The Journalist.*

Matousek, Mark. *Sex, Death, Enlightenment.*

McCarthy, Mary. *Memories of a Catholic Girlhood.*

McConkey, James. *Court of Memory.*

McCready, Karen. *Art Deco and Modernist Ceramics.*

McCullough, David. *Truman.*

McGuane, Thomas. *Ninety-two in the Shade.*

McKenna, Rollie. *A Life in Photography.*

McLeod, Bruce. *Club Date Musicians.*

McPherson, James Alan. *Elbow Room.*

Mehta, Gita. *The River Sutra.*

Mendelson, Edward. *Early Auden.*

Merrill, James. *A Scattering of Salts.*

———. *A Different Person.*

Meyer, Priscilla. *Find What the Sailor Has Hidden.*

Michaels, Leonard. *The Men's Club.*

Middlebrook, Diane. *Anne Sexton.*
Middleton, Faith. *The Goodness of Ordinary People.*
Milford, Nancy. *Zelda.*
Miller, D. A. *The Novel and the Police.*
Miller, Sue. *The Good Mother.*
Miller, William Ian. *Humiliation.*
Milroy, Elizabeth. *Painters of a New Century.*
Monette, Paul. *No Witnesses.*
Montaigne, Michel de. *Essays.*
Moore, Honor. *The White Blackbird.*
Moss, Howard. *Proust's Magic Lantern.*
Mukherjee, Bharati. *The Middleman.*
Munro, Eleanor. *On Glory Roads.*
Nachtigall, Lila E. and Joan Rattner Hellman. *Estrogen: A Complete Guide to Reversing the Effects of Menopause Using Hormone Replacement Therapy.*
Naipaul, V. S. *A House for Mr. Biswas.*
Newhouse, Nancy, ed. *Hers.*
Newman, John Henry Cardinal. *Autobiography.*
Nuland, Sherwin. *How We Die.*
Ohmann, Richard. *English in America.*
Olds, Sharon. *The Father.*
O'Meally, Robert G. *Lady Day.*
O'Reilly, Jane. *The Girl I Left Behind.*
Ostor, Akos. *Vessels of Time.*
O'Toole, Patricia. *The Five of Hearts.*
Ozick, Cynthia. *The Pagan Rabbi.*
Paglia, Camille. *Sexual Personae.*
Paley, Grace. *The Little Disturbances of Man.*
Pemberton, Gayle. *The Hottest Water in Chicago.*
Perenyi, Eleanor. *Green Thoughts.*
Pinsky, Robert, transl. *The Inferno of Dante.*
Pollitt, Katha. *Reasonable Creatures.*
Ponge, Francis. *Le Parti pris des choses.*
Porter, Joe Ashby. *Lithuania.*
Pougy, Liane de. *My Blue Notebooks.*

Poverman, C. E. *Solomon's Daughter.*
Proust, Marcel. *In Search of Lost Time* (6 volumes). Translated
    by C. K. Scott Moncrieff and Terence Kilmartin. Revised
    by D. J. Enright.
Rabb, Jane M., ed. *Literature and Photography.*
Rabinowitz, Peter. *Talking Medicine.*
Rampersad, Arnold. *Langston Hughes.*
Rapoport, Nessa. *A Woman's Book of Grieving.*
Rawlings, Marjorie Kinnan. *Cross Creek.*
——. *South Moon Under.*
——. *The Yearling.*
Reed, Joseph W. *Three American Originals.*
Reed, Kit. *Captain Grownup.*
Richardson, Robert D., Jr. *Thoreau.*
——. *Emerson.*
Ricks, Christopher. *Keats and Embarrassment.*
Rollin, Betty. *First, You Cry.*
Rose, Mark. *Heroic Love.*
——. *Spenser's Art.*
——. *Golding's Tale.*
——. *Shakespearean Design.*
——. *Authors and Owners.*
Rose, Phyllis. *Woman of Letters.*
——. *Parallel Lives.*
——. *Writing of Women.*
——. *Jazz Cleopatra.*
——. *Never Say Goodbye.*
——, ed. *The Norton Book of Women's Lives.*
Rosenberg, Edgar. *From Shylock to Svengali.*
Rosenblatt, Roger. *Children of War.*
Rosenthal, Rob. *Homeless in Paradise.*
Ross, Clifford. *The World of Edward Gorey.*
Rossner, Judith. *Looking for Mr. Goodbar.*
Roth, Philip. *Patrimony.*
Rushdie, Salman. *Midnight's Children.*
Salter, James. *A Sport and a Pastime.*

Sarris, Andrew. *The American Cinema.*

Sauerwein, Leigh. *The Way Home.*

Scalise, Daniele. *Cose del Altro Mundo.*

Scarf, Maggie. *Unfinished Business.*

Scheibe, Karl. *Mirrors, Masks, Lies, and Secrets.*

Schine, Cathleen. *Rameau's Niece.*

Schorr, David, illust. *No Witnesses* by Paul Monette.

———. *Parallel Lives* by Phyllis Rose.

———. *The Fabulists French,* trans. Norman Shapiro.

———. *La Fontaine's Bawdy,* trans. Norman Shapiro.

———. *Songs with a Dying Fall.*

Schwarcz, Vera. *Long Road Home.*

Sendak, Maurice. *Where the Wild Things Are.*

Shames, Laurence. *Florida Straits.*

Shattuck, Roger. *Marcel Proust.*

Sheed, Wilfrid. *Frank and Maisie.*

Shreve, Susan Richards. *Queen of Hearts.*

Shulman, Alix Kates. *Memoirs of an Ex-Prom Queen.*

Shull, Elizabeth, et al. *The Thirteen Colonies Cookbook.*

Simpson, Eileen. *Poets in Their Youth.*

Siry, Joseph. *Unity Temple.*

Skinner, Cornelia Otis. *Our Hearts Were Young and Gay.*

———. *Elegant Wits and Grand Horizontals.*

———. *Madame Sarah.*

———. *Nuts in May.*

Slobin, Mark. *Tenement Songs.*

Slobin, Greta. *Remizov's Fictions.*

Slotkin, Richard. *Gunfighter Nation.*

Smith, Annick. *Heartland.*

Smith, Lee. *Fair and Tender Ladies.*

Solnit, Albert J. and Joseph Goldstein. *Beyond the Best Interests of the Child.*

Sontag, Susan. *Against Interpretation.*

Stegner, Wallace. *Angle of Repose.*

Stein, Gertrude. *The Autobiography of Alice B. Toklas.*

Stein, Richard. *Set Free.*

Steiner, Wendy. *The Scandal of Pleasure.*

Sterne, Laurence. *Tristram Shandy.*

Stone, Robert. *Outerbridge Reach.*

———. *Dog Soldiers.*

———. *A Flag for Sunrise.*

———. *A Hall of Mirrors.*

———. *Children of Light.*

Storrs, Anthony. *Solitude.*

Stowe, William. *Going Abroad.*

Strand, Mark. *Reasons for Moving.*

Strouse, Jean. *Alice James.*

Styron, William. *Sophie's Choice.*

Suleri, Sara. *Meatless Days.*

Swope, Sam. *The Araboolies of Liberty Street.*

Szegedy-Maszak, Andrew. *Atget's Churches.*

Talese, Gay. *Unto the Sons.*

Tanning, Dorothea. *Birthday.*

Theroux, Phyllis. *Night Lights.*

Thurman, Judith. *Isak Dinesen.*

Tololyan, Khachig. *An Index to Gravity's Rainbow.*

Underhill, Lois Beachy. *The Woman Who Ran For President.*

Updike, John. *Rabbit at Rest.*

Ward, Aileen. *John Keats.*

Watkins, John V. and Thomas J. Sheehan. *Florida Landscape Plants.*

Weber, Katharine. *Objects in Mirror Are Closer Than They Appear.*

Weber, Nicholas Fox. *Patron Saints.*

———. *The Art of Babar.*

Weinman, Irving. *Virgil's Ghost.*

Weinstock, Nicholas. *The Secret Love of Sons.*

Welch, James. *Fools Crow.*

White, Edmund. *Skinned Alive.*

———. *A Boy's Own Life.*

———. *Forgetting Elena.*

———. *Caracole.*

————. *Genet.*

Wilbur, Richard. *Advice to a Prophet.*

Williams, Joy. *State of Grace.*

————. *Breaking and Entering.*

Williams, Terry Tempest. *Refuge.*

Wolfe, Linda. *The Professor and the Prostitute.*

Wolff, Geoffrey. *The Duke of Deception.*

Wolff, Tobias. *In Pharaoh's Army.*

Woolf, Virginia. *Mrs. Dalloway.*

Wright, William. *Pavarotti: An Autobiography.*

————. *Lillian Hellman.*

Yergin, Daniel. *Global Insecurity.*

Young-Bruehl, Elizabeth. *Anna Freud.*

Yourcenar, Marguerite. *Memoirs of Hadrian.*

Zhang Jie. *Heavy Wings.*

Zinsser, William. *On Writing Well.*

Zwerdling, Alex. *Virginia Woolf and the Real World.*